India's Development Diplomacy
and Soft Power in Africa

RELATED JAMES CURREY TITLES ON
AFRICA'S INTERNATIONAL RELATIONS

China's Aid and Soft Power in Africa
KENNETH KING

Africa Rising? BRICS – Diversifying Dependency
IAN TAYLOR

Sudan Looks East: China, India and the Politics of Asian Alternatives
DANIEL LARGE AND LUKE A. PATEY (Eds)

*Brazil-Africa Relations: Historical Dimensions and Contemporary Engagements, from the
     1960s to the Present*
GERHARD SEIBERT AND PAULO FAGUNDES VISENTINI (Eds)

India's Development Diplomacy and Soft Power in Africa

Edited by
Kenneth King and Meera Venkatachalam

JAMES CURREY

James Currey
is an imprint of
Boydell & Brewer Ltd
PO Box 9, Woodbridge
Suffolk IP12 3DF (GB)
www.jamescurrey.com
and of
Boydell & Brewer Inc.
668 Mt Hope Avenue
Rochester, NY 14620-2731 (US)
www.boydellandbrewer.com

The publisher has no responsibility for the continued existence or accuracy of
URLs for external or third-party internet websites referred to in this book, and
does not guarantee that any content on such websites is, or will remain, accurate
or appropriate.

British Library Cataloguing in Publication Data

A catalogue record for this book is available from the British Library

ISBN 978-1-84701-274-6 (James Currey paperback)

This publication is printed on acid-free paper

Contents

Part 3: Capacity Building: Shifting Modalities and New Knowledgescapes

Part 4: Skilling, Knowledge Transfer and Indo-African Interactions

Notes on Contributors

Chambi Chachage is the 2018–21 Princeton African Humanities Postdoctoral Research Associate and Lecturer. He holds a BSocSci in Psychological Studies/BA (Hons), MSc in African Studies and AM in History/PhD in African Studies, from the University of Cape Town (UCT), the University of Edinburgh and Harvard University, respectively.

Vincent Duclos is Assistant Professor in the Département de communication sociale et publique (Department of Social and Public Communication) at the University of Québec in Montréal. He is an anthropologist writing about global health, and the transnational circulation of knowledge, medicine and technology. He is currently writing an ethnography of the Pan-African e-Network, tentatively titled "Life at a Distance: Medicine, Markets & Nation in India's Pan-African e-Network". His research has been published in many scholarly journals including *Cultural Anthropology*, *BioSocieties*, *India Review* and *Medical Anthropology Quarterly*.

Mrittika Guha Sarkar is a research scholar at the Centre for East Asian Studies, School of International Studies, Jawaharlal Nehru University (JNU), India. She is also a research assistant at the Centre for Strategic Studies and Simulation, United Service Institute of Indian, in New Delhi. She is associated with the *Routledge Studies on Think Asia* and the *Journal of Indo-Pacific Affairs* (Air University, USA), as an editorial assistant and researcher, respectively.

Kenneth King was Director of the Centre of African Studies and Professor of International and Comparative Education at the University of Edinburgh for many years. He is now Emeritus Professor in its Schools of Education and of Social and Political Studies. His most recent publication is *Education, Skills and International Cooperation: Comparative and Historical Perspectives* (Springer, 2019).

Emma Mawdsley is Reader in Human Geography and Fellow of Newnham College, University of Cambridge, UK. Her research focuses on global development politics, with a particular interest in the UK and India. She is the Director of the Margaret Anstee Centre for Global Development, and currently running the India-UK Development Partnership Forum (IUKDPF), a policy-oriented research project funded by the Foreign, Commonwealth and Development Office (FCDO).

Gerard McCann is Senior Lecturer in Global History and Director of the Centre for Modern Studies at the University of York, UK. He is currently working on two research projects: 'Another world? East Africa and the global 1960s' and 'Afro-Asian networks: transitions in the global south', the approaches of which are distilled in the co-authored 'Another World? East Africa, Decolonisation and the Global History of the Mid-Twentieth Century', *Journal of African History*, 62:3 (2021).

Jacqueline Halima Mgumia is Lecturer in the Department of Sociology and Anthropology at the University of Dar es Salaam (UDSM), Tanzania. She holds a BA degree with a major in Sociology from Albion College, USA; a MA degree in Development Studies from UDSM, Tanzania and a PhD in Anthropology from the University of the Witwatersrand, South Africa.

Jagannath Panda is a Research Fellow and Centre Head for East Asia at the Manohar Parrikar Institute for Defence Studies and Analyses (MP-IDSA), New Delhi, India. He is also the Series Editor for *Routledge Studies on Think Asia*. He is an expert on India-China Relations, China, East Asia, Indo-Pacific security, Indian Foreign Policy and the Korean peninsula.

Supriya Roychoudhury is a researcher with interests at the intersection of transnationalism, development and rights. She holds an MPhil in Geographical Research from the University of Cambridge and an MA in International Relations from the University of Warwick. She is currently a research consultant with the IUKDPF at the Margaret Anstee Centre for Global Studies, University of Cambridge.

Muhidin J. Shangwe is a Lecturer in the Department of Political Science and Public Administration, University of Dar es Salaam, Tanzania. He holds a BA in Political Science and Public Administration, an MA in International Relations from the University of Dar es Salaam and a PhD in International Relations from East China Normal University, People's Republic of China. He is currently working on Chinese soft power in Africa.

Meera Venkatachalam is a Postdoctoral Fellow at the Centre for African Studies, University of Mumbai. Her research is focused on the transregional circulation of religion, people and capital across the Global South, between India and Africa in particular. Recent co-edited publications include *South-South Cooperation: India-Africa Partnerships for Food Security and Capacity*

Building (Palgrave Macmillan, 2021), and *Common Threads: Fabrics made in India for Africa* (ASCL, 2020).

Simona Vittorini is Senior Teaching Fellow in the Department of Politics and International Studies at the School of Oriental and African Studies (University of London). With David Harris (University of Bradford) she is recipient of a research grant from the IUKDPF, a policy-oriented research project funded by the FCDO, to study India's presence in West Africa.

Acknowledgements

This volume originated from two panels organised by Kenneth King and Meera Venkatachalam at the European Conference on African Studies (ECAS), organised by the Africa-Europe Group for Interdisciplinary Studies (AEGIS) in Edinburgh in June 2019. We thank the organising committee of ECAS for making possible the travel and participation of two of our authors. In addition, four others of our twelve contributors were able to be present in Edinburgh. We are grateful to Jaqueline Mitchell of James Currey/Boydell and Brewer, for encouraging us to develop the Edinburgh papers and others into this present volume.

The Binks Trust supported fieldwork on India–Africa development cooperation by Kenneth King and Pravina King in India, Tanzania, Rwanda and Ethiopia during 2018–19. The Manohar Parrikar Institute for Defence Studies and Analyses (MP-IDSA) supported Kenneth King through a fellowship in New Delhi from January to April 2018. Meera Venkatachalam's research has been partially supported by the Research Council of Norway through a collaborative research project entitled 'India's Footprint in Africa', under the Norwegian Programme for Research Cooperation with India (INDNOR). We are also grateful to the Indian Council for World Affairs (ICWA) and the Indian International Centre (IIC) for encouraging our participation in the India–Africa conferences of 2019 and 2020 respectively.

We thank Sunil Khilnani, C.J. Kuncheria and Shobana Shankar for their readiness to review several chapters of our book. Neda Shaikh and Lakshimi Swaminathan kindly assisted with the editorial work in the final stages. And, of course, we are especially grateful to our three reviewers for their helpful commentaries on our manuscript.

Kenneth King and Meera Venkatachalam
May 2021

Abbreviations

AAGC	Asia-Africa Growth Corridor
AASI	Association of African Students of India
ACOTA	Amalgamated Commercial Enterprise of Tanzania
AEGIS	Africa Europe Group for Interdisciplinary Studies
AEI	American Enterprise Institute
AfDB	African Development Bank
Afrexim	African Export Import (Bank)
AI	Artificial Intelligence
AIDS	Acquired Immunodeficiency Syndrome
AIIMS	All India Institute of Medical Sciences
ANC	African National Congress
ARV	Antiretroviral
ASC	African Studies Centre
AU	African Union
AYUSH	Ayurveda, Yoga, Unani, Siddha, Homeopathy
B-2-B	Business to business
BB	Bharat Biotech
BBC	British Broadcasting Corporation
BCE	Before Common Era
BD	Bajrang Dal
BIMSTEC	Bay of Bengal Initiative for Multi-Sectoral Technical and Economic Cooperation
BJP	Bharatiya Janta Party
BRI	Belt and Road Initiative
BRICS	Brazil Russia Indian China South Africa
CAA	Citizenship Amendment Act
CAB	Citizenship Amendment Bill
CBD	Central Business District
CEO	Chief Executive Officer
CEOrt	Chief Executive Officers' Round Table (of Tanzania)
CHNU	Centre Hospitalier National Universitaire
CII	Confederation of Indian Industry

CME	Continuing Medical Education
CNN	Cable News Network
Covid	Coronavirus disease
CT	Computed Tomography
CTI	Confederation of Tanzania Industries
DARPG	Department of Administrative Reforms and Public Grievances
EAC	East African Community
ECAS	European Conference on African Studies
EdCIL	Educational Consultants India Limited
EoI	Embassy of India
EPQI	Expanded Partnership for Quality Infrastructure
ER	External Relations
EXIM	Export-Import (Bank)
FCDO	Foreign, Commonwealth and Development Office
FDI	Foreign Direct Investment
FICCI	Federation of Indian Chambers of Commerce and Industry
FOCAC	Forum on China Africa Cooperation
FOIP	Free and Open Indo-Pacific
FRELIMO	Frente de Libertação de Moçambique
G-20	Group of 20
Gavi	Global Alliance for Vaccines and Immunisations
GCPs	Good Clinical Practices
GMPs	Good Manufacturing Practices
GoI	Government of India
HCI	High Commission of India
HCQ	Hydroxychloroquine
HIPC	Heavily Indebted Poor Countries
HIV	Human Immunodeficiency Virus
HM	Hindu Mahasabha
HRD	Human Resource Development
HSS	Hindu Swayamsevak Sangh
IACCI	Indo-African Chamber of Commerce and Industry
IAFS	India-Africa Forum Summit

IBF	Indian Business Forum
IBSA	India Brazil South Africa
ICC	Indian Cultural Centre
ICCR	Indian Council for Cultural Relations
ICT	Information and Communications Technology
ICWA	Indian Council for World Affairs
IDI	India Development Initiative
IDY	International Day of Yoga
IIC	India International Centre
IIT	Indian Institute of Technology
INR	Indian Rupee
INS	Indian Navy Ship
IOC	Indian Overseas Congress
IORA	Indian Ocean Rim Association
IOR – ARC	Indian Ocean Rim – Association for Regional Cooperation
IPR	Intellectual Property Rights
ISA	International Solar Alliance
ISM	Indian Systems of Medicine
ISRO	Indian Space Research Organisation
IT	Information Technology
ITEC	Indian Technical and Economic Cooperation
IUKDPF	India–UK Development Partnership Forum
IUSSTF	India United States Science and Technology Forum
JBCA	Japan Business Council for Africa
JETRO	Japan External Trade Organisation
JNU	Jawaharlal Nehru University
KACE	Kofi Annan Centre of Excellence
LIMP	Liberalisation, Marketisation, and Privatisation
LoCs	Lines of Credit
LDCs	Least Developed Countries
MCI	Ministry of Commerce and Industry
MDCs	More Developed Countries
MEA	Ministry of External Affairs
MHRD	Ministry of Human Resource Development

MoC	Ministry of Commerce
MoE	Ministry of Education
MoF	Ministry of Finance
MOFA	Ministry of Foreign Affairs
MP- IDSA	Manohar Parrikar Institute of Defence Studies and Analyses
MPLA	Movimento Popular de Libertação de Angola
MSDE	Ministry of Skill Development and Entrepreneurship
MSI	Medium and Small Industry
MSR	Maritime Silk Road
NAI	National Archives of India
NAM	Non-Aligned Movement
NBCL	Nyanza Bottling Company Limited
n.d.	No Date
NDB	New Development Bank
NDTV	New Delhi Television (Limited)
NGO	Non-Governmental Organisation
NIC	National Informatics Centre
NIIT	National Institute for Information Technology
NRI	Non-Resident Indian
NSIC	National Small Industry Cooperation
OCI	Overseas Citizenship of India
OECD	Organisation for Economic Cooperation and Development
OF-BJP	Overseas Friends of the Bharatiya Janta Party
ONGC	Oil and Natural Gas Corporation
ORF	Observer Research Foundation
PAN	Pan-African e-Network
P-2-P	People to People
PE	Patient End
PIB	Press Information Bureau
PIO(s)	Person(s) of Indian Origin
PM	Prime Minister
PPP	Public Private Partnership
PTI	Press Trust of India

RASCOM	Regional African Satellite Communication Organisation
RIS	Research and Information Systems (for Developing Countries)
RSS	Rashtriya Swayamsevak Sangh
Rw.fr.	Rwandan franc
SAARC	South Asian Association for Regional Cooperation
SAGAR	Security and Growth for All in the Region
SCAAP	Special Commonwealth Assistance for Africa Programme
SCRI	Supply Chain Resilience Initiative
SDGs	Sustainable Development Goals
SIDS	Small Island Developing States
SII	Serum Institute of India
SME	Small and Medium Enterprise
SWAPO	South West Africa People's Organisation
SWAYAM	Study Webs of Active Learning for Young Aspiring Minds
TB	Tuberculosis
TCA	Tanzania Cotton Association
TCIL	Telecommunications India Limited
TICAD	Tokyo International Conference on African Development
TRIPS	Trade Related Aspects of Intellectual Property Rights
UAE	United Arab Emirates
UIS	UNESCO Institute of Statistics
UK	United Kingdom
UN	United Nations
UNDP	United Nations Development Programme
UNESCO	United Nations Educational, Scientific and Cultural Organisation
UNGA	United Nations General Assembly
UNSC	United Nations Security Council
USA	United States of America
USD	United States Dollar
VBAB	Vidya Bharati Arogya Bharati

VHP	Vishva Hindu Parishad
VIBHA	Vijnana Bharati
VSO	Voluntary Service Overseas
VTC	Vocational Training Centre
WEF	World Economic Forum
WHO	World Health Organisation
WTO	World Trade Organisation
YIC	Yoga Instruction Course

Glossary

Aayushman (Sanskrit/Hindi)	Longevity
Ahimsa (Sanskrit)	Non-violence
Akhand Bharat (Sanskrit/Hindi)	Literally, 'Entire India'; the undivided Indian subcontinent
Ashtanga Hridaya (Sanskrit)	The essence of eight branches of Ayurveda, a well-known Ayurvedic text
Arogya (Sanskrit)	Free of disease, healthy
Arogya Bharati (Sanskrit)	Indian (global) health (programme)
Aryan (Sanskrit)	From *arya*, meaning pure, referring to ethno-linguistic groups in northern India, and their ancestors
Auqaat (Hindi)	Agency, audacity
Ayurveda (Sanskrit)	Ancient Hindu system of medicine
Baila (Kiswahili)	Dance
Bajrang Dal (Hindi)	Bajrang referring to the mythical Hindu deity Hanumaan; a grassroots right-wing political organisation
Bhaiya (Hindi)	Brother
Bharat (Hindi)	India
Bharati (Sanskrit/Hindi)	Of India, Indian
Bharatiya Janta Party (Hindi)	Indian Peoples' Party
Biryani (Hindi/Swahili)	Rice preparation cooked with meat and vegetables
Brahmin (Sanskrit)	The highest Hindu caste, the hereditary priests
Chakravartin (Sanskrit)	Conqueror of the world
Chapatti (Hindi/Swahili)	Pan fried bread
Charkha (Hindi)	Spinning wheel
Dalit (Hindi)	Oppressed, from *dalaan* meaning broken; people outside the Hindu caste system, the 'untouchables'
Dandi Kutir (Hindi)	Salt Mount museum, commemorating Gandhi's Salt March

Didi (Hindi)	Sister
Dravidian (Sanskrit)	Ethno-linguistic groups in southern India
Duka (n) (Hindi/Kiswahili)	Shop
Fundi (Kiswahili)	Craftsman, pl. *mafundi*
Gurus (Sanskrit/Hindi)	Holy men, religious leaders
Hapshi	Generic term for any African in India, derived from Habesha (Ethiopia)
Hindustan (Hindi)	India
Hindutva (Sanskrit)	Hinduness
Jati (Hindi)	Subcaste, traditionally based on occupation
Jua Kali (Kiswahili)	Informal sector
Karmabhoomi (Sanskrit)	Land where one works, where one is transformed
Karma yoga (Sanskrit)	Selfless service
Mahabharata (Sanskrit)	A Hindu epic
Mahatma mandir (Hindi)	Temple of the Mahatma
Maitrimilani (Sanskrit)	Collective value system
Mandala (Sanskrit)	Circle, referring to formations of centralised states in ancient Indian political theory
Maskini (Kiswahili)	Poor
Mausam (Hindi)	Weather, weather system, from which monsoon is derived
Mhindi (Kiswahili)	Indian; pl. *wahindi*
Muasia (Kiswahili)	Asian; pl. *waasia*
Mwafrika (Kiswahili)	African
Namaste (Hindi)	Indian greeting
Om (Sanskrit)	Syllable referring to the soul, ultimate reality, universe, cosmology
Panchamrit (Sanskrit)	Five sacred foods
Panchsheel (Sanskrit)	Five Pillars
Parivar (Hindi)	Family
Pilau (Hindi/Kiswahili)	Rice preparation
Rajmandala (Sanskrit)	Literally chief state, a reference to India in ancient Indian political theory
Rashtra (Sanskrit/Hindi)	Nation

Rashtriya Swayamsevak Sangh (Hindi)	National Volunteer Organisation, a right-wing Hindu organisation
Saans (Hindi)	Breath
Sabjyata (Sanskrit)	Civilisational linkages
Sammaan (Sanskrit)	Honour/dignity
Samriddhi (Sanskrit)	Shared prosperity
Samvaad (Sanskrit)	Dialogue, engagement
Sangh (Hindi)	Organisation
Sangh Parivar (Hindi)	Family of organisations
Sanskriti (Sanskrit)	Culture
Sarva-bhauma (Sanskrit)	Literally, 'whole world', universal state of being in ancient Indian political theory
Sarva Dharma Sambhava (Sanskrit)	All Faiths are equal
Sattvic (Sanskrit/Hindi)	Balanced
Satyagraha (Sanskrit)	Holding onto truth, a form of non-violent protest associated with Gandhi
Siddha	Traditional medicine originating in Tamil Nadu in South India
Siddi	Descendants of Africans who came to India before the twentieth century
Slok Sangraha (Sanskrit)	Collection of verses
Sowa-Rigpa (Tibetan-Ladakhi)	System of medicine
Suraksha (Sanskrit/Hindi)	Security
Surya Namaskar (Sanskrit)	A Yoga posture which involves praying to the Sun
Swachh Bharat Abhiyaan (Sanskrit/Hindi)	Clean India Programme
Swachh Bharat Diwas (Sanskrit/Hindi)	Clean India Day
Ujamaa (Kiswahili)	Socialist system of villages developed in post-independence Tanzania
Unani (Hindi/Urdu)	System of medicine practised in India, thought to be derived from Persia and Central Asia
Urafiki Utsav (Kiswahili)	Friendship Festival

Vaccine Maitri (Hindi)	Vaccine Friendship
Varna (Sanskrit)	Literally colour/appearance, the four major castes
Vasudaiva Kutumbakam (Sanskrit)	The world is a family
Vibarua (Kiswahili)	Casual labourers
Videsh (Hindi)	Overseas
Vidya (Sanskrit)	Knowledge
Vidya Bharati (Sanskrit)	Indian (global) education (programme)
Vijnana Bharati (Sanskrit)	Scientific Indian (organisation)
Vishva Guru (Sanskrit)	Teacher of the world
Vishvabandhuta (Sanskrit)	World brotherhood
Vishva Hindu Parishad (Hindi)	Global Hindu Family, a political party

Introduction

India–Africa Now:
Changing Imaginaries and Knowledge Paradigms

MEERA VENKATACHALAM AND KENNETH KING

India–Africa relations and decolonisation

India's foreign policy was crafted in the build-up to, and years after, independence in 1947. As India fashioned itself as a burgeoning democracy, mindful of its ethnic, linguistic and religious plurality, it also sought to develop a distinctive position on the global stage. India's first Prime Minister, Jawaharlal Nehru (in office 1947–64), was highly critical of the post-Second World War order, which was defined by the retreat of imperialism, emergence of the liberal capitalist system and the Cold War. The intellectual foundations of Nehru's normative agenda, which sought to govern India's international relations, drew from a variety of sources: British and international socialist ideas, Indian concepts derived from Buddhist ideas and Mahatma Gandhi's philosophy of 'passive resistance' (Hall 2017: 116). India's foreign policy was based on respect for sovereignty and non-violence (Chacko 2013; Hall 2017: 116). Firstly, India vehemently supported decolonisation and independence in the Global South, and remained highly critical of Euro-American neo-imperialism and the economic and political marginalisation of formerly colonised peoples. India's opposition to apartheid and white minority regimes in Africa continued after Nehru's premiership. Secondly, Nehru helped to create a Non-Aligned Movement (NAM) to address Cold War politics, to bridge the divide between the Eastern and Western blocs and to press for universal nuclear disarmament. Ideas of peaceful co-existence on the international stage were enshrined in the 'Panchsheel' (translation: five pillars) agreement made with China in April 1954, and also addressed within the NAM, which brought together many African and Asian nations, most of them recently decolonised.

Indian Prime Ministers after Nehru understood their relations with Africa through the framework of southern solidarity, where multi-ethnic, polyglot countries of the Global South, emerging from colonialism, could cooperate through sharing of developmental experiences and move away from the unequal relationships between countries of the developed North and developing South.[1] Nehru shared close personal friendships with leaders of newly independent African states, such as Kwame Nkrumah of Ghana, Jomo Kenyatta of Kenya and Julius Nyerere of Tanzania. Looked at more closely, though, Indian relations with Africa have consistently interlaced altruism with self-interest. Beginning with Nehru, Indian Prime Ministers have continued to see relations with Africa as crucial to leveraging Indian ambitions in multilateral arenas, most notably India's quest for a permanent seat at the United Nations Security Council (UNSC). India has historically also sought influence in Africa to counter China's economic ambitions in the Indian Ocean region, and more recently after the 2000s to secure raw materials and markets for its economic growth. India's flagship Indian Technical and Economic Cooperation (ITEC) programme, inaugurated in 1964, aimed to share Indian developmental and technical expertise across the Global South: with countries of South Asia, Africa, Eastern Europe, Latin America, the Caribbean and Southeast Asia. Though India had been providing aid in the form of scholarships since 1949 (MEA 2014), it hoped to repair some of the damage it had suffered on the global stage in the aftermath of the border war with China in 1962 through ITEC (Shrivastava 2009: 124–25). ITEC declared itself to be a demand-driven and response-oriented programme, based on the ethos of unconditionality and non-interference in the sovereignty of other nations.

India–Africa relations under Indira Gandhi (1967–77 and 1980–84) continued to develop African solidarity with India. Mrs. Gandhi accorded diplomatic recognition and provided financial and material aid to African liberation movements, like the African National Congress (ANC) of South Africa; the Movimento Popular de Libertação de Angola (People's Movement for the Liberation of Angola, MPLA) of Angola; Frente de Libertação de Moçambique (Mozambique Liberation Front, Frelimo) of Mozambique; and South West Africa People's Organisation (SWAPO) of Namibia (Desai 2009: 416). Under Mrs. Gandhi, attempts were made to engage the Indian diaspora, whom she considered key agents of Indian soft power in Africa. During Rajiv Gandhi's premiership (1984–89), the NAM established the

[1]   The idea of South–South cooperation is widely used retrospectively in the context of Nehruvian and post-Nehruvian Indian foreign policy. However, as a term, it comes into usage only in the late 1970s, and the UN begins to acknowledge it in 1978 (UN n.d.). Only after the 1990s has it gained broader currency in policy circles (Davis 2018).

'Africa Fund' (Action for Resisting Invasion, Colonialism and Apartheid) in 1986 to assist liberation movements in southern Africa. According to one estimate, India donated INR 36 million (USD 4.3 million)[2] by 1977–78 to these liberation movements, while India's initial contribution to the Africa Fund in 1986 was INR 500 million (USD 40.4 million),[3] which included private and individual contributions of INR 25 million (USD 2 million).[4] The Fund made a contribution to ending the invasion of Mozambique, ending colonialism in Namibia and in dismantling apartheid in South Africa (Desai 2009: 417).

Post-Liberalisation India and Africa

India–Africa relations were reinvigorated in the 1990s, after India's experiments with economic liberalisation, which saw the Indian economy grow substantially. In addition to the Government of India (GoI)'s efforts, a number of organisations which initiated private sector exchanges with African stakeholders came into existence. The Indo-African Chamber of Commerce and Industry (IACCI) was established in 1985 as a forum for Indian entrepreneurs with operations in Africa, to facilitate trade and investments in a number of sectors from hospitality to manufacturing and tourism (IACCI n.d.). In 2005, the CII-EXIM conclave on Africa was established jointly by the Confederation of Indian Industry (CII) and the Export Import Bank (EXIM) of India, in collaboration with the Ministry of External Affairs (MEA) (CII-EXIM 2020). The conclave organises trade fairs and exhibitions; networks African and Indian businessmen and government officials; facilitates B-2-B (business-to-business) exchanges, and project opportunities under a public–private partnership model.

The most significant platform to engage African states is the India-Africa Forum Summit (IAFS), organised by the MEA and GoI. The first IAFS, held in New Delhi in 2008, brought together several high-level African delegations and heads of state. Two subsequent summits were held in Addis Ababa (2011) and New Delhi (2015) respectively. IAFS-III saw forty-one African heads of state come to India (MEA 2015). A fourth summit had been scheduled for 2020, but has been postponed on account of the Coronavirus (Covid-19) pandemic. These meetings explored areas of mutual collaboration and engagement. The key areas of common interest were agriculture and food

[2] Historic rates reflected (USD 1 = INR 8.19 in 1978) (Currency Kart 2020)
[3] Historic rates reflected (USD 1 = INR 12.37 in 1985) (Currency Kart 2020).
[4] Historic rates reflected (USD 1 = INR 12.37 in 1985) (Currency Kart 2020).

security, health, education, information technology, climate change and the blue economy (Venkatachalam and Modi 2019). India also sought to boost trade, consolidate its search for raw materials and markets in Africa, and bolster its diplomatic influence vis-à-vis other emerging powers. In 2014, IACCI estimated that India was the ninth largest source of foreign direct investment (FDI) in Africa, largely concentrated in the service and manufacturing sectors. Of the total 187 active concessional lines of credit (LoCs) valued at USD 10.21 billion provided by the EXIM of India in 2014, 133 LoCs, amounting to USD 6.28 billion, were earmarked for Africa (IACCI n.d.). In 2017–18, India's bilateral trade with Africa was valued at USD 63 billion, up from USD 7.2 billion in 2001 (Venkatachalam and Modi 2019).

Prime Minister Narendra Modi's premiership (2014–ongoing) has seen an energetic Africa outreach. Since 2015, India's President, Vice President, and Prime Minister have made twenty-three official visits to Africa (Rej 2019). In 2018, President Ram Nath Kovind was conferred the Condecoracion, the highest honour accorded to a non-citizen by President Teodoro Obiang, during a visit to Equatorial Guinea, in recognition of India's efforts to boost bilateral trade, investments and development cooperation (PIB 2018c). Modi's three-nation tour (to Rwanda, Uganda and South Africa) in July 2018 coincided with the Brazil-Russia-India-China-South Africa (BRICS) summit in Johannesburg. He also addressed the Ugandan parliament – a first for any Indian Prime Minister – where he unveiled the 'Ten Guiding Principles' for India's engagement with Africa (PIB 2018a). He declared that Africa would be at the top of India's priorities, and pledged to enhance development cooperation in a number of sectors, from agriculture, to security and educational capacity building (PIB 2018a). Following Prime Minister Modi's three-nation visit to Africa, India signed numerous bilateral agreements for a renewed engagement on the continent (Viswanathan 2018). In 2018, it also announced eighteen new embassies and consulates in Africa, bringing the total up from twenty-nine to forty-seven (PIB 2018a; Roy Chaudhury 2019).

While Modi's colourful diplomacy seems a departure from previous Indian leaders, there are, in fact, some continuities in terms of policies with the pre-Modi era (Hall 2015; Basrur 2017; Gupta et al. 2018). India's engagement with Africa continues to involve peacekeeping, scholarships and training awards, humanitarian relief and private and public sector investments. While Modi's rhetoric vis-à-vis Africa continues to make references to South–South cooperation, many argue that India's African outreach has evolved into a more pragmatic exercise (Harris and Vittorini 2018). Some clear differences are immediately visible. First, the Modi-led government has increased total Indian foreign aid commitments from INR 70.96 billion

(USD 931 million) under the previous government in 2013–14 to INR 76.6 billion (USD 1 billion) budgeted for 2017–18. These totals do not reflect the EXIM Bank's LoCs, which India considers to be a key component of its foreign assistance (Mullen 2018: 20). Second, Indian foreign aid under Modi has become more mercantilist. There has been a greater focus on economic diplomacy, and the deployment of new models of development assistance which include public–private partnerships, that are more commercial in form. Third, decision-making on foreign aid has become centralised in the Office of the Prime Minister, including a decision to channel less aid through the MEA and more through the Ministry of Finance (MoF) (Mullen 2018: 19). Fourth, the disbursement of aid continues to take into consideration India's regional and global power ambitions in a multipolar world. In 2020, the top recipients of Indian aid were Bhutan (INR 28.02 billion/ USD 372 million),[5] Mauritius (INR 11 billion/ USD 146 million), Nepal (INR 10.5 billion/ USD 139 million), Maldives (INR 5.76 billion/ USD 76 million) and African countries excluding Mauritius (INR 4.5 billion/ USD 59.8 million) (Statista 2020). Indian development assistance under Modi also continues to expand partnerships with countries that have shared diverging historical trajectories and circumstances from India, from the Pacific island states to Francophone Africa, in exchange for diplomatic support at multilateral arenas (Mullen 2018: 21).

India's soft power in Africa

Indian state and non-state actors have used a number of carefully constructed narratives about Indian values, and select cultural resources, to leverage their soft power and influence in Africa and elsewhere. Indian actors frequently advertise values and institutions emblematic of political pluralism, a history of secular co-existence and religious diversity, to emphasise the country's uniqueness (Blarel 2012: 29). Indian politicians have also often promoted an image of the Indian diaspora in Africa as highly successful, conscientious citizens of their adopted homes, in a bid to extend their diplomatic influence and garner goodwill (Xavier 2014; Modi and Taylor 2017). Cultural resources have included Ayurveda (traditional medicine), Bollywood (the Indian film industry), cuisine, fashion, music and dance, meditation and yoga. The Indian Council for Cultural Relations (ICCR), founded in 1950, states as its objectives 'to actively participate in the formulation and implementation of policies and programmes pertaining to India's external cultural relations'

[5]   USD 1= INR 75. 17 in June 2020

(ICCR n.d.). The ICCR funds thirty-seven cultural centres abroad, five of which are located in four African countries, namely Egypt, Mauritius, Tanzania and South Africa (ICCR n.d.).

India's soft power in Africa has also traditionally focused on capacity building, transfer of skills and educational aid (King 2019). As early as 1949, India announced seventy scholarships for students from other developing countries for pursuing studies in India (MEA 2014). Under the ITEC and its sister programmes, the SCAAP (Special Commonwealth Assistance for Africa Programme) and the Technical Cooperation Scheme of the Colombo Plan, more than 160 countries are invited 'to share India's developmental experience acquired over six decades of her existence as a free nation' (MEA 2014). From 2014 to February 2020, 50,813 training slots were offered under the ITEC programme and 13, 838 scholarships were disbursed by the ICCR – these figures include all geographies covered by the scheme, including Africa (MEA 2020). ITEC schemes are run through forty-seven training institutions in India which offer more than 280 training courses in diverse subjects ranging from IT, public administration to election management, entrepreneurship, rural development, parliamentary affairs and renewable energy. Similarly, training programmes on security and strategic studies, defence management, marine and aeronautical engineering, logistics and management, marine hydrography and counter insurgency are also organised for defence personnel. Consequent with the increase in number of participants, the budgetary allocation for ITEC has grown from a modest INR 446,000 (USD 93,700)[6] in 1964–65 to INR 10 million (USD 1.3 million)[7] in 1971–72, and over INR 2 billion (USD 32 million)[8] in 2013–14. In recent years, special courses have expanded to new areas such as election management, government performance management, mid-career training of civil servants, parliamentary studies, urban infrastructure management, fragrance and flavour studies and World Trade Organisation (WTO)–related topics (MEA 2014). The ICCR has established a number of chairs of Indian Studies in overseas institutions (ICCR n.d.), and since 2008, has funded nine hundred scholarships to African students annually (Venkatachalam and Modi 2019). In 2015, at IAFS-III, Prime Minister Modi announced 50,000 scholarships for Africans to study in India over five years (MEA 2015). From 2015 to February 2020, 4,048 IAFS scholarships and training slots have been

---

[6] Historic rates reflected (USD 1 = INR 4.76 in 1964) (Currency Kart 2020)

[7] Historic rates reflected (USD 1 = INR 7.59 in 1972) (Currency Kart 2020)

[8] Historic rates reflected (USD 1 = INR 62.33 in 2014) (Currency Kart 2020)

offered (MEA 2020). The 'Study in India' scheme, launched in 2018, aims to make India a major educational hub by upgrading the country's educational infrastructure; the scheme incorporates public and private universities (PIB 2018b; King, this volume).

Indian capacity building exercises have recently also sought to incorporate the expertise of Indian private sector players, re-affirming as a public–private partnership the flagship Pan-African e-Network; this is now relaunched as India's Global Education (e-VidyaBharati) and Health (e-ArogyaBharati). India has also sought to expand its footprint and collaborate with other countries, such as Japan, through schemes like the Asia-Africa Growth Corridor (AAGC) conceptualised in 2016, to enhance capacity and skills and people-to-people partnership as two of four key pillars, though the venture is yet to become operational (Guha Sarkar and Panda, this volume).

India in Africa: situating scholarly trends and paradigms

There is an abundance of literature on Indian actors in Africa, which captures the modalities of diplomatic engagement and the historical and contemporary trajectories of flows of capital and peoples between the two geographies. This literature focuses on a number of different Indian actors: the Indian diaspora, Indian diplomatic actors, Indian cultural organisations and the Indian private sector. This body of literature engages with five distinct themes.

The first is the manner in which geopolitical and geostrategic concerns govern the India– Africa relationship. This literature has explained India's footprint in Africa against the need for accessing energy and natural resources, securing a seat at the UNSC, promoting Indian businesses and addressing security concerns. The roots of Indian foreign policy – dating back to Prime Minister Nehru's support for multilateralism – have largely guided postcolonial India's quest for influence in Africa (Dubey and Biswas 2016). Scholars have also discussed the evolution of Indian interests in Africa following its conflict with China in 1962 and the growth in India–Africa trade and diplomatic relations in the post-Cold War period (Taylor 2012; Dubey and Biswas 2016). After the Indian economy opened up in the 1990s, India's re-engagement with Africa has been analysed against the backdrop of how a reconfigured sense of southern solidarity has emerged, built on 1) the historic experience of colonial exploitation and a sense of vulnerability to the neoliberal global economic order (Harshé 2019); and 2) an articulation of the principles of mutual respect, solidarity, non-interference and mutually beneficial opportunities (Cheru and Obi 2010; Mawdsley 2011; Taylor 2016).

A second theme is the nature of India's development cooperation in Africa and how India constructs itself as an 'ideal partner' for Africa, by emphasising its positionality as an emerging power, focusing on cost-effective innovation and technology and positioning itself as a leading 'subaltern' nation. This literature has focused on the successes of India's Green Revolution, and highlights its ability to develop Triple A (affordable, available, adaptable) technologies, contrasting these to unsuitable models emanating from the Global North (Cheru and Obi 2010; Modi 2017; Modi and Venkatachalam 2021). The development of India's information and communications technology (ICT), healthcare and pharmaceutical sectors, and what they can bring to Africa, have also been studied (Duclos 2012; Ngangom and Aneja 2016). The main modalities of India's development cooperation with Africa include: technical assistance for capacity building through the extension of concessional lines of credit (LoCs) (Dubey and Biswas 2016; Chakrabarty 2018); foreign direct investment and trade aimed at securing access to natural resources and providing export subsidies for surplus Indian goods (Alden and Verma 2016); and diplomacy through arenas such as the three IAFSs aimed at improving the country's standing in Africa (Taylor 2016; Modi 2017).

A third theme compares India's investments and interests in Africa to several emerging actors such as China, Turkey, South Korea and Indonesia (Cheru and Obi 2010; Gieg 2016; Taylor 2016; Van der Merwe and Taylor 2016; Verma 2017; Harshé 2019; Mthembu 2019; Van der Merwe and Bond 2019). India's investments and diplomacy in Africa are analysed within the context of a broader search for influence in bodies such as BRICS. The conclusions reached by some of these authors is that emerging powers – including India – have become agents for continued uneven development despite their vocal stance against neo-colonisation; and that African elites have merely adapted to, and developed several coping mechanisms, for dealing with emerging powers such as India (Mawdsley 2019).

A fourth strand of historical work addresses how India has promoted its soft power since the 1960s, by showcasing the global popularity of Indian cinema ('Bollywood'), yoga, religious diplomacy (mainly as the birthplace of Buddhism) and the increase of its overseas humanitarian and educational assistance (Blarel 2012; Mullen and Ganguly 2012; Mazumdar 2018). This literature has not specifically focused on the modalities of education and skilling, the purported cornerstones of India's soft power in Africa (King 2019). The ecosystems in which these transfers occur, the organisations which are at the forefront of providing knowledge to African stakeholders, the actual processes of skills transfer, the learnings of individuals involved and the outcomes are not researched or reported – a gap that this volume aims to address.

Fifth, the Indian quest for influence in Africa has also been analysed against the backdrop of historical trade, migration and ideological linkages which have connected Indian Ocean societies for millennia, suggesting a historical continuity with current flows of ideas, capital and peoples (Hawley 2008; Mawdsley and McCann 2011; Venkatachalam et al. 2020). This literature shows how India imagines its relations with Africa, through the lens of the economic and political contributions of the Indian diaspora, and its role in African decolonisation and Indo-African diplomatic collaborations in the postcolonial period (Mawdsley 2011; Taylor 2012; Oonk 2013; Bertz 2015; Dubey and Biswas 2016). A smaller, related body of work has dealt with trajectories of African migrations to India, past and present, and the social matrices into which Africans are received (Basu 2001; Bhatt 2018; Gill 2019).

India in Africa: continuities and discontinuities

This book aims to interrogate how India visualises and deploys its soft power through educational, cultural and skills transfer initiatives to African actors. The volume aims to examine the intricate relationship between India's reimagining of itself as a major power, and its relationship with Africa amid the changing geopolitical and socio-cultural landscape in India. An emergent global multipolar world reordering, which included the end of the Cold War in 1991, the beginnings of the 'War on Terror' in 2001 and the rise of China, led to Indian political elites rethinking their place, amid newly realised economic and security concerns. Over the past three decades, key politico-cultural and economic shifts in India have given rise to a new sense of exceptionalism amongst Indian actors, based on the belief that India's potential contribution to humanity's progress on the world stage could be significant, given the country's own economic and developmental trajectory. India's notion of itself as a major power has developed on account of its own – somewhat controversial – experiments with economic liberalisation in 1991. The economy achieved growth rates of 7.5 per cent between 1994 and 1997. In 2015–16, India was the fastest growing major economy in the world, boasting a 7.5 per cent growth rate, to China's 6.5 per cent (Aiyar 2016). India's growth trajectory was largely a story of the successes of the private sector and a failing public sector. India remains in the bottom half of countries measured by indicators of economic freedom, and social indicators of education, health and nutrition have improved extremely slowly (Aiyar 2016). In 2019, the annual Human Development Index report, which measures improvements to the basic quality of life, ranked India at the 129th position out of 189 countries, one rank above its 2018 ranking (UNDP 2019). India's Gini coefficient, which measures wealth disparities within the population, rose from 32.7 in 1993, to 37.8 in 2011, suggesting that the reforms have failed to tackle inequity (World Bank 2011).

The internal socio-political landscape in India also gradually changed after the 1990s, as the country moved slowly but surely towards the political right (Anderson 2018). The rise of the Hindu religious right was a complex socio-political process, termed 'saffronisation'[9] by some analysts; it saw a reorientation of societal values, institutions and India's reimagination of its own history. The grassroots socio-cultural work of right-wing socio-political parties played a role in this transition, in addition to growing disillusionment with the centrist, secular Congress Party which dominated Indian politics after independence. Many argue that elements which define Indian conservatism – rigid Hindu (and other) religiosities and identities; worldviews conditioned by locality and caste; and a distrust of 'minorities' – were always present in the Indian consciousness and sat uncomfortably alongside the Nehruvian vision of the plural, secular, socialist-leaning post-independence India (Palshikar 2015; Anderson 2018). Although the saffronisation of the Indian imaginary was underway before the Bharatiya Janta Party (BJP) officially formed the government, globalisation and economic growth in the 1990s rendered these saffronised, majoritarian voices louder. The move to the right also coincided with gradual disinvestment in the public sector and the rolling back of the state, with the state acting as the enabler of the burgeoning private sector. Religious conservatism and economic reform were closely linked, and many argue that globalisation, privatisation and neoliberal reforms made Indians 'more Hindu' (Nanda 2009). As Indians began to understand their success as the result of the 'modern' Hindu mindset and the ingenuity of the burgeoning capitalist class, an intertwined 'state-temple-corporate' complex developed in the politico-cultural landscape (Nanda 2009; Palshikar 2015). Narendra Modi's right-wing BJP, associated with the ideology of 'Hindutva' (translation: Hinduness), has been in government since 2014. The professed aim of the BJP is to make India a 'Hindu Rashtra' (Hindu nation). These internal shifts have influenced how Africa is imagined by key Indian actors, and has reconfigured aspects of the India–Africa relationship; some of these aspects are introduced in this volume.

[9]   A term derived from the saffron robes of Hindu holy men.

We identify five key shifts which have reconfigured features of India's soft power and the conceptual lenses which inform India's engagements with Africa. These demonstrate continuities and discontinuities in the place Africa occupies in the Indian geostrategic worldview, and how India imagines its relationship with Africa, over the past seven decades – from independence to the present.

India and emerging power dynamics in Africa

China's influence in Africa has concerned Indian politicians and diplomats ever since the 1960s (Desai 2009). A quick look at how Africa is reported in the Indian press reveals this sense of competition and insecurity vis-à-vis China. Consider, for example, some recent articles in the Indian and international media by Indian authors. 'India's China challenge' reads an article in *The Diplomat* (Rajagopalan 2018). 'Why China's push for Africa should concern India' reads another on the website of the think tank, Observer Research Foundation (Joshi 2018). 'Africa Outreach: Xi Keeps China Ahead of India', with the subtitle going on to qualify that: 'Afro-phobia and racism at home can jeopardise political and diplomatic relations and scuttle the prospects of economic cooperation' (Ramachandran 2018). 'India risks losing Africa to China' reads an opinion in the *Nikkei Asian Review* (Sharma 2018). 'Africa prefers India's non-interfering development model over China' reads another article (Roy Chaudhury 2017). Common to these Indian perspectives is the argument that China is acting as a 'neo-colonial' power in Africa, hungry for resources to fuel its ambitious development agenda; that China needs Africa as a market for Chinese goods, and to absorb excess Chinese labour. The authoritarian Chinese leadership is portrayed as an impediment to the development of good governance in Africa, and its recent 'debt-trap diplomacy' is heavily criticised. China's Belt and Road Initiative (BRI), begun in 2013, which attempts to connect and respace strategic geographies around the 'Middle Kingdom', by constructing an overland Silk Road Economic Belt to interlink Central Asia and Europe, and a Maritime Silk Route between the South China Sea through the Indian Ocean to East Africa, has also generated concern in India circles; hence India has not officially joined the BRI initiative (Wu et al. 2017).

Indian actors have responded by advancing a narrative that India's democratic institutions and layered bureaucracy – despite their inefficiency at times – are a desirable model for African institutions. Indian political analysts and politicians appear to be concerned by the competition in Africa for influence with established and emerging players, such as the United States and China; they are also quick to argue that Indian development cooperation models are unique, and better suited to African realities, and that India is benevolent and non-exploitative in its approach (Mishra 2019). India has also attempted to respace its neighbourhood and spheres of geostrategic interest, as China is attempting through ventures such as the BRI, especially in the Indian Ocean region, by aligning with coalitions of coastal countries with similar concerns. Initiatives such as Project Mausam, concerned with reviving India's age-old sea routes across the western Indian Ocean and eastern and southern Africa, draw their understanding from India's role as a civilisational power in this region (Ministry of Culture 2014). India's vision of 'Security and Growth for All in the Region' (SAGAR), developed in 2015, aims to counter the Chinese Maritime Silk Road, and develop connectivities and strategic partnerships with Indian Ocean littoral states such as Mauritius and Seychelles (Schöttli 2019). India has actively participated in associations such as the Indian Ocean Rim Association (IORA), also known as the Indian Ocean Rim–Association for Regional Cooperation (IOR–ARC), since its inception in 1997. IORA aims to develop cooperation in the areas of trade, the blue economy, disaster management, tourism and safety, between member states that include several East African and African island nations in the western Indian Ocean, and Indonesia and Australia in the east (IORA n.d.). India's geostrategic imagination has seen the incorporation of the Pacific into the sphere of the Indian Ocean, reconfigured as the 'Indo-Pacific', which enlists Australia and Indonesia and other allies in an attempt to counter China's military and economic influence (Saran 2019).

India's civilisational role in the world

The political imagination of the Hindu right has redefined the role that India seeks to carve for itself on the global stage. This imagination is profoundly influenced by a number of ancient Indian strategic thinkers: Kautilya (c. 371–283 BCE), and Ashoka (c. 304–232 BCE) (Basrur 2017:10; Solomon 2012). Both Kautilyan and Ashokan traditions of statecraft suggest that the ultimate goal of a state is to achieve the condition of 'universal being' (Sanskrit: *sarva-bhauma*, literally 'whole world') through expansion, which could be either militaristic or through a civilising mission which involves the export of cultural, religious and existential wisdom. Picking up on the latter theme, Hindutva ideologues have often argued that India has a responsibility to the world to impart knowledge, Indic values and 'enlightenment', a notion which is contingent on an Indian civilising mission, which will eventually lead to the elevation of India's position in the geopolitical order. These ideas reverberate through Modi's foreign policy. Panchamrit (literally, five sacred foods), which form the cornerstones of India's contemporary foreign policy, unveiled in

2015, includes the concept *sanskriti evam sabhyata* (cultural and civilisational linkages) (Basrur 2017: 11).

The Indian right draws upon some ideas propagated by revivalist Hindu *gurus* (holy men) of the late nineteenth and early twentieth century (Hall 2017: 115). The Indian spiritual leader, Vivekananda, who is credited with introducing Hinduism to Western audiences, often referred to India as a *vishva guru* (translation: teacher of the world) (Hall 2018: 14). He argued that 'modern' Hinduism could best synthesise Western materialism with Eastern spirituality, thereby generating a peaceful world (Hall 2018: 14). Vivekananda's philosophy draws from an Indian rendering of 'universal humanism' (which sought to emphasise the commonality between disparate groups in India) and the idea of a Hindu 'exceptionalism' (which regards Hinduism as a unique philosophy and way of life). This idea of India as *vishva guru* is frequently expressed by Indian actors in the context of Indian educational aid to Africa and elsewhere (PIB 2018b). A renewed interest in new modalities of capacity building and training has ensued, informed by the role Indian elites expect the nation to play. Indeed, India often positions itself as an ancient civilisation where religion and modern science were compatible systems of thought. These notions of India as a technologically advanced power grounded in an ancient culture with a responsibility in a chaotic multipolar, neoliberal economic world order, have replaced notions of Third Worldism and southern solidarity which previously informed Indian cooperation with Africa (Venkatachalam, this volume).

The de-territorialisation of the nation state

The Indian political right conceives of India as a boundless 'civilisational nation', rather than a bounded 'nation state'. The political right advertises Indianness as synonymous to a singular, racialised 'Hindu' identity, based on Sanskritic culture, and equated with origins in the subcontinent. These ideas, which sit uncomfortably with non-Hindu minorities in the country, actually expand the definition of 'Indianness' beyond the geographical confines of the nation state and the Indian subcontinent. They have found expression in India's recent diaspora policy, which has moved towards recognising People of Indian Origin (PIO) outside the subcontinent and drawing them into the framework of an imagined community of Indianness, through the granting of Overseas Citizenship of India (OCI) (Modi and Taylor 2017) – a stark departure from the Nehruvian era when the diaspora was encouraged to assimilate into the matrices of their adopted homes (Harshé 2019).

The idea of the bounded nation state has also been reconfigured by the digital revolution and India's competence in ICT (Duclos 2012). Previously, where capacity building and imparting skills required physical relocation to India, today, digital transfers of knowledge enable contact from Indian medical experts with various African locations. Knowledge transfer from India is accessible from transnational zones, and can be accessed for all those who have the requisite infrastructure and need for it (Duclos 2012). Indian capacity building aims to function in a vision of the world in which knowledge appears to flow freely, transcending national borders.

Race in Indo-African relations

A theme which links some chapters of this volume is an analysis of 'race' in Indo-African relations. The racialisation of Asian (Indian) identities under the laboratory of colonialism – which saw Asians constructed as 'intermediaries' between colonised Africans and European colonisers, and portrayed as more 'civilised' and more 'evolved' on a socio-cultural scale than Africans – has been studied extensively (Oonk 2013; Bertz 2015; Mgumia and Chachage, this volume).

Indian notions of race in the colonial era have developed through understandings of other previously existing categories of identification: primarily caste (hereditary, endogamous kinship formations defined by occupational specialisations) and also colour (with lighter skin equated to higher status). More recently, against the backdrop of the Hindutva political project, race has become synonymous with religion and culture (Venkatachalam, this volume). Generally accepted is the notion that ideas of both caste and race in India were reconfigured during the colonial era, against the backdrop of European racism, colourism and the mechanics of colonial administration. Late Victorian colonial stereotypes, which painted Indians as higher on the evolutionary plane than Africans, were internalised by Indian elites. Convoluted, symbiotic notions of the two concepts emerged in the Indian consciousness, as caste hierarchies were superimposed on European racist imaginaries (see essays in Robb 1997) – upper castes were placed within the framework of European modernity, while lower castes and untouchables were portrayed as backward and primitive. Even Gandhi had not been immune to these ideas, and his writings during his early days in South Africa display such racist biases (Vittorini, this volume).

So entrenched was this casteist notion of race in the Indian worldview that it informed Indian anti-racist diplomacy in Africa and the Commonwealth in the early postcolonial era (Davis and Thakur 2016; Davis and Thakur 2018). Nuanced studies of the rhetoric and performance of Indian diplomacy during the Nehruvian era – which was heavily invested in a sense of southern solidarity between Africans and Indians – reveal that this racial solidarity with Africans did not quite mean racial *equality* for Indian political elites (McCann 2019; McCann, this volume), who were mainly upper-caste.

Throughout the colonial era, Indians and Africans came into contact with each other in a number of geographies, from India, Africa, Europe and North America. A myriad of cultural, religious and political encounters led them to continuously reimagine the notion of race and normative relations between each other (see Shankar 2021). But interestingly, conversations between Indian, African and African-American intellectuals about caste and casteism in India, have played a definitive role in how Black Africans in Africa and the African diaspora have come to view India and contemporary Indo-African relations.

Despite its secular and inclusive underpinnings, the Indian national project was largely the artefact of upper-caste Hindu men, such as Gandhi and his followers. Dalits (meaning 'oppressed'), the 'untouchables' who tradition-ally comprised the lowest rung of the Hindu caste system, remained deeply suspicious of the Gandhi-led movement. They believed that Gandhi and his followers had merely reinforced untouchability through their paternalistic rhetoric rather than challenging the systemic and ritual foundations upon which it was built. B.R. Ambedkar, the charismatic Dalit leader and intellec-tual, had studied in the United States, and often equated the Dalit condition to that of African-Americans in that country. Many Indian intellectuals have presented the Dalit struggle akin to a movement for Civil Rights, arguing that upper-caste hegemony in India was the parallel of Euro-American white supremacy in the United States (Prashad 2000; Das 2014; Sampath 2015; Foster 2020). American sociologists have for long sought to explain the plight of African-Americans in the Deep South in terms of the develop-ment of an indigenous caste system which operated much like its counterpart in India (see Immerwahr 2007). In 2020, these arguments resurfaced with Isabel Wilkerson's *Caste: The Origins of Our Discontents*, which explains Afro-American racialised, marginalised subjectivities in terms of Indian notions of caste – with both characterised by fossilised hereditary identities, a lack of social mobility and inherent barriers to equal citizenship (Wilkerson 2020). The Indian government has consistently dismissed arguments that drew par-allels between caste and race in both national and international arenas (Thakur 2016; Davis and Thakur 2018). For Africans who envision diasporic Africans as extended kin and as essential part of the Africana World,[10] similarities

---

[10] A term used to denote geographies with significant populations who derive their ancestry from Africa.

between the Dalit and African-American condition have cemented the perception that race/racism in the Global North and caste/casteism in India are
manifestations of the same phenomenon – somewhat damaging India's moral
standing and reputation in Africa.

The commercialisation of capacity building

The agents that leveraged the instruments of India's soft power, and its aid
to Africa, were previously either state actors, or explicitly acting on behalf of
the state in the pre-liberalisation era. Previously, capacity building worked
within the parameters of a bilateral framework aimed at strengthening the
'collective self-reliance' of emergent states (Duclos 2012: 17). Indian aid was
not meant to have any commercial or non-governmental dimensions at its
inception. For instance, ITEC was conceptualised on the state-to-state transmission of technology and expertise, and the nation state was invested with
the responsibility of looking after health, development and welfare of peoples.
In the post-liberalisation era after the 2000s, aid has been repackaged into
a commercial model, in which the Indian state presents itself as a facilitator
which performs the role of connecting relevant stakeholders. Where the state
was previously directly involved in the welfare of the users of Indian soft
power, now a number of other agencies – the private sector, individual entrepreneurs and diasporic players – may lay claim to the franchise of Indianness
and operate under the banner of the same. The state merely acts as the enabler
of this cooperation, in the hope that this cooperation will lead to economic
benefit and well-being of the stakeholders involved. The Indian state essentially creates the conditions where all stakeholders have equal agency in any
development cooperation exercise.

About this volume

The nine chapters in this book are the result of fieldwork in India, Ethiopia,
Ghana, Kenya, Rwanda, Senegal and Tanzania. The authors approach their
topics from a number of disciplinary perspectives, from History, Political Science, International Relations, Comparative Education and Sociology.

The first part is concerned with India's contemporary geopolitical imaginary, and how Africa fits into that worldview. India continues to make use
of soft power to emphasise its uniqueness as an emerging power in Africa,
as well as draw other like-minded nations to respace the geographical contours which facilitate flows of knowledge, people and capital between India
and Africa. Shangwe (Chapter 1) details the traditional modalities of Indian
soft power, outlining the opportunities and challenges, focusing on a myriad

of Indian agents: cultural flows, the private sector and the diaspora. He questions the idea of the uniqueness of the modalities of Indian soft power, arguing that India's purported 'third way' is in fact similar to the strategies employed by other established and emerging players on the continent. Guha Sarkar and Panda (Chapter 2) examine the newly proposed 'Platform for Japan-India Business Cooperation in Asia-Africa Region' to replace the earlier co-envisioned AAGC, arguing that it offers a new intercontinental context of cooperation on growth and development, between Asia and Africa. They argue that India's interest in Africa is partially – but strongly – driven by competition with China, and that India and Japan seek to both enhance domestic growth and development, as well as protect their national interests in Africa and Asia ahead of a rising Chinese influence.

The second part focuses on India's renewed relationship with Africa against the backdrop of the rise to political dominance of the right-wing ruling BJP, which since 2014 has governed with a parliamentary majority. As the Indian political right seeks to create a new narrative about India's civilisational destiny in the world, the rhetoric, cognitive frames and engagement with Africa with reference to capacity building are undergoing a disruptive transformation from the Nehruvian era. The idea of Africa and the nature of the Indo-African relationship are gradually changing in the Indian imaginary, as shown by Venkatachalam (Chapter 3), transforming from a relationship based on a shared postcolonial solidarity to a hierarchical one, where India's role is understood as an imparter of knowledge and developmental expertise to Africa. While the symbols deployed by Indian actors to promote soft power remain somewhat constant, the frames which legitimise their deployment have changed, as the political right struggles for symbolic ownership of the past. Indian diplomatic missions and diasporic groups have long commissioned statues of Mahatma Gandhi, to symbolise Indian values and national character, from London to Johannesburg to São Paulo. Vittorini (Chapter 4) examines a controversy that erupted at the University of Ghana in response to a statue of Mahatma Gandhi being unveiled there by Indian President Pranab Mukherjee, in 2016. The chapter illustrates how Gandhi is being reclaimed by the Indian political right and adherents of Hindutva as a symbol of India–Africa relations, and South–South cooperation; it also discusses the limitations of India's Gandhi diplomacy in Africa.

The third part illustrates how some aspects of India's demand-driven development compact works with Africa, in the form of its many modalities of skills transfer. Reports on African perspectives on India's soft power and engagements with the continent are few, a deficiency which is addressed by King (Chapter 5). This chapter discusses publicly and privately funded African students in India, as well as returnees in Africa, private sector partners, India–Africa institutional collaborations and non-governmental organisations, with data drawn from fieldwork in India, Tanzania, Rwanda and Ethiopia. Duclos (Chapter 6) examines how the Pan-African e-Network (PAN) holds together at least three different imaginations of an Indian idealised version of the Global South, through a detailed discussion of the initiative. In Chapter 7, Roychoudhury and Mawdsley provide an overview and typology of India's outreach to Africa in the context of the Covid-19 pandemic, examining the key debates and internal justification in India for providing humanitarian assistance to Africa.

Relations between Indians and Africans have often been analysed against the backdrop of racism, which obfuscates the multidimensionality and enrichment that these cultural encounters often bring with them. The fourth part investigates people-to-people relations between Indians and Africans within the context of knowledge transfers. Mgumia and Chachage (Chapter 8) provide a historical and ethnographic account of knowledge transfer between entrepreneurs of Asian and African origins in Tanzania. In doing so, they question the conventional critique, which posits that the emergence of entrepreneurs of Asian descent has been secretive and exclusive to their racial community, leaving out the majority of Tanzanians who are of African origin. They show how relationships have developed among members of both communities, which has led to the transfer of business know-how, skills and capital. McCann (Chapter 9) writes about the evolution of India's educational outreach to Africa, and the experiences of Africans who came to India in the early years after independence, providing a detailed analysis of the challenges faced by them, thereby deconstructing the notion of South–South cooperation in the early postcolonial Indian imaginary.

Bibliography

Aiyar, S.S.A. 2016. 'Twenty-five years of Indian economic reform', *Cato Institute*, Policy Analysis No. 803, 26 October 2016, https://www.cato.org/publications/policy-analysis/twenty-five-years-indian-economic-reform, accessed 28 May 2020.

Alden, C. and Verma, R. 2016. 'India's pursuit of investment opportunities in Africa', in A. K. Dubey and A. Biswas (eds.), *India's and Africa's Partnership: A Vision for a New Future* (New Delhi: Springer), 61–82.

Anderson, E. 2018. 'Hindu nationalism and the saffronisation of the public sphere: An interview with Christophe Jaffrelot', *Contemporary South Asia*, 26/4, 468–82.

Basrur, R. 2017. 'Modi's foreign policy fundamentals: A trajectory unchanged', *International Affairs*, 93/1, 7–26.

Basu, H. 2001. 'Africans in India: Past and present', *Internationales Asienforum*, 32/3–4, 253–74.

Bertz, N. 2015. *Diaspora and Nation in the Indian Ocean: Transnational Histories of Race and Urban Space in Tanzania* (Honolulu: University of Hawai'i Press).

Bhatt, P.M. 2018. *The African Diaspora in India: Assimilation, Change and Cultural Survivals* (London and New York: Routledge).

Blarel, N. 2012. 'India: the next superpower? India's soft power: from potential to reality?', *LSE IDEAS Reports*, SR010, May 2012, http://eprints.lse.ac.uk/43445/1/India_India%27s%20soft%20power%28lsero%29.pdf, accessed 25 December 2019.

Chacko, P. 2013. *Indian Foreign Policy: The Politics of Postcolonial Identity from 1947–2004* (London and New York: Routledge).

Chakrabarty, M. 2018. 'Indian investments in Africa: Scale, trends, policy recommendations', *ORF Online*, Occasional Paper No. 142, February 2018, https://www.orfonline.org/wp-content/uploads/2018/02/ORF_OccasionalPaper_142_India_Africa.pdf, accessed 15 September 2020.

Cheru, F. and Obi, C. (eds.) 2010. *The Rise of China and India in Africa: Challenges, Opportunities and Critical Interventions* (London: Zed Books).

CII-EXIM. 2020. 'Conclave on India-Africa project partnerships', n.d., https://www.ciieximafricaconclave.com/Aboutconclave.aspx, accessed 25 May 2020.

Currency Kart. 2020. 'USD to INR historical exchange rate', n.d., https://blog.currencykart.com/1-usd-to-inr-from-1900-to-2019-historical-exchange-rate/, accessed 2 June 2020.

Das, P. 2014. '"Is caste race?" Discourses of racial Indianisation', *Journal of Intercultural Communication Research*, 43/3, 264–28.

Davis, A.E., and Thakur, V. 2016. 'Walking the thin line: India's anti-racist diplomatic practice in South Africa, Canada, and Australia, 1946–55', *International History Review*, 38/5, 880–99.

——. 2018. 'An act of faith or a new "Brown Empire"? The dismissal of India's transnational anti-racism, 1945–1961', *Commonwealth and Comparative Politics*, 56/1, 22–39.

Desai, N. 2009. 'India and Africa: A new engagement', *India Quarterly*, 65/4, 413–29.

Dubey, A. K. and Biswas, A. (eds.) 2016. *India and Africa's Partnership: A Vision for a New Future* (New Delhi: Springer).

Duclos, V. 2012. 'Building capacities: The resurgence of Indo-African technoeconomic cooperation', *India Review*, 11/4, 209–25.

Foster, K. 2020. 'Dalit and Black solidarity: Interview with Suraj Yengde', *Harvard International Review*, 10 August 2020, https://hir.harvard.edu/dalit-and-black-solidarity-interview-with-suraj-yengde/, accessed 19 September 2020.

Gieg, P. 2016. 'Same same but different? India–Africa relations and Chinese involvement in the continent', *Insight on Africa*, 8/1, 40–58.

Gill, B. 2019. 'In the shadow of illegality: The everyday life of African migrants in Delhi' (Unpublished Ph.D. dissertation, University of Copenhagen).

Gupta, S., Mullen, R.D., Basrur, R., Hall, I., Blarel, N., Pardesi, M.S., Ganguly, S. 2018. 'Indian foreign policy under Modi: a new brand or just repackaging?', *International Studies Perspectives* (0), 1–45.

Hall, I. 2015. 'Is a "Modi doctrine" emerging in Indian foreign policy?', *Australian Journal of International Affairs*, 69/3, 247–52.

——. 2017. 'Narendra Modi and India's normative power', *International Affairs*, 93/1, 113–31.

——. 2018. 'Narendra Modi's new religious diplomacy', in S. Gupta et al., 'Indian foreign policy under Modi: A new brand or just repackaging?', *International Studies Perspectives* (0), 11–14.

Harris, D. and Vittorini, S. 2018. 'Taking "development cooperation" and South–South discourse seriously: Indian claims and Ghanaian responses', *Commonwealth and Comparative Politics*, 56/3, 360–78.

Harshé, R. 2019. *Africa in World Affairs: Politics of Imperialism, the Cold War and Globalisation* (New Delhi: Routledge).

Hawley, C. 2008. *India in Africa, Africa in India: Indian Ocean Cosmopolitanisms* (Indiana University Press: Bloomington).

IACCI. n.d. 'Make Africa your partner', n.d., https://www.indoafrican.org/, accessed 20 May 2020.

ICCR. n.d. 'About ICCR', *GoI*, n.d., https://www.iccr.gov.in/, accessed 2 June 2020.

Immerwahr, D. 2007. 'Caste or Colony?: Indianising Race in the United States,' *Modern Intellectual History*, 4, 275–301.

IORA. n.d. Indian Ocean Rim Association, n.d., https://www.iora.int/en/about/about-iora, accessed 1 November 2020.

Joshi, M. 2018. 'Why China's push for Africa should concern India', *ORF Online*, 10 September 2018, https://www.orfonline.org/research/43917-why-chinas-push-for-africa-should-concern-india/, accessed 28 May 2020.

King, K. 2019. 'India-Africa cooperation in human resource development: education, training, skills', *MP-IDSA*, Occasional Paper No. 51, April 2019, https://idsa.in/occasionalpapers/ind-africa-cooperation-op-51, accessed 28 May 2020.

Mawdsley, E. 2011. 'The rhetorics and rituals of "South-South" development cooperation: Notes on India and Africa', in E. Mawdsley and G. McCann (eds.), *India in Africa: Changing Geographies of Power* (Cape Town: Pambazuka Press).

——. 2019. 'South–South cooperation 3.0? Managing the consequences of success in the decade ahead', *Oxford Development Studies*, 47/3, 259–74.

Mawdsley, E. and McCann, G. (eds.) 2011. *India in Africa: Changing Geographies of Power* (Cape Town: Pambazuka Press).

Mazumdar, A. 2018. 'India's soft power diplomacy under the Modi administration: Buddhism, diaspora and Yoga', *Asian Affairs*, 49/3, 468–91.

McCann, G. 2019. 'Where was the Afro in Afro-Asian solidarity? Africa's "Bandung moment" in 1950s Asia', *Journal of World History*, 30/1–2, 89–123.

MEA. 2014. 'Fifty years of ITEC', *GoI*, n.d., http://www.mea.gov.in/Uploads/PublicationDocs/24148_REVISED_50_yrs_of_ITEC_brochure.pdf, accessed 10 October 2019.

——. 2015. 'India-Africa Forum Summit-III', *GoI*, October 2015, http://mea.gov.in/india-africa-forum-summit-2015/index.html#, accessed 23 April 2020.

——. 2020. 'Performance smartboard, developmental partnerships, capacity building', *GoI*, n.d., https://meadashboard.gov.in/indicators/90, accessed 3 June 2020.

Ministry of Culture. 2014. 'Project Mausam', *GoI*, n.d., https://www.indiaculture.nic.in/project-mausam, accessed 23 December 2019.

Mishra, A. 2019. 'How Indian and Chinese involvement in Africa differs in intent, methods and outcomes', *ORF Online*, 17 September 2019, https://www.orfonline.org/expert-speak/how-indian-and-chinese-involvement-in-africa-differs-in-intent-methods-and-outcomes-55574/, accessed 20 May 2020.

Modi, R. 2017. 'India-Africa Forum Summits and capacity building: Achievements and challenges', *African and Asian Studies*, 16, 139–66.

Modi, R. and Taylor, I. 2017. 'The Indian diaspora in Africa: The commodification of the Hindu Rashtra', *Globalisations*, 14/6, 911–29.

Modi, R. and Venkatachalam, M. (eds.) 2021. *India-Africa Collaborations for Food Security and Capacity Building: South-South Cooperation* (London: Palgrave Macmillan).

Mthembu, P. 2019. *China and India's Development Cooperation in Africa: The Rise of Southern Powers* (London: Palgrave Macmillan).

Mullen, R.D. 2018. 'Indian developmental assistance: The centralisation and mercantilisation of Indian foreign policy', in S. Gupta et al., 'Indian foreign policy under Modi: A new brand or just repackaging?', *International Studies Perspectives* (0), 19–25.

Mullen, R.D. and Ganguly, S. 2012. 'The rise of India's soft power', *Foreign Policy*, 8 May 2012, https://foreignpolicy.com/2012/05/08/the-rise-of-indias-soft-power/, accessed 22 April 2020.

Nanda, M. 2009. *The God Market: How Globalisation is Making India more Hindu* (Delhi: Random House).

Ngangom, T. and Aneja, U. 2016. 'Health is wealth': Indian private sector investments in African healthcare', *ORF Online*, Issue Brief No. 145, June 2016, https://www.orfonline.org/wp-content/uploads/2016/06/ORF_IssueBrief_145_NgangomAneja_Final.pdf, accessed 15 September 2020.

Oonk, G. 2013. *Asian Business Elites in Africa, 1800–2000* (New Delhi: Sage Publications).

Palshikar, S. 2015. 'The BJP and Hindu nationalism: Centrist politics and majoritarian impulses', *South Asia: Journal of South Asian Studies*, 38/4, 719–35.

PIB. 2018a. 'Prime Minister's address at parliament of Uganda during his state visit to Uganda', *GoI*, 25 July 2018, https://pib.gov.in/PressReleasePage.aspx?PRID=1540025, accessed 23 April 2020.

———. 2018b. 'Study in India programme of HRD Ministry launched with the launch of "Study in India Portal" by Smt. Sushma Swaraj and Dr Satya Pal Singh in New Delhi today', *GoI*, 18 April 2018, https://pib.gov.in/PressReleaseIframePage.aspx?PRID=1529560, accessed 23 December 2019.

———. 2018c. 'President Kovind in Equatorial Guinea', *GoI*, 8 April 2018, https://pib.gov.in/PressReleaseIframePage.aspx?PRID=1528258, 23 April 2020.

Prashad, V. 2000. 'Afro-Dalits of the Earth, unite!', *African Studies Review*, 43/1, Special Issue on the Diaspora, 189–201.

Rajagopalan, R.P. 2018. 'India's China challenge in Africa', *The Diplomat*, 31 July 2018, https://thediplomat.com/2018/07/indias-china-challenge-in-africa/, accessed 28 May 2020.

Ramachandran, S. 2018. 'Xi's outreach keeps China ahead of India', *News Outreach*, 27 July 2018, https://www.newsclick.in/africa-outreach-xi-keeps-china-ahead-india, accessed 28 May 2020.

Rej, A. 2019. 'Narendra Modi's re-election as India's Prime Minister: Implications for Africa', *Africa Portal*, 27 June 2019, https://www.africaportal.org/features/narendra-modis-re-election-indias-prime-minister-implications-africa/, accessed 20 April 2020.

Robb. P. (ed.) 1997. *The Concept of Race in South Asia* (Delhi: Oxford University Press).

Roy Chaudhury, D. 2017. 'Africa prefers India's non-interfering development model over China, *The Economic Times*, 23 September 2017, https://economictimes. indiatimes.com/news/politics-and-nation/africa-prefers-indias-non-interfering-development-model-over-china/articleshow/60800978.cms, accessed 28 May 2020.

——. 2019. 'Budget 2019: India to open eighteen new diplomatic missions across Africa', *The Economic Times*, 5 June 2019, https://economictimes.indiatimes. com/news/politics-and-nation/budget-2019-india-to-open-18-new-diplomatic-missions-across-africa/articleshow/70093835.cms, accessed 20 May 2020.

Sampath, R. 2015. 'Racial and caste oppression have many similarities', *The Conversation*, 19 June 2015, https://theconversation.com/racial-and-caste-oppression-have-many-similarities-37710, accessed 21 September 2020.

Saran, S. 2019. 'Is Indo-Pacific a viable geostrategic project?', *ORF Online*, 25 July 2019, https://www.orfonline.org/expert-speak/is-indo-pacific-a-viable-geostrategic-project-53377/, accessed 28 May 2020.

Schöttli, J. 2019. 'Security and growth for all in the Indian Ocean' – maritime governance and India's foreign policy, *India Review*, 18/5, 568–81.

Shankar, S. 2021. *An Uneasy Embrace: India, Africa and the Spectre of Race* (London: Hurst).

Sharma, R.K. 2018. 'India risks losing Africa to China', *Nikkei Asian Review*, 5 September 2018, https://asia.nikkei.com/Opinion/India-risks-losing-Africa-to-China, accessed 28 May 2020.

Shrivastava, M. 2009. 'India and Africa: From political alliance to economic partnership', *Politikon: South African Journal of Political Studies*, 36/1, 117–43.

Solomon, H. 2012. 'Critical reflections of Indian foreign policy: Between Kautilya and Ashoka', *South African Journal of International Affairs*, 19/1, 65–78.

Statista. 2020. 'Indian foreign aid by recipient country', https://www.statista.com/statistics/1060959/foreign-aid-outflow-india-by-recipient-country/, accessed 25 May 2020.

Taylor, I. 2012. 'India's rise in Africa', *International Affairs*, 88/4, 779–98.

——. 2016. 'India's economic diplomacy in Africa', in A. K. Dubey and A. Biswas (eds.), *India's and Africa's Partnership: A Vision for a New Future* (New Delhi: Springer).

Thakur, V. 2016. 'When India proposed a casteist solution to South Africa's racist problem', *The Wire*, published 4 April 2016, https://thewire.in/diplomacy/exploring-casteism-in-indias-foreign-policy, accessed 19 September 2020.

UN. n.d. 'United Nations Day for South-South Cooperation, 12 September', https://
www.un.org/en/observances/south-south-cooperation-day/background, accessed
11 December 2020.

UNDP. 2019. 'Human Development Report 2019', http://hdr.undp.org/en/
content/2019-human-development-index-ranking, accessed 28 May 2020.

Van der Merwe, J. and Bond, P. 2019. *BRICS and Resistance in Africa: Contention,
Assimilation and Co-optation* (London: Zed Books).

Van der Merwe, J. and Taylor, I. 2016. *Emerging Powers in Africa: A New Wave in the
Relationship?* (London: Palgrave Macmillan).

Venkatachalam, M. and Modi, R. 2019. 'A look at how India's Africa strategy is
working', *The Conversation*, 21 March 2019, https://theconversation.com/a-look-
at-how-indias-africa-strategy-is-working-113658, accessed 20 May 2020.

Venkatachalam, M., Modi, R. and Salazar J. 2020. *Common Threads: Fabrics Made-in-
India for Africa*, ASC series 76 (Leiden: ASC publications).

Verma, R. 2017. *India and China in Africa: A Comparative Perspective on the Oil Industry* (London and New York: Routledge).

Viswanathan, H.H.S. 2018. 'PM Modi's Africa tour decoded: A strong imprint in the
continent', *ORF Online*, 30 July 2018, https://www.orfonline.org/research/42856-
pm-modis-africa-tour-decoded-a-strong-imprint-in-the-continent/, accessed 20
May 2020.

Wilkerson, I. 2020. *Caste: The Origins of Our Discontents* (New York: Penguin Random
House LLC).

World Bank. 2011. 'Gini index, India', https://data.worldbank.org/indicator/SI.POV.
GINI?locations=IN, accessed 28 May 2020.

Wu, Y., Alden, C. and Sidiropoulos, E. 2017. 'Where Africa fits into China's massive
belt and road initiative', *The Conversation*, 28 May 2017, https://theconversation.
com/where-africa-fits-into-chinas-massive-belt-and-road-initiative-78016,
accessed 28 May 2020.

Xavier, C. 2014. 'The institutional origins and determinants of India's Africa policy', in
K. Bajpai et al. (eds.), *India's Grand Strategy: History, Theory, Cases* (London, New
York and New Delhi: Routledge), 479–505.

PART 1

The Geopolitical Imaginary and Soft Power

1

India's Soft Power in East Africa: Opportunities and Challenges

MUHIDIN J. SHANGWE

Introduction

Ever since Joseph Nye introduced the idea of soft power in academia in the early 1990s, it has attracted keen interest especially in the emerging economies. Perhaps aware of their hard power deficit, soft power has been embraced as an important element of foreign policy for countries which are looking to charm the world. India has been no exception. Sitting as the world's fifth largest economy, New Delhi is projecting an image of prosperity especially in the developing world. It is not surprising that the African Development Bank (AfDB) president, Akwinumi Adesina, has described India as a developing beacon for the rest of the world (Bhatia 2017). Indeed, in many parts of Africa, India is regarded as a donor country.

This chapter seeks to understand New Delhi's soft power potential in the East African region at a time when India is engaging Africa with rejuvenated rigour. The East African countries referred to here are those forming the East African Community (EAC): Tanzania, Kenya, Uganda, Rwanda, Burundi and South Sudan. The chapter is framed to respond to key questions about India's soft power in East Africa. First, I examine New Delhi's soft power potential. Second, I interrogate the extent to which soft power and related attributes are shaping the relations between India and the East African countries by focusing on the soft aspects of the relationship. Third, I identify and discuss some of the challenges India is facing in its soft power projection in East Africa.

India's soft power project

Nye defined soft power as the power of attraction, stating that 'a country may obtain the outcomes it wants in world politics because other countries – admiring its values, emulating its example, aspiring to its level of prosperity and openness – want to follow' (Nye 2004: 5). Nye went on to identify a country's culture, political values and foreign policy as the main soft power resources. Unlike hard power, which coerces, soft power attracts. This definition has been contested, mostly due to the tendency by states to combine both soft and hard power mechanisms to pursue their national interest. In this chapter, while we are guided by Nye's definition, we will also consider other forms of hard power that we believe partly inform India's ability to attract in the East African region. They include India's trade, investment and development assistance in the region. We are aware of Nye's conceptualisation of soft power, which does not include economic inducement, but we are also mindful of the application of soft and hard power concurrently. Besides, even Nye himself conceded that soft and hard powers 'sometimes reinforce and sometimes interfere with each other' (Nye 2004: 25).

India's soft power resources

In reference to Jain (2018), we consider that India has taken at least four major steps in its soft power promotion: 1) the creation of a public diplomacy division within the Ministry of External Affairs in 2006; 2) the worldwide expansion of the Indian Council for Cultural Relations (ICCR); 3) the Ministry of Tourism's 'Incredible India' campaign; and (4) the creation of the Ministry of Overseas Indians. The manifestation of India's soft power has partly been associated with what has been termed the Indian model, as a soft power resource. As we shall see, the Indian model itself constitutes some of these resources. Ten years ago, American economist, Larry Summers, came up with the term 'Mumbai Consensus' to describe India's development experience. He described it as a democratic developmental state that is driven by people-centred emphasis on growing levels of consumption and a widening middle class (Summers 2010). On the other hand, Amit Ray has cited rapid expansion of high-end, knowledge-intensive sectors as the basis of the Indian model (Ray 2015; see Duclos, this volume). These sectors include information technology, biotech and business/knowledge process outsourcing. This emphasis on high-end, knowledge-intensive sectors explains why, for instance, India's education and health services have added to its soft power. Compared to advanced economies, India offers affordable education, attracting thousands of students from the developing world (King, this volume). Its advanced medical science industry has resulted in a rapid growth in the country's medical tourism.

The following are soft power resources, some of which make up the Indian model.

Cultural values

Home to 1.3 billion people, India has a rich and diverse culture which is crucial in soft power discourse. Its traditional holistic healing system, particularly yoga, has attracted world interest. The yoga impact is such that in 2014, the Indian government created the Ministry of AYUSH (Ayurveda, Yoga and Naturopathy, Unani, Siddha and Homoeopathy). In the same year, the United Nations set 21 June as the International Day of Yoga. Other aspects of Indian culture have also attracted world attention. These include its cuisine, music and film industry, the last popularly known as Bollywood. Indian culture also includes versions of major world religions, namely Buddhism, Christianity, Hinduism and Islam.

In East Africa, Indian cultural influence is striking, so much so that it is probably unwise to continue labelling it as Indian. This cultural visibility has strengthened the view that the region, compared to others in the continent, is better positioned to lead the Afro-Indian dialogue (Chand 2009). In linguistic aspects, the Kiswahili vocabulary has adopted Indian words such as *pilau* (a type of rice dish), *biryani* (a type of rice dish), *chapatti* (a type of bread), *duka* (shop), to mention only a few. Spoken widely in Tanzania and Kenya as an official language, Kiswahili is also spoken in many other parts of the region, including the eastern part of the Democratic Republic of Congo, and in some parts of Uganda, Rwanda and Burundi.

Moreover, India's film industry, Bollywood, has for years attracted a huge following in East Africa. One needs to look no further than how Shah Rukh Khan, arguably Bollywood's most-prized asset, has influenced Diamond Platnumz, currently East Africa's most-decorated Afrobeat singer. The 30-year-old Tanzanian represents a new generation of urban music popularly known as Bongo Flava in Tanzania. Yet, despite the generational gap, the influence of the 55-year-old Khan on the singer is evident. In 2018, he released a song titled 'Baila' (dance), whose video, according to Diamond himself, was inspired by Khan's song 'Saans' (breath), in a 2012 film titled *Jab Tak Hai Jaan* (As long as I live). Diamond has repeatedly expressed his admiration for Khan, stating that he is his biggest influence (see Oduor 2018).

India's cultural presence in East Africa is particularly conspicuous in Tanzania, Kenya and Uganda, the countries with relatively bigger Indian communities. In Kenya, the first-ever Festival of India in Kenya named Urafiki Utsav (friendship festival) was organised by the Indian High Commission in Kenya in collaboration with the Ministry of Culture of India and the Kenyan Ministry of Sports, Culture and Arts in 2016. As part of the celebration, six cultural troupes from India performed in five Kenyan cities.

Since then, according to the High Commission of India (HCI) in Kenya, the Government of India through its Ministry of Culture has distributed grants to sixteen Kenyan organisations promoting Indian culture (HCI Kenya 2019). In Tanzania, cultural activities such as the International Day of Yoga, and festivals such as Namaste[1] have also been organised. In Uganda, the Indian Association in collaboration with the Indian High Commissioner has organised the annual India Day when Indian culture is celebrated. The Ugandan Indian community was also instrumental in the erecting of a Mahatma Gandhi statue at the source of the River Nile in Jinja, unveiled in 1997. In Tanzania, the Gandhi statue sits next to that of Julius Nyerere, the nation's founding father, in the University of Dar es Salaam's prestigious Council Chamber. The 'Gandhi Must Fall' campaign which gripped countries like South Africa, Ghana and more recently Malawi (Vittorini, this volume) has not registered in East Africa.

Moreover, the expansion of the ICCR has sought to promote higher education exchanges within academia in Africa. It has thirty-five Indian Cultural Centres in different parts of the world. Tanzania is the only East African country to host one such centre. The Council also boasts sixty-nine chairs of Indian Studies in various universities across the world. Tanzania and Kenya are two East African countries with these chairs situated in the University of Dar es Salaam and University of Nairobi respectively. The information available on the ICCR website states that the objective of these chairs is to generate interest in India among students in host countries (ICCR 2019a).

India's Foreign policy

Post-independence relations between India and Africa took place in the context of anti-colonialism and South–South cooperation. Under the premiership of Jawaharlal Nehru, India assumed a leading role in the South's attempt to escape global marginalisation. India's central role in the formation of the Non-Aligned Movement (NAM) in 1961 cannot be overemphasised. At the time, Nehru had forged strong ties with Ghanaian leader Kwame Nkrumah and Egypt's Gamal Abdel Nasser. From a soft power perspective, India's anti-colonial posture and promotion of South–South cooperation were seen as legitimate causes and therefore added to its attractiveness. It matched well with Africa's own liberation agenda. To underscore this point, for instance, India recognised the African National Congress (ANC), South Africa's main

---

[1] *Namaste* is a customary greeting practised in India and Southeast Asian countries. In our case, the Namaste festivals are organised to celebrate Indian culture in general.

anti-apartheid movement, as early as 1967 when the organisation was seen as nothing more than a terrorist movement by many Western governments.

Since the 1990s, both East Africa and India have undergone major changes in the direction of embracing a market economy. As a result, economic interests have probably overshadowed previous relations which were based on ideological fraternity. To stimulate its engagement with Africa, India created the India-Africa Forum Summit (IAFS) in 2008 as its official platform to engage Africa. Moreover, New Delhi is also involved in intensified diplomatic initiatives with Africa. During his address to the Ugandan parliament in July 2018, Prime Minister Narendra Modi revealed plans for his country to open eighteen more embassies in Africa by 2021 (MEA 2018a). Before the announcement, India had just twenty-nine embassies in the continent. Significantly, Modi has already visited seven African countries – Kenya, Uganda, Tanzania, South Africa, Rwanda, Mauritius and Mozambique. This is unprecedented for an Indian Prime Minister.

At a foreign policy level, India has been supporting multilateral efforts to deal with diverse problems facing Africa. Its contribution to the UN peace-keeping missions, for instance, stands out. India has 6,000 Blue Helmets in various UN missions, making it the fourth largest contributor (UN Peace-keeping n.d.). East African countries which have benefited from Indian Blue Helmets are Rwanda (1993–96) and South Sudan (since 2005). One op-ed observed that post-independence India enjoys a reputation for being benign, non-violent and fastidiously democratic (Jain 2018). Consequently, India's image in Africa has been that of a peace-loving nation. In one study, respondents who were students of International Relations at the University of Dar es Salaam were asked to rank countries on the basis of whether they posed a security threat to Tanzania (Shangwe 2017). The countries in question were China, India, USA, Britain, Germany and Scandinavia (Denmark, Sweden and Norway). Of the countries posing the 'highest security threat' category India was ranked lowest, suggesting that the South Asian country is viewed positively in this respect.

Political values

Despite its many weaknesses, India boasts a functioning democratic, secular, federal political system. This system has cultivated a sense of nationhood in what is otherwise a culturally diverse country. It is only right to state that this degree of stability is to a certain extent attributed to a political culture of openness and tolerance. With the size of its population, India is usually referred to as the world's largest democracy. It is an image that India wants the rest of the world to see. Many African countries have embraced democracy themselves, and therefore India offers something of a lesson in that direction.

Aspects of India's 'hard power' in East Africa

India's economic presence in East Africa: trade, investment and aid

According to a 2018 joint report by the African Export-Import (Afrexim) Bank and Export-Import (EXIM) Bank of India, trade between Africa and India has increased more than eight-fold from USD 7.2 billion in 2001 to USD 59.9 billion in 2017 (Afrexim Bank 2018). Those figures make India Africa's fourth-largest national trading partner, accounting for more than 6.4 per cent of total African trade in 2017.

Until 2019, according to the African Development Bank, the East African region, including countries in the Horn of Africa, has been the fastest grow-ing region in the continent (AfDB 2019). It was projected that the region would achieve growth of 5.9 per cent in 2019 and 6.1 per cent in 2020. These projections may now appear too ambitious due to the impact of the Coronavirus outbreak. Moreover, the 2017 World Investment Report shows that East Africa received Foreign Direct Investment (FDI) of USD 7.1 bil-lion. Major investors in the region include the UK, the US, UAE, Denmark, Turkey, China and India. On the other hand, according to a 2017 report by the Export-Import Bank of India, from 1996 to 2017, India's cumulative direct investment in the East African region in joint ventures and wholly owned subsidiaries in terms of equity, loans and guarantees issued amounted to USD 316.6 million (EXIM Bank of India 2017).

India–East Africa trade has also grown significantly. According to the report by the EXIM Banks of Africa and India, Tanzania is India's largest trading partner in the region with 19.3 per cent of India's total trade with the region in 2017 (Afrexim Bank 2018). It is important to note that the report includes other countries such as Mozambique and Mauritius as East-ern African countries. The other EAC members are Kenya (15.7 per cent), Uganda (6 per cent), Rwanda (1 per cent), Burundi (0.7 per cent) and South Sudan (0.6 per cent). However, currently, the trade balance between the two areas is heavily skewed in favour of New Delhi. It means India exports more than it imports from these countries. This is in itself a major turnaround in countries such as Tanzania with which India had a trade deficit of USD 15.9 million in 2001. In 2017, India had gone from that deficit to a USD 339.8 million surplus in its trade with Tanzania. The Kenyan market remained the biggest for Indian products in 2017 with a trade surplus of USD 1.68 billion for India. Major East African exports to India include gold, vegetables, fruits, coffee and spices. On the other hand, India's main exports to the region are petroleum products, pharmaceutical products and road vehicles.

On development cooperation, despite the fact that India still receives support from a very small number of partners, it has quietly but effectively become an important member of the community of donors in Africa, even if it does not use the donor–recipient discourse. In a statement by the Minister of External Affairs in response to a question raised in the Indian parliament about the country's engagement with Africa in July 2017, it was revealed that much of the cooperation with Africa is being provided through development partnership assistance schemes such as grant-in aid projects, training and capacity building programmes, lines of credit assistance, humanitarian and disaster relief assistance and familiarisation visits (MEA 2017).

Cooperation that comes in the form of lines of credit (LoCs) has been particularly vital in India's foreign assistance agenda. LoCs target specific projects identified by the Government of India on condition that Indian contractors are substantially involved. According to the EXIM Bank of India (2017), East African countries have been some of the biggest recipients of these LoCs. The Bank's 2017 report shows that with the exception of Uganda, a total amount of USD 1.2 billion had been offered to East African countries in the form of LoCs. Tanzania alone was offered USD 615.2 million in LoCs, making it the region's biggest recipient. The information available on the website of the Indian High Commission in Uganda shows that the country was offered USD 205 million in LoCs (HCI Uganda 2019). The targeted sectors are mainly energy and agriculture.

Training and capacity building

At the Third India-Africa Forum Summit in 2015, Prime Minister Modi announced that India would offer 50,000 scholarships to Africans over the period of five years. Much of India's training and capacity building takes place under Indian Technical and Economic Cooperation (ITEC). Other scholarships are offered by the ICCR which has since 2008 had nine hundred slots for African students (ICCR 2019b). ITEC was established on 15 September 1964, as a bilateral programme of assistance of the government of India. It is a flagship initiative of the Indian government's capacity building effort (ITEC 2019). ITEC's role is mostly in the form of short-term training for African civilians, bureaucrats and military personnel. For instance, under ITEC, 2,369 Tanzanians were trained in India in the period between 2014 and 2019 (The Citizen 2019). Between April and November

2019, a total of 223 Tanzanians were extended ITEC awards (MEA 2020). Although it is challenging to establish exact numbers of East African students who have benefited from ITEC awards and/or ICCR scholarships, it is clear that educational exchanges have gathered momentum as a result of India's increased involvement in Africa. To these figures must be added self-sponsored East African students who have chosen India to pursue their further education.

To put this in perspective, in Uganda it is estimated 600 Ugandans were studying in India in 2019 (HCI Uganda 2019). In Burundi, 447 student visas were issued to Burundian students between 2016 and 2019 (HCI Uganda 2019). Meanwhile, there were about 3,500 Kenyan students studying in fifty institutions throughout India in the same year. In 2017–18 alone, over 400 Kenyan nationals took advantage of training and scholarship programmes in various fields (HCI Kenya 2019). In South Sudan, 200 slots were allocated for the South Sudanese under the ITEC programme for the year 2018-19. According to the Embassy of India (EoI) in South Sudan, that number was raised to 240 for the year 2019–20 (EoI, South Sudan 2019).

Other aspects of India's soft power

India's medical tourism

An article by the Cable News Network (CNN) on 15 February 2019 reported India's plans to make medical tourism a USD 9 billion industry by 2020 (Suri 2019). There has been a surge in the number of Africans going to India to seek medical treatment in recent years. The CNN report shows that the East African countries of Kenya and Tanzania are only surpassed by Nigeria in the list of medical tourists to India. The reason for this surge is that India's medical service industry is attractive for its advanced facilities, skilled doctors and low-cost treatment (Suri 2019).

Indian diasporic populations in East Africa

Long before European conquest of both India and East Africa, Indians and East Africans traded through ancient trade routes. Centuries later when Zanzibar became the capital of Oman in 1832, many Indians who had settled in Oman moved to the East African islands where they enjoyed the protection of the Omani Sultan (Bapumia and Mesaki 2015). Decades later, the British colonial enterprise in East Africa was responsible for bringing in about 32,000 Indians as indentured labourers (WEF 2015). Although it is estimated that only 7,000 chose to stay after their contracts had ended, the path of far stronger connections between East Africa and India had been paved, albeit on the rough terrain of colonialism.

Today, Indians are an integral part of East African demography despite their minority status. India's Ministry of External Affairs (MEA) categorises the majority of them as citizens of their respective East African countries of residence, but also as eligible to apply to be Persons of Indian Origin (PIOs) or Overseas Citizens of India (OCIs). The rest are known as Non-Resident Indians (NRIs), comprising Indians who stay in the region as expatriates. Thus in 2016, East Africa was home to 175,500 overseas Indians, including both PIOs/OCIs and NRIs (MEA 2018b). Countries with the main historical Indian diasporas had the largest numbers of local citizens. Hence, Kenya had 60,000 PIOs/OCIs and 20,000 NRIs, followed by Tanzania with 50,000 PIOs/OCIs and 10,000 NRIs and Uganda with just 6,500 PIOs/OCIs and 23,500 NRIs.[2] East African citizens of African origin seldom distinguish between these categories when they refer to Tanzanian or Kenyan 'Asians' as Wahindi. The role of Indian diasporas in the India–Africa dialogue ranges from facilitating access to African markets for Indian companies (Cissé 2015) to, according to former Indian Vice President Hamid Ansari, providing linkages for development partnerships in general (Kagire 2017).

Colonial legacy as soft power resource?

The complexity of colonialism is such that much as it destroyed and interrupted the social, political and economic fabrics of the colonised people, it also created an identity of shared experiences. The humiliation of colonialism for both Africa and India is still a fresh wound in the collective memory of their people. The fact that India has never been a colonial power goes without saying, of course. This fact may have strengthened the perception of a benign India as mentioned previously. The shared experience in this case points at the British colonial past in the region. Kenya and Uganda were both British colonies, just like India. Tanzania was formerly a mandated territory under British administration. On the other hand, South Sudan was once part of Sudan which was historically jointly governed by Britain and Egypt. In all these countries English is one of the official languages, creating a shared sense of history in those that are part of the Commonwealth. This can be utilised to India's advantage in its soft power push. Many are of the opinion that the use of English as the main medium of

---

[2] The number of Indian citizens in Uganda was dramatically affected by their expulsion by Amin in the early 1970s.

instruction in India has facilitated an inflow of African students, who hail from mainly the Anglophone countries (Modi 2017).

Challenges

So far, our discussion has offered a glimpse of India's soft power. However, several aspects of Indian culture and economic and political values undermine New Delhi's soft power initiative. First, India's social cohesion has proven to be problematic, as much as the country conjures up an image of a multicultural, secular society. Reports of attacks on Muslims by Hindu hardliners are spreading widely. With the rise of Prime Minister Modi of the Bharatiya Janata Party (BJP), there have been fears of India becoming a majoritarian Hindu state, especially with the uptake of the ideology of Hindutva (Hinduness). The 2019 Citizenship Amendment Act (CAA) in particular has been criticised for targeting Muslim minorities, leading to massive protests. This is not an image India wants to sell to the world, much less in East Africa, which has significant percentages of both Muslim and Christian populations. Furthermore, reports of mob violence and racism against Africans living in India are tarnishing the country's image (McCann, this volume). In February 2016 a Tanzanian female student was reportedly beaten and stripped by a violent mob in the city of Bangalore, prompting widespread public condemnation in Tanzania (Al Jazeera 2016).

Second, the Indian model of development has not earned significant admiration outside India. For instance, a survey conducted by Afrobarometer in several African countries in 2016 indicated that the Indian model was the least preferred with only 2 per cent of respondents seeing it as the best one. India stood behind the USA (30 per cent); China (24 per cent); former colonial powers (13 per cent); and South Africa (11 per cent). In fact, 5 per cent of respondents even suggested that their own country's model was better than that of India (Afrobarometer 2016). This belies the promise of the Mumbai Consensus. Moreover, India's economic development has not been consistent, and has failed to convince others of its benefits. Unlike China, India does not boast of high-tech infrastructure, nor does it conjure up an image of a country whose living standards are admirable. Indeed, India's own economic limitations put it at a disadvantage compared to, say, China and the US in that respect.

Third, the Indian communities in East Africa have long been perceived as being closed, having little social interaction with Africans (Prah 2011). This has been attributed on the one hand to a racist colonial policy which racially ranked people: Whites at the top, Asians in the middle and Africans at the bottom; and on the other hand, to Indian racism against Africans. At one point in history, relations between Asians and Africans in East Africa were described to be at the 'shopkeeper-customer or master-servant level' (Ghai and Ghai 1965: 4). Meanwhile, Yasmin Alibhai-Brown, a British journalist who was born and raised in Uganda to an Indian family but left the country just before the expulsion of Asians by Idi Amin in 1972, recounted her experience in the East African country, claiming that most Asians were deeply racist, and saw Africans as inferior people that they could not marry and with whom they could not live as equals (Alibhai-Brown 2002).

Today, this relationship is still a topic of discussion in academic circles. In one incident, this subject was raised by a panellist at a conference organised by the HCI in Tanzania on 18 January 2018, prompting a heated exchange between the panellist and a Mauritian diplomat of Indian descent. The panellist had asked participants to share information of interracial marriages between Africans and Indians. The diplomat saw this as a racial attack on Indians. In another incident on 5 December 2018, the author witnessed racially segregated cafeterias for Indians, Tanzanian Arabs and black Africans at a worksite in Lugoba, Tanzania. The worksite belonged to a Tanzanian company but was run by a management team of Indian expatriates. This continuation of a racially defined relationship does not help the image of the Indian diaspora and Indians in India altogether. It is particularly significant because soft power is about both reality and perception. In fact, one would argue perception is as powerful as the reality when it comes to soft power.

Conclusion

East Africa remains crucial in India's inroads into Africa. Given India's cultural heritage in the region, and the region's proximity to India compared with other parts of Africa, it could be argued that East Africa is the barometer of New Delhi's soft power in the continent. As shown in this chapter, India has managed to stamp its presence in the East African region in economic, political and cultural aspects. The cultural aspect is of particularly great significance in the soft power discourse. For that reason, New Delhi has an advantage over its emerging soft power rivals. However, the Indian model still faces challenges especially when compared with other soft power rivals. The promotion of South–South cooperation is still an attractive agenda for Africa and India's role in that direction will always be appreciated. The adoption of economic diplomacy since the early 1990s by India, however, may have redefined relations with Africa. Yet countries in East Africa have themselves taken a similar direction, meaning that they are aware of the fact that India–Africa relations are not necessarily hinged on the politics of altruism, but rather the promotion of national interest. This is the context under which India's soft power was discussed. The potential of Indian soft power in East Africa and Africa in general will depend on the mutuality of interests of Indians and Africans. However, it is worthwhile to note that only recently have there been coordinated efforts by the Government of India to take full advantage of its soft power potential. While a few gains have evidently been achieved, it remains to be seen how those gains will be sustained given the continuing challenges discussed here.

Bibliography

AfDB. 2019. 'African Economic Outlook (AEO) 2019 – Building today, a better Africa tomorrow', *AfDB*, n.d., https://afdb.org/en/documents/african-economic-outlook-aeo-2019-english-version, accessed 1 December 2019.

Afrexim Bank and EXIM Bank of India. 2018. *Deepening South-South Collaboration: An Analysis of Africa and India's Trade and Investment* (Cairo: Afrexim Bank and EXIM Bank of India).

Afrobarometer. 2015. 'China's growing presence in Africa wins largely popular reviews', 24 October 2016, *Afrobarometer*, https://afrobarometer.org/press/world-development-information-day-chinas-growing-presence-africa-wins-positive-popular-reviews, accessed 1 December 2019.

Alibhai-Brown, Y. 2002. 'Racism and the truth about the Ugandan Asians', *Independent*, 5 August 2020, https://www.independent.co.uk/voices/commentators/yasmin-alibhai-brown/racism-and-the-truth-about-the-ugandan-asians-172084.html, accessed 27 January 2020.

Al Jazeera. 2016. 'Shock in India over mob attack on Tanzanian student', 5 February 2016, https://www.aljazeera.com/news/2016/02/anger-india-mob-attack-tanzanian-student-160205141006483.html, accessed 20 January 2020.

Bapumia, F.G. and Mesaki, S. 2015. 'The minorities of Indian origin in Tanzania', in M. Adam (ed.), *Indian Africa: Minorities of Indian-Pakistani origin in Eastern Africa* (Dar es Salaam: Mkukina Nyota), 351–61.

Bhatia, R. 2017. 'This time for Africa', *The Hindu*, 1 June 2017, https://www.thehindu.com/todays-paper/tp-opinion/this-time-for-africa/article18685157.ece, accessed 1 December 2019.

Chand, M. 2009. 'India: East Africa's twenty-first century ally?', *The East African*, 18 May 2009, https://www.theeastafrican.co.ke/magazine/434746-599062-dvac5p/index.html, accessed 2 December 2019.

Cissé, D. 2015. 'China and India in Africa', *The Diplomat*, 13 November 2015, https://thediplomat.com/2015/11/china-and-india-in-africa/, accessed 1 December 2019.

EoI, South Sudan. 2019. 'India – South Sudan relations', *GoI*, 24 September 2019, http://www.indembjuba.gov.in/india-south-sudan-relation.php, 10 January 2020.

EXIM Bank of India. 2017. *Indian Investments in East Africa: Recent Trends and Prospects*, Working paper no. 68, November 2017 (Mumbai: EXIM Bank of India)

Ghai, D.P. and Ghai, Y.P. 1965. 'Asians in East Africa: Problems and prospects', *Journal of Modern African Studies*, 3/1, 35–51.

HCI, Kenya. 2019. 'Overview', *GoI*, https://hcinairobi.gov.in/pages.php?id=34, accessed 1 December 2019.

HCI, Uganda. 2019. 'Bilateral relations: India-Uganda relations', *GoI*, April 2019, https://hci.gov.in/kampala/?0889?000, accessed 1 December 2019.

ICCR. 2019a. 'ICCR scholarships', *GoI*, n.d., https://www.iccr.gov.in/a2a/iccr-scholarship, accessed 10 January 2020.

——. 2019b. 'Indian Council for Cultural Relations scholarship schemes', *GoI*, n.d., http://a2ascholarships.iccr.gov.in/home/getAllSchemeList, accessed 10 January 2020.

ITEC. 2019. 'About ITEC', *GoI*, n.d., https://www.itecgoi.in/about.php, accessed 1 December 2019.

Jain, D. 2018. 'India's soft power: Prospects and limitations', *Synergy: Journal of Contemporary Asian Studies*, 3 March 2018, http://utsynergyjournal.org/2018/03/03/indias-soft-power-prospects-and-limitations/, accessed 5 June 2019.

Kagire, E. 2017. 'India woos Rwanda, Uganda to expand footprint in East Africa', *The East African*, 3 March 2017, https://www.theeastafrican.co.ke/business/India-woos-Rwanda-Uganda-expand-East-Africa/2560-3835588-svycah/index.html, accessed 10 January 2020.

MEA. 2017. 'Question No.153: Indian aid to African countries', *GoI*, 26 July 2017, https://www.mea.gov.in/lok-sabha.htm?dtl/28705/QUESTION+NO153+INDIAN+AID+TO+AFRICAN+COUNTRIES, accessed 1 December 2019.

——. 2018a. 'Prime Minister's address at Parliament of Uganda his state visit to Uganda', *GoI*, 25 July 2018, https://mea.gov.in/Speeches-Statements.htm?dtl/30152/Prime_Ministers_address_at_Parliament_of_Uganda_during_his_State_Visit_to_Uganda, accessed 9 June 2019.

——. 2018b. 'Population of overseas Indians', *GoI*, n.d., https://mea.gov.in/images/attach/NRIs-and-PIOs_1.pdf, accessed 1 December 2019.

——. 2020. 'Minister of External Affairs Annual Report 2019–2020', *GoI*, n.d., http://www.mea.gov.in/Uploads/PublicationDocs/32489_AR_Spread_2020_new.pdf, accessed 9 June 2019.

Modi, R. 2017. 'India-Africa Forum Summits and capacity building: Achievements and challenges', *African and Asian Studies* (16), 139–66.

Nye, J.S. 2004. *Soft Power: The Means to Success in World Politics* (New York: Public Affairs).

Oduor, M. 2018. 'Diamond explains why he copied scenes from Indian video for his new song "Baila"', *Ghafla!*, 18 July 2018, http://www.ghafla.com/ke/diamond-explains-why-he-copied-scenes-from-indian-video-for-his-new-song-baila/, accessed 8 June 2019.

Prah, K.K. 2011. 'On records and keeping our eyes on the ball', *Centre for Consciencist Studies and Analyses*, 24 July 2011, https://consciencism.wordpress.com/history/documents/kwesi-k-prah-responds/, accessed 27 January 2020.

Ray, A.S. 2015. 'The enigma of the "Indian Model of Development"', *Centre for International Trade and Development (JNU)*, Discussion Paper 15–01, February 2015, https://www.jnu.ac.in/sites/default/files/DP01_2015.pdf, accessed 1 December 2019.

Shangwe, M.J. 2017. 'China's soft power in Tanzania: Opportunities and challenges', *China Quarterly of International Strategic Studies*, 3/1, 79–100.

Summers, L. 2010. 'India and the global economy', *Remarks at the Asia Society, Mumbai*, 15 October 2010, http://larrysummers.com/wp-content/uploads/2015/07/India-and-the-Global-Economy_10.15.2010.pdf, accessed 1 December 2019.

Suri, M. 2019. 'Medical tourism in India could be a booming $9 billion industry by 2020', *CNN*, 15 February 2019, https://edition.cnn.com/2019/02/13/health/india-medical-tourism-industry-intl/index.html, accessed 1 December 2019.

The Citizen. 2019. 'India High Commission celebrates ITEC', 21 March 2019, https://www.thecitizen.co.tz/News/India-High-Commission-celebrates-Itec/1840340-5035820-sc5kbw/index.htm, accessed 1 December 2019.

UN Peacekeeping. n.d. 'Troop and police contributors', *UN*, https://peacekeeping.un.org/en/troop-and-police-contributors, accessed 1 December 2019.

WEF. 2015. 'Fifteen facts about the Indian diaspora in Africa', *WEF*, 25 June 2015, https://www.weforum.org/agenda/2015/06/15-facts-about-the-indian-diaspora-in-africa/, accessed 10 January 2020.

2

Between Business and Balance: India–Japan in Africa vis-à-vis China

MRITTIKA GUHA SARKAR AND JAGANNATH PANDA

Introduction

Academic scholarship and dominant knowledge paradigms constructed Africa as being marred with political instability, poverty, disease and the incapacity to govern itself. However, a change in the geopolitical locus from West to East has accorded Africa with primacy and enabled the global system to view the region as a potential hub for trade, business, technological development, infrastructural connectivity and geostrategic interests. Africa today, as a resource centre and an emerging global market, provides opportunities for developed and developing countries such as Japan, China and India to engage and invest for the enhancement of their own foreign policy goals of economic expansion and strategic advancement.

It is in this regard that China has been rapidly increasing its footprints in Africa through trade and investment in ensuring infrastructural and sustainable development. On the other hand, India and Africa have been natural partners for decades. They have engaged through ancient trade routes and cultural exchanges; anti-colonial and nationalist movements; establishing Afro-Asian solidarity especially after the Bandung Conference in 1955; and finally, as developmental partners in the purview of current developments. Japan's keen interest in Africa should also not be discounted, as it is based on sustainable development through aid, infrastructure, technology transfers and innovation. However, while China's attractive and sustained investments in Africa have been allowing it to become Africa's largest trading partner, India and Japan find their interests and initiatives competing with China's, not only to protect their respective interests but to envision a fine balance in the face of increased Chinese engagement. While Japan and India as like-minded partners advocating a 'rule-based order' have successfully upgraded their 'Comprehensive Economic Partnership' to a 'Special Strategic and Global Partnership' through cooperation and collaboration, a key motivation for the same remains their mutual apprehensions about China's growing regional influence (Chacko and Panda 2019). As China expands its economic and strategic sway in Africa, a changing trend is witnessed in India's and Japan's engagement with the region which, through a business-oriented partnership, albeit at a planning stage, focuses on economic growth and technological progression, leading to a change in the earlier aid-oriented outlook towards the region.

This chapter highlights the envisioned India–Japan partnership in Africa vis-à-vis China's Africa policy and argues that while India and Japan's policies in Africa are often pitted against China's, the formers' interests in the region remain without any conditionalities. In fact, an India–Japan partnership in Africa reiterates their Special Strategic and Global Partnership, while setting the tone for a rule-based and inclusive 'Free and Open Indo-Pacific'. Further, with the onset of Covid-19, a partnership prioritising their engagement in an emerging region like Africa by focusing on the changing economic and health landscape of the region through a business model would enhance the scope of their regional (if not global) Indo-Pacific partnerships, establishing themselves as infrastructure and connectivity promoters.

Tracing a business partnership in Africa

Though at a nascent stage, the India–Japan partnership in Africa has mostly been aimed at augmenting India's and Japan's national interests while promoting a 'liberal and value-based order' in the Indo-Pacific, ensuring a region devoid of autarkic and unilateral policies. India's engagement with African states has been increasing since the opening of the Indian economy in the 1990s. The reiteration of enhanced ties has been visible during the three India–Africa Forum Summits (IAFS) held in 2008, 2011 and 2015 (Wagner 2019), through a desire to strengthen trade, economic cooperation and investment linkages including socio-cultural ties. The first two rounds of the summits in 2008 and 2011 highlighted the multi-aligned partnership between India and Africa and recognised key areas of convergence. Focusing on enhanced cooperation, the summits discussed climate change, trade development, piracy, terrorism, nuclear disarmament and United Nations (UN) reforms (see MEA 2008; MEA 2011; Bhatia 2011), extending the canvas of India–Africa cooperation to be comprehensive.

As the first India–Africa summit set the tone for a more robust partnership between India and Africa, the second summit deliberated on deeper economic engagement, with initiatives such as 'Duty Free Tariff Preference Scheme' by India focusing on trade enhancement; forming an India–Africa

Business Council by concentrating on business-to-business (B-2-B) and people-to-people (P-2-P) cooperation and identifying priority areas of partnership. While the launch of IAFS-I built on several earlier Indian initiatives with Africa, such as Team-9[1] and Focus Africa, New Delhi's engagement with the African region remained largely limited. Thus, India and Africa committed to cooperate in the fields of agriculture, infrastructure, human resource development, capacity building and enhancement in the lines of credit (LoCs) during the IAFS-II. This enabled India to build an altruistic image, which, through a benevolent and non-intrusive approach (a key arch in Indian foreign policy), aimed towards sustainable development and growth in Africa. However, India's goodwill approach has lost out on a strategic front to emerging players such as China, which increased its strategic outreach in Africa by utilising significant economic opportunities (Trigunayat 2019).

In this regard, a key shift was witnessed in India's approach towards Africa in the third India–Africa summit held on 26–29 October 2015. Continuing its trend of enhancing the LoCs to the African countries and increasing the aid and assistance towards infrastructure, agriculture, health and capacity building, India capitalised on its policy of 'Arc of Prosperity' through a 'Business Alchemy' between itself and Africa (MEA 2015). Highlighting a more geo-economic approach towards Africa, the third India-Africa Forum Summit committed to cooperate in the areas of trade and industry through:

1) Establishment of small and medium enterprises (SMEs) and medium and small industries (MSIs) in order to promote employment and generate income for people of both sides.

2) Promotion of public–private partnerships (PPP) by encouraging Indian businesses to set up skill development units in African industrial zones, aiming to train African engineers, technicians, managers and workers.

3) Providing special attention to events such as the business exhibition, Focus Africa conferences as well as the India-Africa Business Forum to facilitate business cooperation between India and Africa.[2]

---

[1] Team-9 or the Techno-Economic Approach for Africa-India Movement, established in 2004, is a regional cooperation mechanism between the governments of India and eight West African countries, namely Burkina Faso, Chad, Côte d'Ivoire, Equatorial Guinea, Ghana, Guinea-Bissau, Mali and Senegal. The initiative focuses on transfer of technology, know-how and knowledge management (MEA 2004).

[2] The Business Exhibition at IAFS-III was centred around 'Innovation, ingenuity and inventiveness', providing a platform for Indian and African business leaders to interact with each other. 'Focus Africa' was an economic initiative started in

It was during the India-Africa Forum Summit (IAFS) III that Prime Minister Modi announced a concessional credit line of USD 10 billion over the next five years, in addition to its ongoing credit programme to Africa. IAFS-III unveiled a new phase in the India–Africa economic ties which is aiming for sustainable growth, carried out not just through an upgrade in modern energy services, healthcare, education and poverty eradication, but also through enhanced cooperation in institution building, establishment of public–private partnerships, infrastructure and connectivity and development of small and medium industries as the four major pillars of the economic partnership.

A similar geo-economic approach was emphasised during Prime Minister Narendra Modi's state visit to Uganda on 24–25 July 2018. Undertones of a reinvigorated India–Africa partnership were reiterated by Modi while he listed the ten principles which would guide India's engagement with Africa. According to him, Africa would remain as one of India's top priorities through sustained and regular interaction and exchanges. It would commit to a developmental partnership as per African priorities, where preferential access to Indian markets and industry would be ensured to invest in Africa. India and Africa would fight together against climate change, for free and open oceans and maritime lanes; strengthen cooperation and mutual capabilities in combatting terrorism and extremism; ensure a free, stable and secure cyberspace and support the UN to uphold peace. The India–Africa partnership would be built on cooperation not competition, which would ensure an inclusive, secure and developed Indian Ocean. Further, propounding that Africa should become a nursery for its youth, India would not want the region to become a theatre of rivalry. Lastly, through their historical links of fighting colonialism, India and Africa would ensure a just, representative and democratic global order that has a voice and a role for the one-third of the humanity that lives in Africa and India (MEA 2018a).

While the India–Africa ties have witnessed a markedly geo-economic outlook under the Modi administration, it is the strategic undertones of national interest which should not be discounted. India has been utilising a more pragmatic and comprehensive approach to fulfil its own national goals of economic growth and technological progress. Thus, India's policies towards

---

March 2002 by the Indian government to increase the trade and business relations between India and Africa (MoC 2013); the India-Africa Business Forum is an initiative to establish B-2-B relations with a sectoral focus on areas such as infrastructural projects between India and Africa, agricultural growth and transformation in Africa, partnership between India and Africa for energy and sustainable development, and economic and capital development and affordable healthcare in Africa (MEA 2015).

Africa, viewed through a geo-economic lens, stand in tandem with its initiatives of 'Make in India', 'Digital India', 'Skill India' and 'Aayushman Bharat' (National Health Protection Scheme) which aim at redefining India as an economic power. At the same time, India's policies in the region synergise with Africa's Agenda 2063, which aspires to transform the continent into a global powerhouse by the year 2063. However, India's policies towards Africa under Prime Minister Modi have been acknowledging China's growing presence in Africa in terms of infrastructure and energy resources. Nonetheless, it is not to say that India's policies are conditioned by China's connectivity ambitions of the Belt and Road Initiative (BRI) and Maritime Silk Road (MSR). It is in this regard that T.S. Tirumurti, (former Secretary of Economic Relations, Ministry of External Affairs), stated during the Africa Day round-table discussion at the Manohar Parrikar Institute for Defence Studies and Analyses (a New Delhi-based think tank) that:

> India's partnership with Africa is based on a model of cooperation which is responsive to the needs of African countries. It is demand-driven and free of conditionalities. It is based on our history of friendship, historical ties, and a sense of deep solidarity. As the Prime Minister has underlined, African priorities are our priorities (Tirumurti 2019).

If anything, India under the current government has been taking pro-active steps to strengthen its outreach in Africa. What is significant about India's approach towards Africa is its utilisation of unique developmental models to prevent the continent from turning into a hub of power politics. For instance, India is using its 'Skill Diplomacy' programme in particular African countries to support entrepreneurship training to create jobs (Pandey 2017; MEA 2019). In fact, this was reiterated during the knowledge exchange workshop organised by the Skills Ministry and The National Skill Development Corporation in New Delhi on 30 October 2017 where Rwanda, Nigeria, Ethiopia, Senegal, Tanzania and Ghana participated to strengthen the engagement between Asia and Africa (MSDE 2017). Similarly, the government is also taking concrete steps to upgrade the connectivity between India and Africa by establishing digital infrastructures such as e-VidyaBharati and e-ArogyaBharati Networks in at least eighteen countries in Africa to provide quality tele-education and tele-medicine facilities by connecting selected Indian universities, institutions and super speciality hospitals to African counterparts (MEA 2018b).

These initiatives will become a greater requisite in the post-Covid-19 period as both India and Africa experience an economic crisis with rising unemployment and disruptions in supply chains, as well as an unprecedented health crisis due to the global pandemic. Thus, India and Africa have planned to expand their multi-faceted partnership not only to combat Covid-19 jointly, but also to address the prevalent global challenges. As they reiterated during the webinar 'Mapping Next Steps in India-Africa Partnership: Pandemic & Beyond', which brought together eminent diplomats, experts and leaders, both India and Africa are committed to working together in the areas of tourism, medicine, agriculture, manufacturing, governance, science and technology, space, education and mining to ensure sustainable development (Roy Chaudhury 2020). Additionally, India has donated essential medicines worth USD 50 million to Nigeria and other African countries (Odutola 2020). More importantly, India and Africa have preferred to define their partnership by seeking to address the challenges of the changing world by cooperating to counter climate change, extremism and transnational crimes, while collaborating in the areas of counter-terrorism and maritime security.

However, economic and business relations between India and Africa have still not realised their true collaborative potential. The trade between India and Africa, which reached its peak during the year 2014 at USD 71.5 billion, dropped to a level of USD 49.6 billion in 2016 and only increased to USD 62.66 billion in 2018.

A similar trend can be witnessed in business, where despite devising policies to encourage small, medium and large industries to invest in Africa, only few large industries such as ONGC Videsh, Oil India Limited, Tata Steel and Tata Power have been putting money into countries such as Congo, Egypt, Ivory Coast, Libya, Mozambique, Sudan, South Africa and Zambia. A way forward might be for Indian enterprises to find suitable business partners to create a new African model of business, which would enable expanding the linkages and enhancing the economic growth. Like-minded countries such as Japan could play a great role through triangular partnerships in Africa in enhancing B-2-B links. This would provide a new impetus for sustainable development through successful and bolstered business linkages and enhanced economic progress.

Tokyo's Africa reach and the envisioned India–Japan partnership

Japan, since 1993 has been partnering with Africa through aid and assistance and has been regularly holding the Tokyo International Conference on African Development (TICAD). However, since TICAD IV in 2008, a progressive fine-tuning has been noticeable in Japan's approach towards

Africa from 'aid' to 'business'. This was further strengthened in TICAD VII, held in August 2019 (TICAD 2019). Shifting away from its image as an 'aid giver', Japan, especially through TICAD VII, has been taking pragmatic steps to ensure a 'mutually beneficial' relationship. Its 'Public-Private Business Dialogue' between Japan and Africa, and its initiative of 'accelerating economic transformation and improving business environment through private sector development and innovation', reiterate its commitment to bolstering economic and primarily business relations with Africa. For this reason, TICAD VII launched the Japan Business Council for Africa (JBCA) to promote Japanese companies' businesses in Africa through public–private partnerships. It further organised the Second Japan-Africa Public-Private Economic Forum and launched a bilateral committee for improvement in the business environment in seven countries through enhanced investment by the private sector. Further, Japan has been promoting African start-ups and is collaborating with private funds for African entrepreneurs by utilising the technological know-how in Japanese organisations such as JETRO (Japan External Trade Organisation). It is moreover promoting Japanese SME businesses and sustainable development goals (SDGs) in Africa and supporting the formulation of digital public goods to accelerate innovation in public and private sectors (Sasaki 2019).

However, a change in Japan's approach towards Africa should not be viewed solely in economic terms; the strategic underpinnings of the move should also be acknowledged. Japan as a rational power is concerned about its own national interests in securing and sustaining economic growth and prosperity. Faced with a shrinking economy and an aging population, Japan has been bolstering efforts through its TICAD summits to sustain and strengthen its trade and investment in Africa to ensure economic progress (Eyinla 2018). Thus, with this shift in status from an 'aid giver' to business partnership, Japan is not just ensuring access in Africa to secure its energy supplies, it has also been establishing an avenue for industrial and business cooperation. In other words, Japan is using its overseas investment and aid programmes as a tool to secure and strengthen its own national interests and goals of economic development. At the same time, Japan is being cautious about China's rapidly rising influence in the region, which can be seen as an obstacle to expanding the former's footprints. Thus, Japan is using its economic initiatives to preserve and strengthen its diplomatic and economic power in Africa.

In the post Covid-19 period, as the Japanese economy shrinks at its fastest rate while battling the pandemic, the changed leadership in Japan, under Prime Minister Yoshihide Suga, will want to advance Tokyo's economic relations with Africa further by taking forward Shinzo Abe's legacy. Moreover, as Japan looks towards diversifying its supply chains away from China, greater investments in Africa through strengthened business relations might only supplement Japan's regional as well as domestic interests.

The above sketches the convergent approaches and initiatives of both India and Japan towards Africa and further increases the impetus for a greater India–Japan partnership in the region. It is for this reason that India and Japan aim to promote innovation and investment, develop industrial human resources, ensure debt sustainability and invest in quality infrastructure to enhance connectivity and strengthen industries.

As a highly developed economy, and as a technology, finance and business powerhouse, Japan suitably synergises with India as a developing nation. Japan's sectors of research and development, finance and design, cutting-edge technology and know-how create a perfect combination for quality and prosperity. Essentially, under the leadership of Modi, Indian foreign policy narratives have undergone radical changes, imbibing a more nationalist character. A new level of confidence has been built with Tokyo. An India–Japan partnership in Africa must also factor in India's strategic and economic strides. Though the consequences of the pandemic have slowed down the Indian economy, India, according to a study by *The Lancet*, is set to overtake Japan by 2050 to become the third largest economy in the world (Financial Express 2020). India's national narrative under Modi is thus focused on economic growth and technological progression with the schemes mentioned earlier. Thus, technology and economic power are two areas that could exemplify India–Japan strategic cooperation in Africa.

Essentially, an India–Japan partnership in Africa had been earlier envisioned through an ambitious proposition termed the Asia-Africa Growth Corridor (AAGC). The AAGC scheme, (now remodeled as the Platform for Japan-India Business Cooperation in Asia-Africa Region), was officially discussed between Prime Minister Narendra Modi and former Japanese Prime Minister Shinzo Abe during the India-Japan Annual Summit Meeting held in Tokyo in 2016 (MEA 2016). The crux of the meeting between the countries remained the necessity to realise the growing strategic convergence between India and Japan in the Indo-Pacific region by establishing a chain of industrial corridors and networks in and between Asia and Africa. However, contrary to its ambitious expectations, AAGC has witnessed little progress since its introduction. In fact, the AAGC was neither mentioned in the India-Japan Joint Statements, nor in the statements by Modi's state visit to Uganda in 2018 nor by Shinzo Abe during the TICAD VII held in 2019. An apparent modification in approach in India and Japan's earlier model of investment and engagement in Africa was further underlined during the TICAD VII where Japan's business-oriented policies reduced the emphasis on the AAGC, by subsuming any cooperation with India under its vision for a 'Free and Open Indo-Pacific (FOIP)' (Aiyar 2019). While such a changed trend might be viewed as an instrumental hurdle in the enhancement of India–Japan partnership in Africa, it could also be perceived as a timely makeover, focusing on a bolstered economic and business-oriented partnership in the region.

The China balance

While envisioning a greater partnership between India and Japan in Africa, neither country overlooks the economic and strategic influence of China in Africa. A reiteration of the same is demonstrated in the trade links of the three countries with Africa, where China successfully dwarfs the combined trade of India and Japan. China's Africa engagement has especially been institutionalised after the establishment of the Forum on China-Africa Cooperation (FOCAC) in 2000 (Yu 2010). FOCAC has helped the 'China-Africa strategic partnership' to be pushed to another level through effective channels of communication between the two sides, collective dialogue and practical cooperation between China and Africa (Yang 2012). Today, China remains the largest trading partner for Africa with a trade of USD 208 billion as compared to USD 66.76 billion and USD 17.2 billion dollars for India and Japan respectively for the year 2019. Similarly, China's aid and investment in Africa significantly overpower the Indian and the Japanese counterparts.

According to the American Enterprise Institute (AEI), in 2005–18 there were a total of approximately 10,000 Chinese companies present in Africa, investing up to USD 300 billion dollars (AEI 2019) in many infrastructural and developmental projects, as opposed to 597 Indian companies and 796 Japanese companies. While both India and Japan acknowledge China's growing economic and strategic outreach in Africa, they also hold apprehensions regarding the huge debt burdens of middle-income countries (MICs) and least developed countries (LDCs) in Africa through China's infrastructural projects coupled with opaque interest rates. As China is monopolising big infrastructural projects such as railways in Kenya and Ethiopia, as well as dams, roads, airport construction and telecommunications in many regions of the continent, a potential for increased debts is making the region vulnerable to unsustainable infrastructural development (Nyabiage 2019a). This has the potential to negatively affect the market scenario and act as a hurdle for India and Japan to penetrate into the African markets for investments (Nyabiage 2019b).

It is, thus, in the interest of both India's and Japan's Africa policies to advocate for sustainable and quality infrastructure to realise a 'win–win' scenario. Proposing a rule-based order and transparency, and discouraging unilateral policies in the region, both India and Japan witness key convergences between their ideals and values, while necessitating both the countries partnering in Africa. Further, India and Japan can play a great role in partnering with each other to provide valued risk management, ensuring human security and promoting local employment as an alternative model to China's risk-prone one. An India–Japan partnership in Africa based on the values of peace and stability would enable Africa to prosper through quality infrastructure and sustainable policies. Japan has pledged 300 billion yen (USD 2.8 billion) at the 'Second Africa-Japan Public-Private Conference for High-Quality Infrastructure', held on 27 August 2019, for transparent infrastructure development in Africa. Further, Japan has been teaming up with the African Development Bank (AfDB) to advance infrastructure and enable private-sector company participation through its 'Enhanced Private Sector Assistance Initiative' (AfDB 2019).

Similarly, India's policies towards Africa have been focusing on a business-oriented partnership between India and Africa that has been underpinned by sustainable growth. India has invested USD 10 billion in the continent for development, which prioritises infrastructure and connectivity, poverty eradication, education, employment, better healthcare and advancement in energy development (MEA 2015). It is essential to acknowledge that the India–Japan 'Special Strategic and Global Partnership' is based on quality infrastructure and sustainable development. This was reiterated in India's and Japan's Vision Statement, announced on 29 October 2018. This statement restated the synergy between India and Japan through their collaborative developmental projects in the Indo-Pacific region, especially in the continent of Africa through the 'Platform for Japan-India Business Cooperation in Asia-Africa Region'.

The India–Japan partnership in Africa also suggests a South–South cooperation and a triangular partnership. India and Japan's developmental measures in Africa, reflecting their commitment to South–South cooperation, also signify their aim to strengthen their respective positions in the region as advocates for infrastructure and development in developing countries. On the other hand, their triangular partnership is reflected in the collaborative efforts undertaken by India and Japan, such as the plans to develop a cancer hospital in Kenya and more. India and Japan are already a part of triangular cooperation with several countries in the Indo-Pacific; this was emphasised by Japan's former Ambassador to India, Kenji Hiramatsu, after the Japan–India summit held from 28-29 October 2018, as he provided concrete examples of New Delhi and Tokyo working in third countries such as Bangladesh, Myanmar, Sri Lanka as well as in Africa, for connectivity and infrastructural development (Embassy of Japan in India 2018). As aforementioned, a B-2-B approach between India and Japan in Africa could be utilised to enhance the global partnership between New Delhi and Tokyo in the region. This has been further reiterated by Gurjit Singh[3] in his article 'India, Japan and the Asia-Africa Growth Corridor' where he propounded:

> The B-2-B engagement enables such ideas to be discussed. Indian compa-
> nies' primary interest in Africa is in infrastructure. They need to work with
> those who have invested in and trade in Africa and can bring them in closer
> engagement with Japanese companies so that a mutuality of interests can
> be established. The B-2-B connect among Indian and Japanese companies
> needs to be diversified, keeping Africa in focus. The Japan External Trade
> Organisation (JETRO) and the Confederation of Indian Industry (CII),
> among others, have tried to network companies through meetings in India,
> Uganda and Nigeria over the last year (Singh 2019).

It is also significant to acknowledge that a developing region of Africa would require quality infrastructure which would be cost-effective and disaster resistant. Shifting from China's approach towards connectivity and infrastructural projects, the Indian and Japanese business mode of development, focusing on quality and sustainability, would not just add value to the economy but also to society in Africa by creating local employment, enhancing the skillset and building capability and improving the standard of living. In other words, an India–Japan partnership in Africa would enhance connectivity between Asia and Africa through its business-oriented model, in a pragmatic sense.

India–Japan cooperation in Africa in a post-Covid 19 period

In a post Covid-19 period, the kind of a business cooperation between India and Japan in Africa mentioned above would be needed more than ever. Covid-19 has inevitably, and to a great extent, altered the economic situation of Asia as well as Africa. At the same time, the pandemic has illustrated the drawbacks of overdependence on Beijing, leading to a call to diversify away from China-centric supply chain networks. The newly proposed Japan–India–Australia-led Supply Chain Resilience Initiative (SCRI) can offer added stimulus, if its execution is thought out clearly. It could hold significant potential for advancing many of India's and Japan's shared policy goals in the

---

[3]   Former Indian ambassador to Germany and former diplomat to Japan.

post-pandemic period: boosting national and regional economies, creating employment, building alternate and resilient global supply chains as well as reducing their dependence on China. Notably, China has been facing a backlash for its role in global commerce, as its Covid aid diplomacy has received mixed signals in several parts of the globe, including in Africa. This is only likely to increase the risks associated with the BRI projects in Africa, while impacting Chinese trade and other investments in the region. In fact, according to Wang Xialong, director-general of the Chinese foreign ministry's international economic affairs department, about a fifth of the BRI projects aiming to boost trade and investment across Asia, Africa and Europe had been 'severely affected' (Nyabiage 2020), while African countries like Sierra Leone and Tanzania cancelled Chinese projects and loans on account of debt concerns (Venkateswaran 2020).

For India and Japan, this situation presents an opportune moment to demonstrate willingness and capacity to collaborate with Africa through a business-oriented model which focuses on economic growth post Covid-19 through sustainable development. Further, both the countries need to have a multidimensional collaboration with Africa in handling the challenges brought about by the pandemic through supplying medicines, masks and other medical equipment needed to counter Covid-19. This has the possibility not only to expand India and Japan's diplomatic and developmental outreach in the region, but to also enhance a purposive partnership factoring the Indo-Pacific to exhibit their shared regional and global leaderships and enhance the status of both the countries as responsible and reliable Indo-Pacific powers and global stakeholders.

Conclusion

In response to China's increasingly active and unilateral actions in the Indo-Pacific region, India and Japan envisioned the AAGC to uphold quality and sustainable infrastructure. Although the AAGC was a product of India and Japan's synergistic policies of the 'Act East' and the Expanded Partnership for Quality Infrastructure (EPQI), vouching for an open, fair and transparent order, it has now been remodelled. Both India and Japan have struggled to execute such a cross-continental initiative as it requires sustained financial back-up, official and non-official planning and, notably, a concrete 'third-country' cooperation framework suiting their bilateral partnership. However, the non-execution of such a framework or initiative has not really acted as an obstruction to a greater India–Japan partnership in Africa. It instead has set the tone for a new business-oriented partnership between the two special strategic partners in the region.

Greatly synergic to each other's business-oriented partnership with Africa, enhanced triangular business ties involving the public as well as the private sector can act as an impetus for India and Japan to realise their national goals through investments in Africa. Further, with the backdrop of an economically and strategically rising China, partnership remains a way to secure and sustain India and Japan's diplomatic overtures and strategic influences in the region. However, it remains important for India and Japan to strike a balance in the business environment if they are to challenge China's strong foothold. As convergent interests of major players in the region can turn into conflicts, it will also be vital for India and Japan to expand their business partnership in Africa and enhance their global partnership in the Indo-Pacific, without turning the region into a hub of power rivalry.

Bibliography

AEI. 2019. 'China global investment tracker', n.d., https://www.aei.org/china-global-investment-tracker/, accessed 2 December 2019.

AfDB. 2019. 'Japan and African Development Bank announce $3.5 billion in support of Africa's private sector development', 30 August 2019, https://www.afdb.org/en/news-and-events/press-releases/japan-and-african-development-bank-announce-35-billion-support-africas-private-sector-development-29588, accessed 1 February 2020.

Aiyar, P. 2019. 'Japan's push for `quality engagement´ with Africa', *The Hindu*, 7 September 2019, https://www.thehindu.com/news/international/japans-push-for-quality-engagement-with-africa/article29362661.ece, accessed 2 December 2019.

Bhatia, R. 2011. 'India-Africa summit: From agreement to action', *The Hindu*, 9 June 2011, https://www.thehindu.com/opinion/op-ed/indiaafrica-summit-from-agreement-to-action/article2088135.ece, accessed 1 December 2019.

Chacko P. and Panda, J. 2019. 'Regionalising India-Japan relations in the Indo-Pacific', in K. Springer, *Implementing the Indo-Pacific: Japan's Region Building Initiatives*, Perth USAsia Centre, August 2019, https://perthusasia.edu.au/events/past-conferences/defence-forum-2019/2019-indo-pacific-defence-conference-videos/keynotes-and-feature-presentations/pu-134-japan-book-web.aspx, accessed 1 December 2019.

Embassy of Japan in India. 2018. 'Ambassador Hiramatsu Attended Regional Connectivity Conference', 1 November 2018, https://www.in.emb-japan.go.jp/files/000414829.pdf, accessed 30 November 2020.

Eyinla, B.M. 2018. 'Promoting Japan's national interest in Africa: A review of TICAD', *Africa Development*, Council for the Development of Social Science Research in Africa, XLIII/3, 107–22.

Financial Express. 2020. 'India may pip Japan to become third largest economy by 2050 after China, US', 11 October 2020, https://www.financialexpress.com/economy/india-may-pip-japan-to-become-3rd-largest-economy-by-2050-after-china-us/2102977/, accessed on 30 November 2020.

MEA (Ministry of External Affairs)Times 2020b. 2004. 'Ministerial Meeting of Team-9 countries, Joint statement', GoI, 1 March 2004, https://mea.gov.in/bilateral-documents.htm?dtl/7425/Ministerial+Meeting+of+TEAM9+Countries+Joint+Statement, accessed 2 December 2019.

——. 2008. 'Joint press conference following the conclusion of first India-Africa Forum Summit 9th April 2008, Vigyan Bhavan, New Delhi', GoI, 9 April 2008, https://www.mea.gov.in/media-briefings.htm?dtl/4075/, accessed 1 December 2019.

——. 2011. 'Second Africa-India Forum Summit 2011: Africa-India framework for enhanced cooperation', GoI, 25 May 2011, https://mea.gov.in/bilateral-documents.htm?dtl/34/Second+AfricaIndia+Forum+Summit+2011+AfricaIndia+Framework+for+Enhanced+Cooperation, 1 December 2019.

——. 2015. 'Third India-Africa Forum Summit', GoI, 29 October 2015, http://www.mea.gov.in/Uploads/PublicationDocs/25981_framework.pdf, accessed 1 December 2019.

——. 2016. 'India-Japan joint statement during the visit of Prime Minister to Japan', GoI, 11 November 2016, https://mea.gov.in/bilateral-documents.htm?dtl/27599/IndiaJapan+Joint+Statement+during+the+visit+of+Prime+Minister+to+Japan, accessed 2 December 2019.

——. 2018a. 'Address by foreign secretary at the Regional Connectivity Conference: South Asia in the Indo-Pacific context', GoI, 1 November 2018, https://www.mea.gov.in/Speeches-Statements.htm?dtl/30556/Address+by+Foreign+Secretary+at+the+Regional+Connectivity+Conference++South+Asia+in+the+IndoPacific+Context, accessed 2 December 2019.

——. 2018b. 'Prime Minister's address at parliament of Uganda during his state visit to Uganda', GoI, 25 July 2018, https://mea.gov.in/Speeches-Statements.htm?dtl/30152/Prime_Ministers_address_at_Parliament_of_Uganda_during_his_State_Visit_to_Uganda, accessed 2 December 2019.

——. 2019. 'Inaugural address by secretary (ER) at India-Africa Higher Education and Skills Development Summit', GoI, 27 August 2019, https://mea.gov.in/Speeches-Statements.htm?dtl/31771/Inaugural+Address+by+SecretaryER+at+IndiaAfrica+Higher+Education+and+Skills+Development+Summit, accessed 2 December 2019.

MoC (Ministry of Commerce). 2013. 'Focus Africa programme', GoI, March 2004, https://commerce.gov.in/writereaddata/publications/africa_cr_nov2003.pdf, accessed 1 December 2019.

MSDE (Ministry of Skill Development and Entrepreneurship). 2017. 'Skill India and World Bank organise a "knowledge sharing workshop" for African delegates', GoI, https://nsdcindia.org/sites/default/files/Press_Release_Africa_India_Knowledge_Exchange_Mission_English.pdf, accessed 2 December 2019.

Nyabiage, J. 2019a. 'Japan keen to do business in Africa as China extends reach on continent', *South China Morning Post*, 30 August 2019, https://www.scmp.com/news/china/diplomacy/article/3024955/japan-keen-do-business-africa-china-extends-reach-continent, 2 December 2019.

———. 2019b. 'Japan seeks to counter China in Africa with alternative 'high-quality' development', *South China Morning Post*, 18 August 2019, https://www.scmp.com/news/china/diplomacy/article/3023243/japan-seeks-counter-china-africa-alternative-high-quality, accessed 2 December 2019.

———. 2020. 'Pandemic takes the shine off China's Belt and Road Initiative as African partners struggle with coronavirus', *South China Morning Post*, 28 June 2020, https://www.scmp.com/news/china/diplomacy/article/3090850/pandemic-takes-shine-chinas-belt-and-road-initiative-african, accessed on 30 November.

Odutola, Abiola. 'COVID-19: India donates $50 million worth essential medicines to Nigeria, others', *Nairametrics*, 18 July 2020, https://nairametrics.com/2020/07/18/covid-19-india-donates-50-million-worth-essential-medicines-to-nigeria-others/, accessed 30 November 2020.

Pandey, M. 2017. 'Modi diplomacy at work; African nations looking up to India for entrepreneurship tips', *India Today*, 24 December 2017, https://www.indiatoday.in/mail-today/story/modi-diplomacy-african-nations-looking-india-entrepreneurship-tips-1115223-2017-12-24, accessed 2 December 2019.

Roy Chaudhury, D. 2020. 'India, Africa favour new dimensions to multifaceted partnership in post-Covid world order', *The Economic Times*, 27 May 2020, https://economictimes.indiatimes.com/news/politics-and-nation/india-africa-favour-new-dimensions-to-multifaceted-partnership-in-post-covid-world-order/articleshow/76037917.cms?from=mdr, accessed 30 November 2020.

Sasaki, N. 2019. 'Africa commerce succeeds through new partnerships, *Japan Times*, 27 August 2019, https://www.japantimes.co.jp/news/2019/08/27/business/economy-business/africa-commerce-succeeds-new-partnerships/#.XeVydTIzZQK, accessed 2 December 2019.

Singh, G. 2019. 'India, Japan and the Asia Africa Growth Corridor', *Gateway House*, 17 January 2019, https://www.gatewayhouse.in/japan-aagc/#_ftn6, accessed 1 February 2020.

TICAD. 2019. 'TICAD 7 Yokohama 2019, the seventh Tokyo International Conference on African Development', *Government of Japan*, https://ticad7.city.yokohama.lg.jp/english/ accessed 2 December 2019.

Tirumurti, T.S. 2019. 'Remarks by Shri T. S. Tirumurti, Secretary (ER) at Africa Day round-table discussion in IDSA on: "India-Africa partnership in a changing world"', *MP-IDSA*, 29 May 2018, https://idsa.in/keyspeeches/remarks-shri-ts-tirumurti-india-africa-partnership, accessed 2 December 2019.

Trigunayat, A. 2019. 'Evolution and importance of India-Africa relations; from Gandhi to Modi', *Financial Express*, 2 April 2019, https://www.financialexpress.com/india-news/evolution-and-importance-of-india-africa-relations-from-gandhi-to-modi/1535979/, accessed 1 December 2019.

Venkateswaran, L. 2020. 'China's Belt and Road initiative: implications in Africa', *ORF Online*, 24 August 2020, https://www.orfonline.org/research/chinas-belt-and-road-initiative-implications-in-africa/, accessed 12 February 2021

Wagner, C. 2019. 'India's Africa policy', *Stiftung Wissenschaft und Politik (SWP)*, Research Paper 9, July 2019, https://www.swp-berlin.org/fileadmin/contents/products/research_papers/2019RP09_wgn_Web.pdf accessed 1 December 2019.

Yang, J. 2012. 'Take the new type of China–Africa strategic partnership to a new high', *Embassy of the People's Republic of China in the Federal Democratic Republic of Ethiopia*, 18 July 2012, http://et.china-embassy.org/eng/zfgx/t952597.htm, accessed 2 February 2020.

Yu, G.T. 2010. 'China's Africa policy: South-South unity and cooperation', in L. Dittmer and G.T. Yu (eds.), *China, the Developing World and the New Global Dynamics*, (Bouler: Lynne Rienner), 129–56.

PART 2

The Indian Political Right and the Reconfiguration of Soft Power in Africa

3

The Indian Political Right, Soft Power and the Reimagining of Africa

MEERA VENKATACHALAM

Indian state and non-state actors, from the Nehruvian to the Modi eras, have used similar cultural resources in their deployment of soft power in Africa, from yoga to Bollywood (Shangwe, this volume). They have also emphasised as India's strengths a value system based on political pluralism, diversity and non-violence (Blarel 2012: 29), virtues sometimes embodied through the figure of Mahatma Gandhi (Vittorini, this volume). The gradual rise of the right-wing BJP in India has coincided with the dethroning of the Nehruvian vision of the nation as a secular, multi-faith, pluralistic society. Along with this broader shift, India's normative agenda, which defines intrinsic value systems developed by the nation, and its place and role on the global stage has also changed (Hall 2017). A reinvention of Indian culture and reconceptualisation of the nation's past civilisational role in the world has ensued, which is changing the rationale for India's engagement with Africa – against the backdrop of the BJP's 'Hindutva' ideology. This chapter seeks to illustrate how ideas derived from Hindutva define the cognitive frames which inform understandings of certain elements of Indian soft power in Africa. These ideas are contributing to the redrawing of India's normative agenda on the global stage, and also reconfiguring the India–Africa relationship from one governed by southern, postcolonial solidarity to a more hierarchical relationship.

Hindutva and its tenets

Hindutva (translation: Hinduness) itself is not a coherent ideology, but a curious blend of Hindu cultural nationalism of the colonial era; ideas from nineteenth century revivalist Hindu movements, and pseudo-scientific notions of race and eugenics developed by regimes on the brink of the Second World War in Europe. The ruling BJP and a number of other socio-cultural organisations and political parties – such as the Rashtriya Swayamsevak Sangh (RSS), Vishva Hindu Parishad (VHP), Bajrang Dal (BD) and Hindu Mahasabha (HM), among others – are collectively organised into the Sangh Parivar (family of organisations) that broadly subscribes to the ideology of

Hindutva. Its adherents largely conceive of India as a Hindu civilisational nation, which they believe developed a unique moral, socio-economic and technological order (Bajpai 2014: 131). The 'founding fathers' of Hindutva, Vinayak Damodar Savarkar (1883–1966) and Madhav Sadashiv Golwalkar (1906–73), argued that Hindu India had fallen in stature due to centuries of subjugation by Muslim and Christian powers. Intrinsic to their ideological project was to rebuild Hindu civilisation, erase the humiliation of a millennium of 'foreign' (non-Hindu) rule and spread the enlightening message of Hinduism throughout the world (Basrur 2017: 10; Basrur 2018: 7–8). Hindutva's arguments construct a monolithic Hindu identity, based on a common geographical origin, Sanskrit-derived languages, culture, common laws and rites, sometimes ignoring the nuanced patchwork of class, caste, tribal, religious and ethno-linguistic identities present in India (Khilnani 1997: 161). Many have pointed out that this worldview, fixated on political power, militancy and culture, stems from an upper-caste Hindu conceptualisation of the early twentieth century, when colonial India was undergoing tumultuous socio-political realignments internally (Harriss et al. 2017: 8).

The contemporary Hindutva political imaginary envisions three great global threats: Islam (denoting Islamic 'domination' of precolonial India), the Christian West (referring to British colonialism) and China (Bajpai 2014: 133–34). The threat from these forces to India is not only militaristic, but is also derived from their cultural machinery, which could dilute Hindu civilisation and values. Central to the Hindutva project is a Hindu *mission civilisatrice* (civilising mission), where foreign cultures – both in the immediate neighbourhood of India and beyond – are made to recognise the value of India's ancient (Hindu) wisdom (Bajpai 2014: 131). The implicit notion of this Hindu *mission civilisatrice* finds expression in some elements of India's soft power strategy in Africa. The previous rhetoric of southern solidarity and cooperation which characterised India's imagining of early postcolonial India's relations with Africa continue to exist, albeit feebly, alongside newly emerging discourses of India's role as an imparter of a unique civilisational wisdom.

Saffronisation[1] of public culture

From the 1980s, Hindutva's frames of reference were internalised by both elites and the masses (Palshikar 2015), leading to the widespread normalisation of 'banal Hindutva' (Harriss et al. 2017: 7–13). The normalisation of

---

[1]   A political term referring to the ideological and socio-cultural project of the BJP and the Sangh, with saffron being the colour of the BJP and the sacred robes of Hindu holy men.

'banal Hindutva' was a result of the grassroots cultural activism of the Sangh Parivar, as well as a disillusionment with the policies of previous Congress and Congress-led governments, which were accused of Hindu exclusion at the cost of appeasement of religious and other minorities (Ganguly 2015). In the 1990s, as India experimented with pro-market reforms, public spaces became infused with a neo-religious Hindu aura – temple construction and renovation often sponsored by diasporic Indians, the renewal and invention of ritual and public displays of religious festivals, and the prominence of new religious leaders or *gurus* as the religious and symbolic currency of the new India (Nanda 2009). The cultural processes, termed 'saffronisation', have been thriving for four decades, and are normalised irrespective of whether the BJP – or the non-majoritarian Congress – is in power (Anderson 2018). Public opinion in now tilted towards Hindutva, and the BJP now occupies the centre ground in the political landscape.

Nowhere is this saffronisation more apparent than in the educational apparatuses of the state. Since 2014, a series of changes have been made by the Ministry of Human Resource Development (MHRD).[2] The BJP seeks to create a national unity based on the idea of a common Hindu lineage for all Indians. To this end, an entirely new curriculum based on Hindutva rein- terpretation of history has emerged, downplaying the legacy of key secular figures of a liberal disposition in Indian history, omitting the contributions of 'foreign' (i.e., non-Hindu) dynasties. In 2016, Jawaharlal Nehru's and Mahatma Gandhi's[3] contributions to history were underplayed from school text books in Rajasthan (Ahmad 2018). In 2017, textbooks in the Mahar- ashtra state omitted all mention of the (Muslim) Mughals (Hussain 2017). There have been attempts to incorporate Hindu religious texts such as Vedas and Upanishads in the upper secondary school curriculum during the present tenure of the BJP in Uttar Pradesh, where Muslims form about 20 per cent of the population (Ahmad 2018).

The notion that Hindu civilisation bequeathed to the world advanced science and technologies has found mainstream acceptance. The 2019 Indian Science Congress celebrated a story in the Hindu epic Mahabharata about a

[2]   As of 2020, reconfigured as the Ministry of Education (MoE).

[3]   The symbolism of Mahatma Gandhi is employed by the Hindu Right in con- flicting ways. Internally, he is portrayed as a 'soft' leader, who did not champion the cause of Hindus wholeheartedly – by allowing partition which divided In- dia and created Pakistan, and by pandering to Ambedkar's demands for separate electorates for lower castes which 'split' the Hindu community in independent India. However, many Indian governments, including the Modi government, have used Gandhi as a symbol of India–Africa ties, in acknowledgement of his years in South Africa (see Vittorini, this volume).

woman who gave birth to a hundred children, citing that Hindu civilisation had developed advanced reproductive technologies thousands of years ago. The Vice Chancellor of Andhra University in Visakhapatanam declared that 'stem cell research was done [in India] thousands of years ago' (Kumar 2019). The Vijnana Bharati (VIBHA), the science wing of the RSS, has promoted the view that Hindu spirituality/knowledge is the precursor of modern science. VIBHA receives generous government funding and is active in twenty-three states; it has 20,000 initiated members and 100,000 volunteers – including many in the highest echelons of Indian science – to spread its views (Kumar 2019).

Race, Hindutva and Africa

Hindutva ideologues, past and present, have developed ideas about 'race' based on precolonial concepts of otherness rooted in the socio-cultural matrices of the sub-continent and European racialised imaginaries and hierarchies of the colonial period, which would come to inform their relationship with Africa. Indians came to understand race and racial difference in the colonial era through already existing identities – as defined in the caste or *varna* (colour) system. Each *varna* comprises innumerable *jatis* (or subcastes, alluding to occupational specialisations). Over generations, some *jatis* have risen in status through capital and ritual accumulation, while others have fallen in status. New occupational groups have been incorporated into the system and others have died out. Caste became entrenched in legal frameworks and governance strategies engineered by the British from the early nineteenth century, and was used as an instrument of social control. That caste was known as *varna* (Sanskrit: colour, appearance) alluded to the fact that colour, status and hierarchy were intimately linked, and that caste endogamy, ritual behaviour and social practices had resulted in distinct groups of people who were believed to share certain physical characteristics, a view which sat comfortably with crude colour-based scientific racism of the colonial era.

The view that some Indians were 'Aryans' acquired currency due to the scholarship of German linguist and orientalist Friedrich Max Müller (1823–1900). Max Müller argued that linguistic similarities between (northern) Indic (Aryan), Central Asian and European languages, meant that these populations occupied a common homeland in their distant past, and were dispersed through migration (Thapar 1996: 5–6). The original proto-Aryan homeland, according to Max Müller, was most likely in Central Asia, where a proto-Indo-European language was spoken. The Aryan invasion theory saw certain groups in India stress their Indo-European heritage, to emphasise their civilisational prowess and historical genealogy during the colonial era. But the Sangh Parivar has reversed the Aryan invasion theory, to privilege ancient India as the birthplace of Indo-European civilisation, by arguing that Aryans originated in India (and not Central Asia), thereby taking their civilisational wisdom beyond the subcontinent through their migrations out of India (Ahmad 2018). Indeed, the idea that the Aryans and Dravidians (the linguistic groups found in central and southern peninsular India) were the two major racial types of the subcontinent became deeply entrenched – even though these differences are beginning to hold much less currency for the contemporary Hindutva political project, which emphasises religion as a marker of the Indic race. Dalits occupied an ambiguous space in the Hindutva imagination: perched at the bottom of the Vedic caste system, they were still Hindu as far as upper-castes were concerned, though they lacked the adequate ritual and cultural capital which made them 'Hindu'. Thus the contours of caste, colour and cultural capital worked to define an Indian race in the late colonial era, from which the Hindutva imagination borrowed.

In addition, certain British colonial stereotypes – which depicted India as stagnant and having 'fallen' from a previous civilisational zenith, and therefore higher in the hierarchy than, say, Africa (with the exception of Egypt and South Africa) – are internalised in the Hindutva worldview. The colonial enterprise labelled India and Indians as 'civilised and teachable' while Africans were not (Davis 2018: 248). Further, views on 'race' were shaped by global discourses of the pre- Second World War era, from crude pseudo-scientific racism and an obsession with 'racial purity'. Indeed, many of these views were mainstream in the late Victorian age among colonised, 'liberal' Indian elites who were not of a Hindutva disposition, and later came to champion the vision of a secular, plural India – Mahatma Gandhi himself was guilty of uncritically reproducing derogatory stereotypes about Africans during his time in South Africa (Vittorini, this volume).

Hindutva ideologues wrote very little about Africans, and when they wrote about Africa, it was largely in the context of Hindu communities living on the continent. Ironically, this silence about Africans tells us a great deal. M.S. Golwalkar, the second leader of the RSS, explained the predicament of Hindus in East Africa as such:

> In the past our people there, for the most part, did not actively sympathise with the aspirations of the native African people while they were struggling against the White colonialists. They also did not spend out of their earn- ings for promoting the welfare of the local population, for their education or for enlightening them in the tenets of Hinduism. The religious vacuum

prevalent there was filled in by the Christian and Islamic missionaries. The upshot of all these lapses on our part was that when the Africans became free, they were dominated by Christian and Islamic propaganda which soon made them lose sympathy for Hinduism or for Hindus in general. They therefore set about to displace the Hindus from their positions of strength and resources (Golwalkar 1996: 266).

Two ideas are striking. First, the assumption that Africans existed in a 'religious vacuum' prior to the advent of Christianity and Islam, in that they did not have a 'religion' of any sort. Religion is conflated with civilisation and culture in the Hindutva worldview, and the implicit assumption is that if Africans lacked a 'religion', they also lacked a 'civilisation'. Second is the explicit reference to the missed opportunity of engineering a Hindu civilisational mission, which would have been beneficial to Africans.

Indeed, the imagination of Indians and Africans as monolithic entities continues to pervade in the discourses about anti-black racism in India (Davis 2018) and in the Indian government's responses to racist incidents. Racist attacks against African students in recent years in India have attracted condemnation from across the continent and from African diplomats stationed in India (Modi and D'Silva 2016). Indian officials, including Modi's former Minister of Foreign Affairs, the late Sushma Swaraj, were quick to condemn them as 'law and order incidents', vehemently denying racist motivations. Such attitudes were revealing of a broader mindset associated with the Indian political right. First, the denial of overt anti-black racism (towards Africans) is part of a broader strategy which disacknowledges casteist discrimination perpetuated by upper castes against Dalits, and is a failure to recognise the complex ways in which caste, colour, privilege and power intertwine. Second is the Hindutva rendering of race as both a given biological category, as well as an overarching ideology, where acquiring attributes of 'civilisation' (or cultural capital associated with upper castes) could be earned, thereby elevating marginalised positionalities albeit without disturbing rigidly hierarchical social structures.

Hindutva in Modi's foreign policy

Hindutva ideologues often quote a number of ancient Indian strategic thinkers, such as Kautilya (also known as Chanakya) (*c.* 371–283 BCE). Kautilya authored the *Arthashastra*, a treatise on kingship that demonstrates what conforms to 'offensive realism' today (Basrur 2017: 10). Kings and states are caught in perennial conflict, and true security comes only from the attainment of *sarva-bhauma* (literally: whole world) or universal empire (Basrur

2017: 11). This Kautilyan concept finds articulation in the Indic-flavoured 'transcendental globalism', of Savarkar and Golwalkar, in their descriptions of Hindu India's civilisational duty on the global stage (Hall 2017: 124). Kautilya argued that in the pursuit of *sarva-bhauma*, unregulated territorial expansion – which could lead to insecurities and decline – was undesirable. Instead, the method to achieve the desired state of *sarva-bhauma* ought to be peaceful. In stark contrast to the *realpolitik* embodied by Kautilya is the figure of the Mauryan Emperor, Ashoka (*c*. 304–232 BCE) (Solomon 2012), whose trajectory and achievements are also discussed extensively by some Hindutva ideologues (Savarkar 2003). During his reign, Ashoka transformed from a belligerent conqueror committed to military expansion to a prophet of Buddhism espousing values of peace, non-violence, tolerance and universalism. Ashoka was appropriated first by the Nehruvian regime, which emphasised his virtues of peacefulness and tolerance, and his status as the first unifier of the new polyglot, postcolonial nation (Hall 2017: 117). The reign of Ashoka, the *chakravartin* (conqueror of the world), saw much of the subcontinent, southeast and east Asia come under the influence of Indo-Buddhist culture, not through conquest or confrontation, but through evangelising, diplomatic and cultural flows and trade. This aspect of Ashoka's career is emphasised by Hindutva ideologues: the state of world domination was achieved *because* of a series of military conflicts and masterful *realpolitik*, which enabled his U-turn and transformation into a peaceful figure. Thus, the Hindutva imaginary, drawing selectively from both diametrically opposed traditions of statecraft, strongly links the realisation of Kautilyan *sarva-bhauma*, with an Ashokan civilising mission, where India imparts knowledge and civilisational values to the rest of the world.

Modi is very much the product of Hindutva institutions (such as the RSS) as well as a symbol of a new Hindutva order.[4] His own political compass is a patchwork of his interpretations of Hindutva, in dialogue with the more entrenched ideas of the doctrine. The emergent 'Modi Doctrine' (Hall 2015) demonstrates more continuities than departures from previous leaders: in the *modus operandi* of Indian diplomatic machinery and the general understanding of India's place in the world. One school of thought argues that the impact

---

[4]   Modi's tenure as Chief Minister of Gujarat (2001–14) saw the establishment of pro-business regimens designed to strengthen investments in the state. Modi also presided over the worst spell of communal riots in Gujarat in 2002 (Harriss et al. 2017: 13–14). This led to international condemnation – Modi's human rights' record became a focal point for not just the Indian Supreme Court, but many international regimes which instituted visa bans against the then Chief Minister (Miller and Sullivan da Estrada 2017: 32–33).

of Hindutva on Modi's foreign policy has been minimal (Gupta et al. 2018). These scholars suggest, however, that other changes are evident after Modi's ascent to power. First, his tenure has seen the centralisation of foreign policy decision-making in the Prime Minister's Office. Second, religious diplomacy plays an important role, though the version of Hinduism that Modi has adopted in foreign affairs is more inclusive than the version at home. Third, India's foreign economic policy has adopted a recognisable, nationalist tone – embodied by initiatives like 'Make in India' which encouraged Indians to produce goods and services in India rather than import them (Gupta 2018: 18). Fourth, the regime remained preoccupied with a 'Neighbourhood First' focus in foreign policy, tending to concentrate on the nation states of the Indian subcontinent and China (Gupta et al. 2018: 1). 'Act East', focused on southeast Asia, and engagements with regions such as Africa were secondary to the neighbourhood.

Modi often invokes India's 'glorious heritage' and expects it to play a 'leading role' in the world. He often employs the phrase *vasudaiva kutumbakam*, which loosely denotes the interconnectedness of the world and that the world is one family. He emphasises that India stands for *vishvabandhuta* (world brotherhood) and peace. In April 2015, the BJP's national executive, led by Modi, presented Panchamrit (literally, five sacred foods), that is, the five pillars of his foreign policy: *sammaan* (dignity, honour); *samvad* (engagement, dialogue); *samriddhi* (shared prosperity); *suraksha* (regional and global security) and *sanskriti evam sabhyata* (cultural and civilisational linkages) (Basrur 2017: 11). The development of cultural and civilisational linkages involves a reimagination of history, where India is placed centre stage.

The quest for *sarva-bhauma*

What space does Africa occupy in the Hindutva religious and political cartography? Kautilyan thought envisions the world as a complex set of *mandalas*, or circles – best encapsulated as political ecosystems. These mandalas share differing degrees of affiliation and antipathy towards the *rajamandala* (the Kautilyan kingdom, the core of civilisational India in the Hindutva reading) and between themselves, which necessitate different modalities of strategic action (Modelski 1964). Savarkar's and Golwalkar's religious cartography defined three spaces: 1) Akhand Bharat or the Indian subcontinent; 2) a Hindu-Buddhist Asia, consisting of southeast, east and central Asia; and 3) an Indo-European sphere which shared cultural similarities with ancient Vedic 'Aryan' India (Stolte 2016: 51–2). The presence of large Hindu diasporic groups in East Africa means that it occupies an ambiguous space, positioned marginally within the confines of a civilisational India, though securely connected to the *rajamandala*. In his 1937 address to the Hindu Mahasabha (a socio-political organisation and party founded in 1915), Savarkar's understanding of what he termed 'Greater Hindustan' appeared to include Africa and Mauritius. He offered a message of 'sympathy and loving remembrances to those of our co-religionists and countrymen abroad who have been building a greater Hindustan without the noise of drums and trumpets in Africa, America, Mauritius and such other parts of the world … holding out as remnants of the ancient world empire of our Hindu race' (Savarkar n.d.). While Savarkar is clearly making references to branches of the Mahasabha started in Africa by the Hindu diaspora, he is also suggesting that Africa was once within the remit of ancient India's *sarva-bhauma*, or universal empire.

In the early years of the Modi regime, an initiative emerged which sought to respace the geopolitical landscape with references to the Indian Ocean (Bajpai 2014). Project Mausam (named after the monsoon weather system) was conceived primarily as a socio-cultural initiative, aimed at creating India-centric networks which would develop infrastructures for the movement of capital, ideas and cultural resources derived from Indic knowledge frames (Ministry of Culture n.d.). A website dedicated to the project declares that 'Project Mausam aims to understand how the knowledge and manipulation of the monsoon winds have shaped interactions across the Indian Ocean and led to the spread of shared knowledge systems, traditions, technologies and ideas along maritime routes' (Ministry of Culture n.d.). While considerable attention was given to celebrating the trading and cultural links of antiquity and the recent past, the project also attempted to 1) re-connect and re-establish communications between countries of the Indian Ocean world, which would lead to an enhanced understanding of cultural values and concerns, and 2) focus on understanding national cultures in their regional maritime milieu (Ministry of Culture n.d.). The Project also sought recognition from UNESCO. Some commentators envisioned Mausam as a counter-strategy to China's Beijing-centric Belt and Road Initiative (BRI), which sought to redraw the map of the world based on Han Chinese conceptions of the Middle Kingdom's pre-eminence (Baruah 2018).

Similarly, the BJP conceives of India as a civilisational state. The overseas Indian diaspora are key players in this vision. While all Indian governments after the 1990s have attempted to engage the diaspora to encourage foreign investment and trade, the BJPs' relationship with the diaspora has been informed by a revisiting of history, a particularly 'Hindu' history, which has reframed the ideal Indian diasporic subject as a cultural actor within the framework of an international civilisational Hindu network (Modi and Taylor 2017). As of 2014, the overseas wing of the BJP, known as the Overseas Friends of the BJP (OFBJP) planned to open branches in Ethiopia, Kenya, Rwanda, Uganda, Zambia and Zimbabwe (India Today 2014). As of 2020, they have a lively online presence in addition to these countries, in Nigeria (OFBJP Nigeria n.d.). The aims of the OFBJP include winning support for the BJP's foreign policy amongst the diaspora and to 'correct' narratives about the Modi administration generated by the liberal/secular intelligentsia believed to dominate the media. By contrast, the opposition Congress Party, which is organised into the Indian Overseas Congress (IOC) outside India, does not have a significant, organised presence in Africa at the time of writing (IOC n.d.). The OFBJP's success in Africa is owed to the prior existence of networks of Indian associations on the continent, which espoused the ideology of the Sangh Parivar. *Shakhas* (branches) of the RSS – known as the Hindu Swayamsevak Sangh (HSS) overseas – were established in Kenya as early as 1947 by diasporic Indians (Andersen and Damle 2018). As of 2015, the HSS was present in thirty-nine countries worldwide (Mukherji 2015). Most activities of the HSS and OFBJP overlap – such as organising Hindu religious festivals, humanitarian work amongst the host community, fundraising drives for cultural projects of right-wing parties in India and receiving high-profile BJP members abroad. Thus, global communities of Hindutva adherents are well established today due to transregional migrations (see Bhatt 2020), the online cultural and pedagogical work of the HSS and, more recently, the OFBJP.

Vishva guru of the world: exporting Indic wisdom

Make India *vishva guru* (again)

In their attempts to define normative power, Hindutva thinkers reject Nehruvian tenets, drawing upon certain discourses of universal humanism propagated by revivalist Hindu *gurus* and political activists of the late nineteenth and early twentieth century (Hall 2017: 115). Vivekananda, who founded the Ramakrishna Mission in Kolkata (Hall 2018: 14), and is credited with 'introducing' Hinduism to Western audiences, often referred to India as a *vishva guru* (teacher of the world). Vivekananda had also argued that Hinduism – and by extension India – has a particular role to play by synthesising Western materialism with Eastern spirituality, thereby generating a peaceful world. India was a spiritual 'dynamo' capable of ending the 'fanaticism and religious wars' that 'mar the life of man and the progress of civilisation' (Hall 2018: 14). Though Vivekananda was not associated with the Hindutva movement in his lifetime, his 'universal humanism' coupled with a Hindu exceptionalism was appropriated and improvised into more aggressive doctrines by Hindutva ideologues, such as Deen Dayal Upadhyaya (1916–68).[5] Such Hindutva ideologues have also argued the need for evangelism – of Indic wisdom, not literal conversion to Hinduism.

In 2018, India announced the 'Study in India' scheme, aimed at revamping the Indian educational machinery and attracting foreign students to Indian institutions. The Study in India scheme is meant to build upon and complement the efforts of the Indian Council for Cultural Relations (ICCR) and Indian Technical and Economic Cooperation (ITEC), and involve private educational institutions. Africa was identified as a key market (see King, this volume). Echoing Vivekanandan ideas, officials from the then MHRD declared that:

> The quest for knowledge has always been fundamental to India's culture and civilisation. Throughout our history, India has made seminal contributions to human thought, philosophy and development (PIB 2018b).

They continued:

> India has been known to the world as 'Vishva Guru'. Knowledge-seekers and curious minds from across the world came here to study in universities like Nalanda, Takshashila, Vikramshila, Pushpagiri and Somapura. These globally renowned seats of learning not only stood at the crossroads of many civilisations but influenced and enriched those civilisations.
>
> As you are aware, we have revived the Nalanda University. Ancient Nalanda was a centre of excellence, devoted to the study of philosophy and Buddhism and was also a centre for the advancement of science and technology.
>
> In fact … 'Study in India' is not new. It existed since ancient times and Indian centres of learning produced world-famous alumni such as Megasthenes, Hiuen Tsang, Fa Hien, and Al-Barauni, all of who went on to spread the word, far and wide, and wrote treatises based on India's knowledge systems.
>
> Our objective should be to once again make India the world's 'Vishva Guru' (PIB 2018b).

[5] Upadhya's 'Integral Humanism' propagates a unified national consciousness which seeks to aggressively assimilate all 'minorities' into a single cultural and socio-political framework, engineering economic trajectories of progress based on indigenous Hindu realities and rejecting grand narratives emerging from Western thought.

AYUSH

The Ministry of AYUSH[6] (an acronym for Ayurveda, Yoga and Naturopathy, Unani, Siddha, Sowa-Rigpa and Homeopathy, the alternative systems of medicine recognised by the Government of India) was established in 2014. The aim of the Ministry is to 'ensure the optimal development and propagation of AYUSH systems of health care' (PIB 2018a). AYUSH's activities involve: popularising Indian traditional systems of medicine globally; promoting quality assurance of other forms of drug and non- drug therapies of the Indian Systems of Medicine (ISMs); the development of Good Manufacturing Practices (GMPs) and Good Clinical Practices (GCPs) guidelines; and framing rules and guidelines for export promotion schemes like quality certifications for ISM products and encouraging yoga professionals to popularise ISM treatments through quality benchmarks (James and Bhatnagar 2019: 4). Since 2016, there have been dedicated celebrations for 'World Homoeopathy Day'; 'Unani Day'; 'Ayurveda Day' and 'International Day of Yoga' in India. Information about these have been disseminated through diplomatic missions overseas.

In 2019, international delegations from thirty different countries, including Ghana, South Africa and Tanzania, attended a meeting organised by AYUSH in collaboration with the World Health Organisation to develop benchmarks and international terminologies for Ayurveda, Siddha and Unani (Indus Dictum 2019). As part of the Third India-Africa Forum Summit (IAFS-III) in New Delhi, India and Africa agreed to collaborate in this sector. In February 2018, thirty-one participants from eleven African countries attended an AYUSH training programme. The efforts of the Ministry of AYUSH have seen the inclusion of alternative medicine into the ICCR and ITEC schemes. Under the AYUSH scholarship scheme, fifty scholarships are provided globally for undergraduate, postgraduate and diploma courses in Ayurveda, Unani, Siddha and Homeopathy (James and Bhatnagar 2019: 12), of which twenty are reserved for non-BIMSTEC[7] countries, including in Africa (ICCR 2019). The Ministry of AYUSH also proposes to establish a number of chairs in non-Indian universities: one Unani Chair was established at the University of the Western Cape in South Africa (PIB 2015), while an Ayurveda Chair is planned for Mauritius (Republic of Mauritius 2016).

---

[6]   India has always recognised alternative health systems, and the AYUSH systems of health were previously incorporated under the Ministry of Health.

[7]   Bay of Bengal Initiative for Multi-Sectoral Technical and Economic Cooperation, including Bangladesh, Bhutan, India, Myanmar, Nepal, Sri Lanka and Thailand.

The medical systems collectively referred to as AYUSH have been developed over centuries of transregional contact and incorporation in the Indian subcontinent and beyond. However, they are represented as being infused by a common flavour, either compatible with Vedic knowledge or having borrowed heavily from it. The term Sowa-Rigpa is reported to be 'derived from the Bhoti [a Tibetic language spoken in Ladakh] language', and is described as an 'ancient Indian medical system which enriched the entire trans-Himalayan region'. Further, the website claims that Sowa-Rigpa spread 'along with Buddhism to neighbouring countries', and that it 'can be perceived to be more close or having similarity with Ayurveda philosophy/principles of India', 'since more than 75 per cent of the texts of Sowa-Rigpa are taken from Ashtanga Hridaya, one of the most famous Ayurveda texts, and 75 per cent of the medical therapies are derived from Ayurveda' (Ministry of AYUSH n.d. a). Naturopathy, which has its origins in Germany, is described as 'having references in the Vedas and other ancient texts', representing it as similar to Ayurveda, and alluding to aspects of the common civilisation shared by Indo-Aryan/European peoples. The names of Vincent Priessnitz (1799–1851) and Louis Huhne (1835–1901) are mentioned in the context of hydrotherapy and the origins of naturopathy, along with a number of other prominent German naturopaths. The website declares naturopathy to be compatible with ancient Indian systems of healing (Ministry of AYUSH n.d. b). The Unani system, introduced by the Arabs and Persians in the eleventh century, we are told, has its origins in Greece, and that 'Unani medicines incorporated the best of traditional systems from Egypt to China, and the Delhi sultans provided extensive patronage to Unani scholars' (Ministry of AYUSH n.d. c). We are told that the birthday of Hakim Ajmal Khan, the renowned Unani medical practitioner and educationist who also played an important role in India's freedom struggle, is observed as Unani Day every year (Ministry of AYUSH, 2019a). That Unani thrived at the zenith of an outward-looking Islamic civilisation in India, which incorporated influences from the Middle East to Central Asia and beyond, and that Hakim Ajmal Khan was a Sufi, goes unmentioned. While the internationalisation of alternative systems of healthcare may seem like a benign idea, the homogenisation of these holistic therapies into a cultural corpus representing the entirety of alternative 'Indian medical systems' is a reflection of a wider political agenda.

Yoga

In 2014, the United Nations General Assembly (UNGA) approved by consensus a resolution establishing an International Day of Yoga (IDY) to be held each year on 21 June, as a result of Modi's persistent personal diplomacy on the global stage. For Modi, 21 June 2015 was 'the beginning of a new era that would inspire humanity in its quest for peace and harmony' (Miller and Sullivan da Estrada 2017: 44). He also declared that yoga could reduce violence between nations and bring 'a dramatic reduction in conflicts and misunderstandings within families, communities and between nations' (Miller and Sullivan da Estrada 2017: 45). The Modi government organised yoga-related events across India and, through its overseas missions, around the world (Miller and Sullivan da Estrada 2017: 43). IDY has been commemorated across Africa, and several interactive tutorials – including 'Yoga with Modi' sessions which feature an animated figure bearing the likeness of the Prime Minister performing *asanas* (yoga postures) – were posted on the Facebook page of the Indian Consulate General in Durban in June 2018 (India in South Africa, Facebook 2018).

Critics of this move have argued that Modi has fashioned IDY based on a specific, Hinduised understanding of yoga's origins (Miller and Sullivan da Estrada 2017: 45; Gautam and Droogan 2018).[8] Meanwhile, Hindu nationalist groups, including the BJP and RSS, attempted to reclaim yoga as part of India's past glory, hailing from an era prior to the presence of Christian and Muslim communities. Some Indian Muslim groups opposed the institutionalisation of IDY, and objected to certain practices, such as chanting *om* and a posture known as *surya namaskar*, which they interpreted as 'praying to the sun' (Miller and Sullivan da Estrada 2017: 45). In the lead up to the 21 June celebrations in 2015, the Ministry of AYUSH released a booklet (and a video) laying out a *Common Yoga Protocol*. Observers noted that while the *Protocol* omitted *om* and the *surya namaskar*, it contained prayers in Sanskrit, the ritual language which has historically been the preserve of the Hindu elite. The 4th edition of the *Protocol* declared yoga to be an immortal cultural outcome of the 'Indus-Saraswati Valley civilisation', dating back to 2700 BCE (Ministry of AYUSH 2019b).[9] Some described the *Protocol* as 'a narrowly conceived

---

8   India's official promotion of yoga predates Modi's leadership. The ICCR has been instrumental in disseminating yoga through its overseas centres for decades, and yoga formed a major visual theme of the cross-ministerial 'Incredible India' tourist campaign, launched in 2002. However, the form has never received as much active patronage as it has during the Modi regime (Miller and Sullivan da Estrada 2017: 43).

9   Saraswati refers to a sacred, mythical river mentioned in the Vedic texts. The ancient Indus Valley civilisation in contemporary Pakistan is referred to as the Sindhu (Indus)-Saraswati civilisation by Hindutva historians, based on their belief that the erstwhile Sarasvati flowed through Indus Valley cities, where they believe a formidable 'Hindu' civilisation was developed. The quest for the exact

definition of yoga' that captured 'one Hindu understanding of yoga's aims' and ignored a variety of other aims that Hindu and non-Hindu traditions have historically attributed to yoga (Jain 2015). Further, it is pointed out that historical research has indicated that modern yoga is very much a product of the twentieth century, and 'incorporated methods from military calisthenics, modern medicine, the physical culture of gymnasts, body builders and con-tortionists' (Jain 2015).

ITEC regularly conducts Yoga Instruction Courses (YICs) for Yoga trainers from all over the world in six institutes, as of early 2020 (ITEC n.d. a). From 4 February 2019 to 3 March 2019, ITEC conducted a special YIC for participants from Senegal, Gambia, Cape Verde and Guinea Bissau (ITEC n.d. b). The ITEC website describes the course thus: 'YICs have been specially designed so that within one month, a person feels comfortable and sufficiently knowledgeable to be able to teach yoga, in a positive non-harmful manner, which imbibes ancient knowledge of India' (ITEC n.d. b). It further says that at the S-VYASA institute (where this course was conducted), the YIC aims to inculcate a value system among students, through *maitrimi-lani*, or the chanting of *slok sangraha* (verses) from the Bhagavad Gita. It also propounds the Vivekanandan concept of *karma yoga* (selfless service) to the community, and to lead a balanced, simple and wholesome life. The objective of the course is to inculcate values of honesty, sincerity, integrity, punctuality and morality, and to emphasise the importance of traditional [Hindu] values. Participants are all called *bhaiyas* (brothers) and *didis* (sisters), and are taught 'the value of rising early' in the morning as well as 'universal brotherhood'.

Conclusion

The rhetoric used to describe India's relationship with Africa has been redefined, since language of postcolonial solidarity has been replaced by a hierarchical discourse (Davis 2018) based on internal reconceptualisation of India as an emerging power with a newly configured role on the global stage. Inserting 'race' into the frames of analysis – as much as political scientists have resisted doing so – while attempting to map the evolving trajectory of India–Africa relations, provides some valuable insights into changing Indian imaginings of Africa. Imperial histories of race and colonial hierar-chical renderings of the same were, and are, crucial in the conceptualisation

---

geographical location of the river Saraswati has preoccupied some historians for a while, and some initiatives have been dedicated to recreating/restoring the river in northern India (see Agarwal 2019).

of India–Africa relations from the colonial era to the present. In their interactions with each other, Indians and Africans internalised these imperialist stereotypes and built upon them. Crucially, these stereotypes came to inform the contrary practices of the enactment of solidarity and ideas of racialised hierarchies.

The symbols, enactment and *modus operandi* of India's soft power in Africa may seem unchanged from Nehru to Modi – with yoga, music, food, Bollywood and educational aid the main elements. And analysing the tangible outcomes of Modi's policies may suggest that there is little difference from his predecessors, and that India's Africa policy is defined by a sense of pragmatism where self-interest is paramount (Gupta et al. 2018). But upon interrogating the relationship between culture, identity and foreign policy (Michael 2018: 62), and upon deconstructing how cultural resources, ideological presuppositions and symbolic gestures are employed by Indian actors, it becomes evident that a paradigm shift is underway in the way Indians understand India–Africa relations. This article has tried to show how India's imagination of its role on the global stage is changing, and how Africa fits into that imagination, based on contemporary re-renderings of race, postcolonial solidarity and 'progress', many of which derive from the worldview of the Indian political right and Hindutva's ideological project, in particular.

Bibliography

Agarwal, M. 2019. 'Bring back the ancient Saraswati river', *Mongabay*, 19 July 2019, https://india.mongabay.com/2019/07/upcoming-elections-in-haryana-boost-efforts-to-revive-the-ancient-saraswati-river/, accessed 2 January 2020.

Ahmad, H. 2018. 'Saffron: The changing colours of Indian education', *Polemics and Pedantics*, 4 April 2018, https://www.polemicsnpedantics.com/single-post/2018/04/03/Saffron-The-Changing-Colors-of-Indian-Education, accessed 23 December 2019.

Andersen, W.K. and Damle, S. 2018. 'How the RSS operated in foreign countries in general and the USA in particular', *The Scroll*, 9 August 2018, https://scroll.in/article/889509/how-the-rss-operates-in-foreign-countries-in-general-and-the-usa-in-particular, accessed 10 November 2020.

Anderson, E. 2018. 'Hindu nationalism and the saffronisation of the public sphere: An interview with Christophe Jaffrelot', *Contemporary South Asia*, 26/4, 468–82.

Bajpai, K. 2014. 'Indian grand strategy: Six schools of thought', in K. Bajpai, S. Basit and V. Krishnappa (eds.), *India's Grand Strategy: History, Theory, Cases* (New Delhi: Routledge), 113–50.

Baruah, D. 2018. 'India's answer to the Belt and Road: A road map for South Asia', *Carnegie India*, 21 August 2018, https://carnegieindia.org/2018/08/21/

india-s-answer-to-belt-and-road-road-map-for-south-asia-pub-77071, accessed 23 December 2019.

Basrur, R. 2017. 'Modi's foreign policy fundamentals: A trajectory unchanged', *International Affairs*, 93/1, 7–26.

——. 2018. 'Modi, Hindutva and foreign policy', in S. Gupta et al. (eds.), 'Indian foreign policy under Modi: A new brand or just repackaging?', *International Studies Perspectives* (0), 7–11.

Bhatt, C. 2000. '*Dharmo rakshati rakshitah*: Hindutva movements in the UK', *Ethnic and Racial Studies*, 23/3, 559–93.

Blarel, N. 2012. 'India: The next superpower? India's soft power: From potential to reality?', *LSE IDEAS reports,* SR010, May 2012, http://eprints.lse.ac.uk/43445/1/India_India%27s%20soft%20power%28lse10%29.pdf, accessed 25 December 2019.

Davis, A.E. 2018. 'Solidarity or hierarchy?: India's identification with Africa and the postcolonial politics of race', *India Review*, 17/2, 242–62.

Ganguly, S. 2015. 'Hindu nationalism and the foreign policy of the Bharatiya Janta Party', *Transatlantic Academy*, 2014–15 Paper Series 2, 19 June 2015, https://www.gmfus.org/publications/hindu-nationalism-and-foreign-policy-indias-bharatiya-janata-party, accessed 2 January 2020.

Gautam, A. and Droogan, J. 2018. 'Yoga soft power: How flexible is the posture?', *Journal of International Communication*, 24/1, 18–36.

Golwalkar, M.S. 1996. *Bunch of Thoughts* (Bangalore: Sahitya Sindhu Prakashan, third edn).

Gupta, S. 2018. 'India's trade engagement: The more things change, the more they remain same', in S. Gupta et al., 'Indian foreign policy under Modi: A new brand or just repackaging?', *International Studies Perspectives*, 14–19.

Gupta, S., Mullen, R.D., Basrur, R., Hall, I., Blarel, N., Pardesi, M.S., Ganguly, S. 2018. 'Indian foreign policy under Modi: A new brand or just repackaging?', *International Studies Perspectives* (0), 1–45.

Hall, I. 2015. 'Is a "Modi doctrine" emerging in Indian foreign policy?', *Australian Journal of International Affairs*, 69/3, 247–52.

——. 2017. 'Narendra Modi and India's normative power', *International Affairs,* 93/1, 113–31.

——. 2018. 'Narendra Modi's new religious diplomacy', in S. Gupta et al., 'Indian foreign policy under Modi: A new brand or just repackaging?', *International Studies Perspectives* (0), 11–14.

Harriss, J., Jeffrey, C. and Corbridge, S. 2017. *Is India Becoming the 'Hindu Rashtra' Sought by Hindu Nationalists?*, Simons Papers in Security and Development No. 60, School for International Studies (Vancouver: Simon Fraser University).

Hussain, S. 2017. 'Maharashtra education board omits Mughal empire from its history textbooks', *Home Grown*, 8 August 2017, https://homegrown.co.in/article/801529/education-board-omits-mughal-empire-from-maharashtra-history-textbooks, accessed 30 December 2019.

ICCR. 2019. 'Annual report 2017-18', *GoI*, n.d., https://www.iccr.gov.in/sites/default/files/Annual%20reports/Annual-Report_2017-2018.pdf, accessed 28 January 2020.

India in South Africa (Durban), *#yogawithmodi*, Facebook. 2018. 27 June 2018, https://www.facebook.com/cgidbn/videos/1757315660990559, accessed 2 January 2020.

India Today. 2014. 'After Uganda, the BJP to open office in Kenya, other African nations', 7 September 2014, https://www.indiatoday.in/world/story/bjp-overseas-office-kenya-other-african-nations-207641-2014-09-07, accessed 1 November 2020.

Indus Dictum. 2019. 'AYUSH Min & WHO to develop standardised terms, benchmarks for Ayurveda, traditional medicine', *Indus Dictum*, 25 November 2019, https://indusdictum.com/2019/11/25/ayush-min-who-to-develop-standardized-terms-benchmarks-for-ayurveda-traditional-medicine/, accessed 23 December 2019.

IOC. n.d. https://www.iocongress.org/, IOC, n.d., accessed 1 November 2020.

ITEC. n.d. a. 'Health and Yoga', *GoI*, n.d., https://www.itecgoi.in/institute_list.php?salt3=08e05c39682019-2020&salt=2b6435b6b826, accessed 30 January 2020.

——. n.d. b. 'SWAYAM: Swami Vivekananda Yoga Anusandhana Samsthana, 2018-19', *GoI*, n.d., https://www.itecgoi.in/courses_listinst.php?salt6=2ef9306ead141&salt9=40dfc50458&salt3=797e8254c42018-2019, accessed 28 January 2020.

Jain, A. 2015. 'On International Yoga Day, Yoga is just politics by other means', *Quartz India*, 21 June 2015, https://qz.com/india/433356/on-international-yoga-day-yoga-is-just-politics-by-other-means/, accessed 1 January 2020.

James, T. C. and Bhatnagar A. 2019. 'Together towards a healthy future: India's partnerships in healthcare', *RIS*, http://www.ris.org.in/sites/default/files/Together%20Towards%20a%20Healthy%20Future-India%E2%80%99s%20Partnerships%20in%20Healthcare.pdf, accessed 20 December 2019.

Khilnani, S. 1997. *The Idea of India* (London: Hamish Hamilton).

Kumar, S. 2019. 'Hindu nationalists claim that ancient Indians had airplanes, stem cell technology, and the internet', *Science*, 13 February 2019, https://www.sciencemag.org/news/2019/02/hindu-nationalists-claim-ancient-indians-had-airplanes-stem-cell-technology-and, accessed 26 July 2019.

Michael, A. 2018. 'India's foreign policy and Hindutva: The new impact of culture and identity on the formation and practice of Indian foreign policy 2014–17', in M. Rehman (ed.), *The Rise of Saffron Power: Reflections on Indian Politics* (Oxford and New York: Routledge), 62–83.

Miller, M.C. and Sullivan da Estrada, K. 2017. 'Pragmatism in Indian foreign policy: How ideas constrain Modi', *International Affairs*, 93/1, 27–49.

Ministry of AYUSH. 2019a. *Fifty Days to go: Fourth Unani Day*, Facebook, 23 December 2019, https://www.facebook.com/moayush/posts/3085957334962840, accessed 2 January 2020.

——. 2019b. 'Common Yoga protocol', *MEA, GoI*, May 2019, http://mea.gov.in/images/pdf/common-yoga-protocol-english.pdf, 2 January 2020.

——. n.d. a. 'Introduction of Sowa-Rigpa', *GoI*, n.d., 9 December 2019, https://main.ayush.gov.in/about-the-systems/sowa-rigpa/introduction-sowa-rigpa accessed 10 October 2020.

——. n.d. b. 'Naturopathy', *GoI*, n.d., 26 February 2016, https://main.ayush.gov.in/about-the-systems/naturopathy, accessed 10 October 2020.

——. n.d. c. 'Unani: Introduction', *GoI*, n.d., 25 February 2016, https://main.ayush.gov.in/about-the-systems/unani/introduction, accessed 10 October 2020.

Ministry of Culture. n.d. 'Project Mausam', *GoI*, n.d., https://www.indiaculture.nic.in/project-mausam, accessed 23 December 2019.

Modelski. G. 1964. 'Foreign policy and international system in the ancient Hindu world', *American Political Science Review*, 58/3, 549–60.

Modi, R. and D' Silva, R. 2016. 'Liminal spaces: Racism against Africans in India', *Economic and Political Weekly*, October 2016/41, 18–20.

Modi, R. and Taylor, I. 2017. 'The Indian diaspora in Africa: The commodification of the Hindu rashtra', *Globalisations*, 14/6, 911–29.

Mukerji, A. 2015. 'Rashtriya Swayamsevak Sangh 'shakha' spreads its wings to thirty-nine countries', 21 December 2015, *Times of India*, https://timesofindia.indiatimes.com/india/Rashtriya-Swayamsevak-Sangh-shakha-spreads-its-wings-to-39-countries/articleshow/50260517.cms, accessed 1 November 2020.

Nanda, M. 2009. *The God Market: How Globalisation is Making India More Hindu* (Delhi: Random House).

OFBJP Nigeria. n.d. *Overseas Friends of the BJP Nigeria*, Facebook, n.d., https://www.facebook.com/BJPOFnigeria, accessed 1 November 2020.

Palshikar, S. 2015. 'The BJP and Hindu nationalism: Centrist politics and majoritarian impulses', *South Asia: Journal of South Asian Studies*, 38/4, 719–35.

PIB. 2015. 'Ministry of AYUSH', *GoI*, n.d., https://pib.gov.in/newsite/PrintRelease.aspx?relid=134031 accessed 28 January 2020.

——. 2018a. 'Study in India programme of HRD Ministry launched with the launch of "Study in India Portal" by Smt. Sushma Swaraj and Dr SatyaPal Singh in New Delhi today', *GoI*, 18 April 2018, https://pib.gov.in/PressReleaseIframePage.aspx?PRID=1529560, accessed 23 December 2019.

——. 2018b. 'Achievements of the Ministry of Ayush', *GoI*, n.d., http://pibarchive.nic.in/4YearsOfNDA/Comprehensive-Materials/AYUSH.pdf, accessed 23 December 2019.

Republic of Mauritius. 2016. 'AYUSH's capability to interact with modern medicine highlighted by President of the Republic', *Government of Mauritius*, 13 April 2016, http://www.govmu.org/English/News/Pages/AYUSH%E2%80%99s-capability-to-interact-with-modern-medicine-highlighted-by-President-of-the-Republic.aspx, accessed 28 January 2020.

Savarkar, V.D. 2003. *Essentials of Hindutva* (New Delhi: Bharati Sahitya Sadan).

——. n.d. 'Hindu Rashtra Darshan', *Maharashtra Pratnik Hindusabha*, n.d., http://savarkar.org/en/pdfs/hindu-rashtra-darshan-en-v002.pdf, accessed 4 January 2020.

Solomon, H. 2012. 'Critical reflections of Indian foreign policy: Between Kautilya and Ashoka', *South African Journal of International Affairs*, 19/1, 65–78.

Stolte, C. 2016. 'Compass points: Four Indian cartographies of Asia', in M. Frey and N. Spakowski (eds.), *Asianisms: Regionalist Interactions and Asian Integration* (Singapore: NUS Press), 49–74.

Thapar, R. 1996. 'The theory of Aryan race and India: History and politics', *Social Scientist*, 24/1–3, 3–29.

4

Modi and the Mahatma:
The Politics of Statues and the
Saffronisation[1] of India–Africa Relations

SIMONA VITTORINI

Public monuments are never merely symbolic. They do matter. They are expressions of power and authority. They make claims to represent a community and are means through which communities express their values and collective past. More often than not, they quickly become part of the familiar landscape and we become oblivious to them. But there are times when historical monuments attract affective energies and become objects of political action and violent contestation. At the end of May 2020, the death in the USA of George Floyd at the hand of a police officer sparked a wave of 'Black Lives Matter' (BLM) protests across the world to demand racial justice and condemn police brutality. Statues commemorating colonial conquest and racial subjugation turned into objects of hatred and became targets of defacement. In the US the rage was mainly directed at Confederate monuments. But across Europe, protesters attacked the symbols of the continent's racist colonial past.

These protests come almost five years after the 'Rhodes Must Fall' Campaign of 2015 that resulted in the removal of the statue of Cecil Rhodes from the campus of the University of Cape Town. Only a year later, in September 2016, some lecturers and students of the University of Ghana, in Legon (Accra), signed a petition demanding the removal of a statue of Mohandas Karamchand Gandhi that had been gifted by the then Indian President Pranab Mukherjee only a few months earlier. Referring to a number of racist remarks that Gandhi had made about Black South Africans when he lived in South Africa (1893–1914), the petitioners claimed that Gandhi was a racist. They also drew attention to Gandhi's campaigns 'against the efforts of the Dalits, The Black (sic) "Untouchables" of India' and his acceptance of the hierarchical caste system, calling the gift 'a slap in the face' that undermined

---

[1] Saffron is the colour of the robes worn by Hindu ascetics and devotees. The term 'saffronisation' refers to the process of glorifying Hindu cultural heritage promoted by right-wing Hindu nationalist organisations.

Ghana's 'struggle for autonomy, recognition and respect' (Change.org 2016). The controversy quickly gained international attention partly because it grated against the common representation of Gandhi as a symbol of peace and civil disobedience that inspired anti-colonial and civil rights movements even after his death, but also because it was one of many protests on university campuses in Africa and elsewhere against the enduring symbols of colonial oppression. The Government of Ghana quickly agreed to remove the statue 'to avoid the controversy … becoming a distraction from our strong ties of friendship' with India (Ashutosh 2014). Finally, two years later, in December 2018, the statue was quietly removed overnight from the Legon campus and in February 2019, Ghana's Ministry of Foreign Affairs and Regional Integration and the Indian High Commissioner to Ghana held an official ceremony to mark the relocation of the statue to the Kofi Annan Centre of Excellence for Training in Information and Technology (KACE) in downtown Accra, bringing to an end a 'misconceived perception about the legacy of the Indian freedom fighter' (Lartey 2019).

As diplomatic gifts go, however, the Gandhi statue was not an unconventional present. India may have many nationalist heroes (Sardar Vallabhai Patel, Subhas Chandra Bose, B.R. Ambedkar and Jawaharlal Nehru) but it has only one father of the nation, M.K. Gandhi. As such, he has become one of the most powerful and exploited symbols of India, representing anything from the anti-colonial struggle to the principle of non-violence and, most recently, cleanliness. True, in the wake of the 'Rhodes Must Fall' movement, a statue of Gandhi had been defaced in Johannesburg (BBC 2015), but statues of the Mahatma have regularly been gifted by the Indian government and have been staples of its soft-power strategy.

There was something else. Even though, historically, India's presence in Ghana goes back a long way (even before the West African country obtained independence), it was the friendship between India's first Prime Minister, Jawaharlal Nehru, and Ghana's first post-independence leader, Kwame Nkrumah, which cemented the relations between these two countries. According to Chandhoke (2016), Nehru and Nkrumah were like-minded souls, friends and comrades. Besides admiring each other, Nkrumah and Nehru shared ideas of solidarity among fellow colonial and postcolonial countries and of radical cosmopolitanism (Lartey 2019). Nkrumah's walks from the presidential lodge, Flagstaff House, along Jawaharlal Nehru Road to the Indian High Commission[2] were emblematic of this personal bond between these two leaders. So why gift a statue of Gandhi and not one of Nehru?

[2]   Interview with former Ghanaian High Commissioner to India and government minister, Mike Ocquaye, Accra, 27 June 2015.

This chapter does not aim to establish if statues should fall or not. It is not necessarily even about how to deal with Gandhi's complicated personal history and legacy,[3] important as they may be. It is more about the importance of statuary and public iconography and about the use of Gandhi as an icon to promote India's attractiveness to the world and the implications and significance of this for India–Africa relations.

The chapter starts from the assumption that the gifting of the statue of Gandhi to the Legon university campus in Accra, far for being a random act of diplomatic generosity, was symbolically important. It places this event within the broader strategy of Indian Prime Minister Modi's government to reclaim symbolic ownership of the Mahatma and his legacy. Two additional points will be made here. First, this strategy of re-appropriation of Gandhi's legacy is consistent with Hindutva's[4] domestic agenda of making India Hindu and with its *modus operandi* of symbolic appropriation of India's nationalist imagination. Second, this is also suggestive of a concurrent saffronisation of India's foreign policy (Hall 2019). The gifting of the statue of Gandhi to the University of Legon therefore must be seen within the broader Hindutva project of reforming (Jayal 2019: xi) India's national imaginary, as a symptom of its attempt at recasting its foreign policy and rewriting the history of India–Africa relations.

Making India Hindu

Gandhi was a controversial figure in life and as he is in death, but since Indian independence, as the only father of the nation among a constellation of anti-colonial heroes, he has become one of the most powerful and exploited symbols of India. Paintings of Gandhi have graced the walls of many public offices and schools; his statues have been erected in many squares in towns and in villages alike across the breadth of India; buildings, streets and airports have been named after him. He has also been commemorated countless times in stamps in India and abroad, and he is prominently displayed on the obverse of India's rupee banknotes of all denominations (from 10 to 2000 rupees) in what is known as the Mahatma Gandhi (New) Series and in many commemorative coins too.

Gandhi's symbolic potential has been so evocative that public personalities and politicians often invoke him. To be associated with India's most iconic

---

[3] See, for instance, Rao (2015, 2016); Mishra (2018); Sagar (2019).

[4] Hindutva is the version of Hindu ethnic and cultural nationalism held by a number of Indian organisations, including the Bharatiya Janata Party, the party to which the current Prime Minister belongs.

political figure always brings the promise of increased legitimacy and credibility. India's current Prime Minister – Narendra Modi – has publicly paid his
respects to Gandhi and sought association with this iconic figure on various
occasions. During his time as Gujarat Chief Minister (2001–14), cultivating
the legacy of Gandhi became part of a strategy to transform his image, and
to craft a distinct leadership style (Jaffrelot 2013). In those years, he became
a regular visitor to Gandhi's Sabarmati Ashram – one of Gandhi's residences
on the banks of the Sabarmati river in Gujarat – and he also presided over the
construction of the Mahatma Mandir and Dandi Kutir in Gandhinagar – a
monumental convention centre and Gandhi memorial built in the shape of a
mound of salt to commemorate Gandhi's Salt Satyagraha (Shah 2018) – the
240-mile march to the coast of Gujarat where in 1930 Gandhi set out to
break the British salt tax by manufacturing his own salt (Payne 1969: 392).

Since coming to power in Delhi in 2014, Modi has continued to capitalise on Gandhi's public stature. As Prime Minister, he made Gandhi the
face of the Swachh Bharat Abhiyaan – his flagship 'Clean India Campaign'
programme that, significantly, was launched on the anniversary of Gandhi's
birth (2 October) in 2014. Gandhi's iconic wire-rimmed spectacles are the
main symbol of this government programme. They are often accompanied
on various publicity material by a silhouette of a marching Gandhi, stick
in hand – a reminder of one of his most popular representations during the
Salt March – or by an image of the father of the nation holding a broom and
hunched over sweeping the floor. Significantly, Gandhi's birthday – India's
only non-religious national holiday dedicated to a political figure – has since
been celebrated as Swachh Bharat Diwas (Clean India Day) (Bhatia 2018).

Beside the grandiose, two-year, government-sponsored celebrations
of Gandhi's 150th birth anniversary, most significantly, and perhaps also
most disturbingly, Modi has even taken to impersonating Gandhi himself
(Ministry of Culture 2019). In 2017, on his visit to Sabarmati Ashram in
Ahmedabad to mark the centenary of its foundation, Modi posed in front
of the photographers spinning at the *charkha* (spinning wheel) in an obvious
attempt at staging one of the most iconic images of the leader of the nationalist movement (Financial Express 2017). Modi's insistence on abstinence
from alcohol and his dedication to celibacy, vegetarianism and spiritual practice (in the form of daily yoga and participation in religious pilgrimages) are
also an indication of this personification.

Popular mass politics are not possible without invoking figures that have
left an indelible print on the national political landscape. Every major political movement has a pantheon of so-called 'patron saints' linked to the birth
of the nation or the collectivity they represent. Their role is to give their

'blessings' to whatever policy is being pursued and to legitimise those who invoke them. The legitimisation is achieved by creating a direct line of descent from those saintly figures, showing that the current leaders are the bearers of the 'sacred' flame passed down by the original founders (Kertzer 1996).

This is a common practice in contemporary politics. Yet, Modi's extraordinary appropriation of the legacy and symbolism of Gandhi is at odds with what historically Hindu nationalist forces have stood for. The Sangh Parivar – literally the 'family of the organisations', an umbrella body organised around the Rashtriya Swayamsevak Sangh (RSS) which includes the ruling BJP and other socio-cultural and missionary bodies like the Vishva Hindu Parishad (VHP) – has always been vehemently opposed to the Indian National Congress and especially to Gandhi, his views and his legacy. The RSS was born in 1925 in reaction to Gandhi's appeals to Hindu-Muslim unity that were seen as attempts at appeasing and emboldening the Muslim community. For Golwalkar, one of the RSS's most influential ideologues, Gandhi's most famous political tool – *ahimsa* (non-violence) – 'was to be rejected as perverse' (Golwalkar 1996: 272) and was considered responsible for the emasculation of India (Van der Veer 1994: 96). Not to mention, of course, Nathuram Godse, Gandhi's assassin, who was a former member of the RSS and of the Hindu Mahasabha, another political organisation that ascribed to the ideology of Hindu nationalism.

The fact is that the Sangh Parivar's pantheon of patron saints is poorly populated by figures who really made a mark on India's political history. It includes gods and goddesses (Ram, Hanuman and Ganga Mata); historical figures (Maharana Pratap and Shivaji); its own founding fathers (M.S. Golwalkar, K.B. Hedgewar, Deendayal Upadhyaya and S.P. Mookherjee); and current and past political leaders (A.B. Vajpayee, L.K. Advani and, of course, now Modi). However, the Sangh Parivar's contribution to the independence movement was chequered, if not characterised by collaboration with the colonial powers. The ideologues and functionaries of the Sangh Parivar's ideological fountainhead – the RSS – played no role in the articulation of the idea of India post-independence and left no mark in the creation of the constitution of independent India (Jaffrelot 1996; Jayal 2019: xv).

Often in established and consolidated democracies, the arrival of a new regime is not accompanied by collective or governmental acts of radical iconoclasm. On the contrary, to establish their hegemony, the new forces in power will strive to appropriate and expand the existing symbolic capital by changing the 'cultural framework within which political authority can define itself and advance its claims' (Geertz 1985: 25) and by re-inscribing it with their own ideology and political commitments.

What we are, therefore, witnessing since the BJP came to power in 2014 is a Hinduisation of India's public sphere. To redefine the paradigms of India's national imagination, to replace the ideological foundation of post-independence secular Nehruism and to make India Hindu (Vittorini 2009: 159) have been the long-term goals of the Sangh Parivar (Jaffrelot 1996: 77). A Hindu Rashtra (Hindu Nation) is quickly materialising in India under Modi (Anderson and Jaffrelot 2018: 474).

In the last three decades, and even more so with the election of Modi for a second consecutive term in 2019, an amount of key legislation has been passed and Hindu nationalist forces have penetrated the state and federal institutions, permeating a variety of spaces. (Anderson and Jaffrelot 2018). After returning to power with a much larger coalition, the Modi government also finally achieved two of its three core pledges: the abolition of the state of Jammu and Kashmir's special status through Article 370 (BBC 2019) and the Supreme Court ruling last November 2019 that agreed to set up a trust to oversee the construction of a temple dedicated to the Hindu god Ram on the disputed site in the Hindu holy city of Ayodhya where a mosque once stood (Times of India 2019). At the time of writing, the passage in the lower chamber of Parliament (the Lok Sabha) of the Citizenship Amendment Act – which promises to fast-track requests of Indian citizenship on the basis of an applicant's religion but excluding Islam (PIB 2019) – represents another step toward this government's successful imposition of Hindutva.

But nations do not exist primordially. They are manufactured through an ongoing and contested process that establishes 'the hegemony of a particular imaginative construct' (Foster 1997: 9). Nationalism, in fact, is no other than a mobilisation system (Apter 1965). Hindutva is the expression of an ethnic form of nationalism according to which the Indian nation is defined in terms of ethnicity and that is predicated on the inculcation and reaffirmation of Hindu culture and heritage. Since its inception, Hindu nationalism has been primarily a programme of social engineering and of cultural awakening. It has relied on the grassroots activism and groundwork of its various organisations, primarily of the RSS – whose main interest has always been in character building and the transformation of society from below rather than obtaining political power (Jaffrelot 1996).

Because 'we can relate to the larger political entity only through abstract symbolic means' (Kertzer 1988: 7), in order to make India Hindu, Hindutva forces have relied on the possibilities of the politics of the spectacle to create (the illusion of) a collectivity (Hansen 2004: 21), drawing upon a vast reservoir of popular national histories and religious myths, symbols and imagery (Hansen 2004: 25).

Hindutva as a programme of social engineering seeks to transform the symbolic capital of India's nationalist movement through the three key strategies of encroaching, appropriation and erasure. On the one hand, it strives to legitimise its own ritual and symbolic capital (and hence ideology) by insinuating, for instance, its heroes into the national space. On the other, it hijacks the pantheon of sacred martyrs, and appropriates the calendar of already existing national rituals, while also instituting a new 'calendar of rearranged festivals' (Assayag 1998:142). Their argument is that this 'heritage' does not belong to one political section only, and that the Congress does not have the moral exclusivity over it (Kertzer 1996: 86). The appropriation of Gandhi's legacy and symbolism by the current administration is a case in point of this *modus operandi*. And lastly, the Sangh Parivar also operates through a strategy of erasure. Their historical imagination is populated by figures it admires 'as well as those it reviles, such as Nehru' (Jayal 2019: xv). Modi's contempt for Nehru and anything Nehruvian is well documented. As Khilnani (2014) has suggested, if the arrival of Modi has brought with it a rewriting of the history of India, Nehru will not be a leading chapter anymore. The various attempts at dismantling some premier Nehruvian institutions of postcolonial India, such as the Planning Commission; the abandoning of the proposed refurbishing of Nehru's former residence; and the repeated attempts at transforming Jawaharlal Nehru University (one of India's premier higher education institutions) must also be seen in this light (Mukhopadhyay 2016).

Saffronising India's foreign policy

Many have observed that, since being elected, Modi has imparted great dynamism to India's foreign policy (Bajpai 2015; Hall 2015). Affectionately referred to as the Non-Resident Prime Minister, in his first one hundred days in power Modi clocked up an impressive number of overseas miles and successfully put India firmly back on the global agenda. Yet, despite this frenetic diplomatic activism, there have not been many substantial changes to New Delhi's foreign policy. Many now agree that India's economic development, its relationship with its immediate neighbourhood, its aspiration to become a major global player and its promotion of India's 'natural' soft power (that derives from its cultural and civilisational heritage), are largely still the elements of India's strategic agenda (Bajpai 2015; Basrur, 2017; Hall 2019).

However, what Modi has done since coming to power has been to provide an alternative view of India's foreign policy, not by replacing the older version with a new approach based on realism or even pragmatism, but by reinventing Indian foreign policy's ideological foundation and grounding it in Hindu nationalist ideology (Hall 2019: 18). Key to the consolidation and communication of this alternative foreign policy approach is the usage of a new language 'shaped by India's civilisational ethos' (Modi at the 2017 Raisina Dialogue, in Hall 2019: 10) and also heavily infused with Hindi or even Sanskrit terms.

A shift from, indeed an erasure of, the Nehruvian-inspired foreign policy is what has distinguished this new idiom. To signal the advent of a more autochthonous and authentic foreign policy, Panchamrit (literally, the five sacred foods, a term borrowed from Hindu devotional practice) has taken the place of the Nehruvian doctrine of Panchsheel (that referred to the five principles of mutual respect for each other's territorial integrity and sovereignty; mutual non-aggression; non-interference; mutual benefit, and peaceful co-existence). *Sammaan* (dignity), *samvaad* (dialogue), *samriddhi* (shared prosperity), *suraksha* (regional and global security) and *sanskriti evam sabhyata* (cultural and civilisational links) are now the five pillars guiding India's foreign policy under Modi (BJP 2015). Gone are also any references to Non-Alignment, Afro-Asian solidarity, Third-Worldism and strategic autonomy (Hall 2019). India is now Bharat[5] and concepts of *vasudhaiva kutumbakam* (a Sanskrit term meaning 'the world is one family') and *vishva guru* (literally, world teacher[6]) are the new key symbolic representations of India in the world (Narayan 2014; Business Standard 2018).

Thus, this saffronisation of India's foreign policy (Hall 2019) also occurs through a complex set of symbolic practices and through the phenomenon of symbolic encroachment, appropriation and erasure described above. These shifts are also clearly visible in the ways in which India–Africa foreign policy has evolved under Modi.

A Nehru-free India–Africa

Initially, when Modi took office in 2014, Africa did not figure prominently in his foreign policy agenda. However, after some initial hesitation and mixed signals, he brought new impetus to what appeared to be languishing India–Africa

---

[5]   The Republic of India is referred to in Article One of the Constitution both as India and Bharat. Hindu nationalists have long preferred the use of the Sanskrit term, Bharat. Very recently, a petition was moved to the Supreme Court of India to amend the Constitution and replace the word 'India' with 'Bharat' to redress India's colonial oppression and instil a sense of patriotic pride. On 2 June 2020 the Supreme Court declined to entertain the plea.

[6]   The term refers to the notion of India's sense of destiny to play a leading role in the world based on its unique civilisational heritage (see Hall 2019, Chapter 5).

relations. The larger and more spectacular than usual India-Africa Forum Summit (IAFS) of 2015 (MEA 2015) can be seen as an attempt to recalibrate India's relationship with the African continent. Modi's assertion, at the 52nd meeting of the African Development Bank in 2017, that he had 'made Africa a top priority for India's foreign and economic policy' (Dhoot 2017) further confirmed this shift in priorities. Modi's extensive Africa outreach since then has clearly addressed, head-on, the lack of high-level visits at the bilateral level, one of the most glaring lacunae in India–Africa relations till then.[7] Equally, the Indian government decision to open eighteen new Indian Missions in Africa before 2021 (a move that would raise the total number of New Delhi's African missions from twenty-nine to forty-seven, an increase of about 60 per cent) signalled New Delhi's commitment to strengthen its links with Africa (PIB 2018).

Despite instilling India–Africa relations with a renewed dynamism, in terms of substance since Modi came to power there have hardly been any significant changes in direction in any policy areas. Even the 'Ten Guiding Principles for India-Africa Engagement', unveiled by Modi while addressing the Ugandan Parliament in 2018 (MEA 2018a), which aimed at delineating a new coherent and strategic Africa policy and was hailed as the closest thing to New Delhi's 'white-paper' or vision document on Africa (Viswanathan and Mishra 2019: 1–2), simply reiterated earlier policies and directing principles. Elements that have historically characterised the relations between the two regions – an emphasis on political equality, mutual benefit, sovereignty, non-interference, win–win cooperation, a shared past of colonial subjugation and developing country status – all continue to feature prominently in official publications, declarations and speeches.

This may suggest that the Panchsheel doctrine of Nehruvian heritage – rather than the new doctrine of Panchamrit – is still driving India–Africa relations. However, at a more symbolic level, some key changes have become clearly visible. India–Africa policy under Modi has been reshaped in two significant ways. These are in line with his government's attempt at making India Hindu and at recasting India's foreign policy in Hindu nationalist thought through the strategies delineated in the previous section.

---

[7] From 2014 to 2019 there have been nearly thirty high-level visits (President, Vice President and Prime Minister) from India to as many African countries and at the ministerial level all fifty-four African states received a visit from India. Thirty-two African heads of state or government travelled to India in the same period (Viswanatham and Mishra 2019: 5).

On the one hand, Gandhi has been squarely placed at the heart of India–Africa relations in the same way that the father of the nation has become Modi government's iconic national mascot in India's domestic politics (Thakur and Davies 2016). Gandhi's personal history, his philosophy and his legacy are used to strengthen the bonds between India and the African continent. Gandhi's formative years in South Africa feature prominently in most official declarations and speeches in a variety of descriptions. Africa has been called Gandhi's *karmabhoomi*, the land that 'transformed a Mohandas into the Mahatma' (Modi's speech during his visits in South Africa 2016, in Rajeshwari 2016), the soil that 'gave greater clarity to his life's mission' (India's Vice President Venkaiah Naidu on his visit to the Comoros in 2019, Vice President of India 2019), where 'he found his true calling' (Modi during his visit to South Africa, in Sharma 2016), the 'birthplace of *satyagraha*' (Sharma 2016). Similarly, Gandhi's 'universal and timeless values' (Modi's address to the Ugandan Parliament, MEA 2018a), his 'quest for liberty, dignity, equality, opportunity for every human being' (MEA 2018a), and his methods of passive resistance are constantly invoked.

Of course, this is not the first time that Gandhi's African past has been used to illustrate the bond between India and the African continent. What is remarkable is that Modi is going to extraordinary lengths to associate himself and New Delhi's revamped Africa policy with Gandhi. In the same way that the Gandhi icon is used to sponsor a number of government programmes in India, so too convention centres,[8] technology parks[9] and heritage centres[10] across Africa, have been named after him, this despite Gandhi not being a national figure or having any direct historical connection with these African countries.

The celebration of Gandhi's 150th birth anniversary has been an occasion for launching a series of initiatives across Africa: the 'India for Humanity' programme in Malawi (inspired by Mahatma Gandhi's service to humanity) (Tokale 2018); essay and painting competitions; a philatelic exhibition

---

[8] New Delhi has promised to build twenty-one convention centres in Africa. The first one – the USD 56 million Mahatma Gandhi International Convention Centre – was unveiled in Niamey (Niger) by External Minister S. Jaishankar in January 2020 (Business Standard 2020). The next eight will be erected in Uganda, Zambia, Malawi, The Gambia, Burkina Faso, Togo, Gabon and Liberia. They will be built entirely with the help of Indian grants and using Indian firms (Roy Chaudhury 2018).

[9] Such as the Mahatma Gandhi IT and Biotech Park, in Grand-Bassam, Côte d'Ivoire, which was inaugurated in 2019 (MEA 2019a).

[10] Such as in Uganda (MEA 2018b).

in South Africa; the release of commemorative stamps (in Ghana, Senegal, South Africa); and, of course, the unveiling and garlanding of statues.

Just as Modi has taken to impersonating Gandhi in India, he used his 2017 visit to South Africa to re-enact Gandhi's transformation into the Mahatma. On the day marking the 125th anniversary of the birth of Satyagraha, Modi – in a carefully choreographed event, rich in symbolism – retraced Gandhi's momentous train journey of 1893. At Pentrich station in Durban, he boarded a train similar to the one from which Gandhi was famously thrown out, and he travelled on to Pietermaritzburg, the place where Gandhi started his life-long commitment to non-violent protest and where he experienced his political awakening.

On the other hand, the elevation of Gandhi as the main architect of India–Africa relations has come at the expense of the erasure of Nehru, his thought and legacy. There is no doubt that the long history of political solidarity between the two regions can be traced back to Gandhi – who spent his formative years in South Africa and for whom India's independence was not to be considered complete until Africa was free from the colonial shackles. But, significantly, it was India's first Prime Minister, Jawaharlal Nehru, who invested earnestly in putting India on the global map by carving a role for New Delhi as the leader of the postcolonial world. This led to the creation of the Non-Aligned Movement (NAM) at the 1955 Bandung Conference and laid the foundation of a long-lasting solidarity with Africa. The strong ideological considerations (broadly India's forthright support of liberation movements in the continent, steadfast commitment to Afro-Asian solidarity, South–South fraternity, non-interference and the planning for a more equitable world) that formed the core of Nehruvian thought cemented India–Africa relations throughout the decades (Harris and Vittorini 2018).

Although it is true that Nehru-style South–South partnership is increasingly becoming less relevant and that principles of solidarity and mutual benefit are now used as a tool to leverage commercial ventures (Harris and Vittorini 2018: 365), the ideas of Nehruvianism and alternative global norms, sovereignty and economic development have not disappeared altogether (Hall 2017). Till recently, in the official and unofficial discourse about India–Africa links, Nehruvian thought has figured prominently. India has continued to use the language of solidarity, articulating notions of an 'accumulated sense of history' and special affinity with Africa (Harris and Vittorini, 2018: 366).

But since coming to power, Modi, on various occasions, has taken considerable steps to distance himself as much as possible from his revered predecessor. At the third IAFS Nehru was conspicuous by his absence. A picture of Nehru with the Egyptian leader Gamal Abdel Nasser appeared briefly during the Summit's opening ceremony, but India's first Prime Minister was never mentioned in any of the official literature released before and after the Summit. Most unusually, in his opening speech at the third IAFS, Modi did not refer to Nehru and refrained from using terms dear to Nehruvianism in describing India's relations with the South. This shift in register caught a number of African leaders unawares. While a clearly well-briefed Senegalese President mentioned *vasudhaiva kutumbakam* in his speech, the President of South Africa, Jacob Zuma, referred to Nehru (and Indira Gandhi) as 'visionary leaders', and other African leaders spoke of Nehru in glowing terms whilst addressing the summit (Vittorini 2016).

Modi's snubbing of Nehru should not be surprising. India's first Prime Minister encapsulates all that the Modi brand of national-populism (McDonnel and Cabrera 2018) stands against. Nehru was an erudite thinker; he belonged to the Western-educated, English-speaking elite; he was a believer in reason and modern science, and preferred history over mythology.

Conclusion

There are two ways of looking at the incident of the Gandhi statue in Ghana. The first one, and perhaps the most obvious, is as an act of iconoclasm. There is a rich literature on monuments and monumental iconoclasm (Verderey 1999). According to this literature, acts of monumental iconoclasm are often symptomatic of, and harbingers of, deep social changes that demand a re-conceptualisation of the symbolic capital of the community of belonging and that introduce novel ancestral lineages and new heroes (Khilnani 2014) to be recruited into the services of the new regime. This way, old monuments are torn down and new ones are erected.

The 'Gandhi must fall' protest was directed against the University of Ghana and its governance body, decrying a lack of consultation with staff and students, and articulated a 'cry for belonging' (Shringapure 2015). Deploring the lack of statues dedicated to 'African heroes and heroines, who can serve as examples of who we are and what we have achieved as a people' (Change. org 2016), the protesters demanded the iconographic decolonisation of the University's public spaces and, drawing attention to Gandhi's racism and casteism, denounced the monument (and Gandhi) as an object of oppression and domination, branding, by extension, India as a neo-colonial power in Africa: 'It is better to stand up for our dignity than to kowtow to the wishes of a burgeoning Eurasian super-power' (Change.org 2016). For Chandhoke (2018), the petitioners not only rejected Gandhi; they rejected India too.

Yet, despite tracing its genealogy directly to other Gandhi statue con-troversies and other African protest movements against symbols of colonial domination,[11] the #GandhiMustFall protest was uniquely peculiar. First, the protest did not demand the removal of a statue that had occupied the public space for a long time and that belonged to a previous domestic political regime. On the contrary, the statue of Gandhi had not only been recently erected, but it also formed part of the symbolic repertoire of a foreign power. Second, and more baffling, there was no real act of iconoclasm. Despite the protest and the fact that the petition quickly attracted international attention, the statue was not defaced, it was not toppled by protesters and, most signifi-cantly, it was not forcefully removed nor was its pedestal or the vacated space used to erect another statue. As was mentioned above, the statue was quietly removed from the university campus and then relocated, a year and half later, outside the premier symbol of India's South–South development cooperation (Harris and Vittorini 2018) – the Kofi Annan Centre for Excellence in Accra. Unveiled for the second time in the presence of Ghana's Minister for For-eign Affairs and Regional Integration and the Indian High Commissioner to Ghana, this second ceremony attracted much less attention and certainly little protest (Radio Univers 2019).[12]

Another way to look at this incident is to use the act of erecting the mon-ument (rather than the act of destruction or its removal) as the point of departure. An analysis of this kind still continues to be premised on the power of public monuments as symbolic sites of political meaning (Whelan 2002: 508) but is broader in scope. Every statue makes implicit political statements (Jeffrey 1980) and diplomatic gift-giving is rarely a mundane

11 The #RhodesMustFall movement, which gained momentum across South Africa and beyond after 2015, preceded the #GandhiMustFall movement. Pro-testers called for the removal of the statue of Cecil Rhodes, the British imperialist and businessman, after whom Rhodesia was named. Rhodes, for them, was a sym-bol of the institutional structures that enabled the continued marginalisation of peoples of African descent in post-apartheid South Africa.

12 A similar fate befell the statue of Gandhi that was supposed to be erected at Ginnery Corner in Blantyre, Malawi. A petition – signed by about 3,500 con-cerned citizens under the 'Gandhi Must Fall Movement' (#GandhiMustFall) – demanded that the Malawian and Indian governments halt the construction of the statue, accusing Gandhi of having been a racist. They were critical of what they saw as India's attempt to 'spread its imperial influence in Malawi' (Rampal 2018). The petitioners won the injunction and the statue was not erected at Ginnery Corner. Instead, it was moved inside the Mahatma Gandhi Convention Centre, which it is still under construction (Faiti 2019).

act of generosity. These diplomatic material exchanges reflect the politics of the donor and serve precise political purposes. It is the value system of the donor at a particular time that 'define the nature of gifts exchanged' (Muraleedharan 2017: 7).

Gandhi's contribution to India's image abroad is unparalleled. But since Modi took office, Gandhi has been brought out of the archive, becoming perhaps India's most powerful soft power tool (Mitra 2019). By recasting the image of the father of the nation in the popular imagination as the mascot of the Swachh Bharat campaign and the symbol of sustainable living and development, Modi has successfully rebranded Gandhi for the twenty-first century, making his principles relevant to deal with contemporary global challenges. At a special commemorative event to mark the 150th anniversary of the Mahatma's birth – titled 'Leadership Matters: Relevance of Gandhi in the Contemporary World' – organised and hosted by Modi while in New York for the United Nations General Assembly in 2019, the Indian Prime Minister said that Gandhi's principles provide a moral compass for the world grappling with the challenges of terrorism, climate change and corruption (MEA 2019b).

But India's Prime Minister has done more than just rebrand Gandhi as 'cool' (Mitra 2019). With Modi, as Ashis Nandy (2008) noted in a controversial article more than a decade ago, 'Gandhi himself has been given a saintly, Hindu nationalist status'. In fact, by erecting and unveiling monuments in honour of India's father of the nation, by naming countless government initiatives after him, by even attempting to impersonate Gandhi on a number of occasions, Modi is not just simply seeking association with India's most prominent national icon.

On the contrary, this chapter has suggested that Modi's appropriation of Gandhi, of his legacy and his symbolic potential and the concomitant erasure and elimination of Nehru from India's public life and historical memory, are part of the BJP's broader project of reshaping India's national imagery (Jayal 2019: xi-xii) and of establishing – in India and abroad – the hegemony of those values and ideas that are at the heart of Hindutva, altering the foundational values of India foreign policy (Hall 2019) and refashioning the symbolic landscape of India–Africa relations.

Bibliography

Anderson, E. and Jaffrelot, C. 2018. 'Hindu nationalism and the saffronisation of the public sphere', *Contemporary South Asia*, 26/4, 468–82.

Apter, D.E. 1965. *The Politics of Modernisation* (Chicago: University of Chicago Press).

Ashutosh. 2014. 'The appropriation of Gandhi', *The Indian Express*, 13 October 2014, https://indianexpress.com/article/opinion/columns/the-appropriation-of-gandhi/, accessed 19 December 2019.

Assayag, J. 1998. 'Ritual action or political reaction? The invention of Hindu nationalist processions in India during the 1980s', *South Asia Research*, 18/2, 125–48.

Bajpai, K. 2015. 'Continuity with zeal', *India Seminar*, April 2015, http://india-seminar.com/2015/668.htm, accessed 17 December 2019.

Basrur, R. 2017. 'Modi's foreign policy fundamentals: Trajectory unchanged', *International Affairs*, 93/1, 7–26.

BBC. 2015. 'Mahatma Gandhi statue vandalised in Johannesburg', 13 April 2015, https://www.bbc.co.uk/news/world-africa-32287972, accessed 10 January 2020.

——. 2019. 'India strips Kashmir of special status', 5 August 2019, https://www.bbc.co.uk/news/world-asia-india-49231619, accessed 19 December 2019.

Bhatia, A. 2018. 'As Swachh Bharat Abhiyan turns four this Gandhi Jayanti, here's what is lined up to mark Swachh anniversary', *NTDV*, 1 October 2018, https://swachhindia.ndtv.com/swachh-bharat-abhiyan-turns-four-gandhi-jayanti-heres-lined-mark-swachh-anniversary-25377/, accessed 1 November 2019.

BJP. 2015. 'Resolution on foreign policy passed in BJP national executive meeting at Bengaluru, Karnataka', 3 April 2015, https://www.bjp.org/en/pressreleasesdetail/295596/-b-Resolution-on-Foreign-Policy-passed-in-BJP-National-Executive-Meeting-at-Bengaluru-b-Karnataka-, accessed 15 December 2019.

Business Standard. 2018. 'PM Modi invokes 'Vasudhaiva Kutumbakam' at World Economic Forum', 23 January 2018, https://www.business-standard.com/article/news-ani/pm-modi-invokes-vasudhaiva-kutumbakam-at-world-economic-forum-118012300901_1.html, accessed 4 March 2020.

——. 2020. 'Jaishankar inaugurates first convention centre in Niger made by India in Africa to honour Gandhi', 22 January 2020, https://www.business-standard.com/article/pti-stories/jaishankar-inaugurates-first-convention-centre-in-niger-made-by-india-in-africa-to-honour-gandhi-120012201410_1.html, accessed 20 October 2020.

Chandhoke, N. 2016. 'Rooted cosmopolitanism: Jawaharlal Nehru and Kwame Nkrumah', in M. Ajei (ed.), *Disentangling Consciencism: Essays on Kwame Nkrumah's Philosophy* (Lanham: Lexington Books), 303–12.

——. 2018. 'When Gandhi's statue is removed in Ghana', *The Hindu*, 24 December 2018, https://www.thehindu.com/opinion/lead/when-gandhis-statue-is-removed-in-ghana/article25814427.ece, accessed 4 March 2020.

Change.org. 2016. 'Gandhi's statue at the University of Ghana must come down', *Change.org*, 12 September 2016, https://www.change.org/p/the-members-of-the-university-of-ghana-council-gandhi-s-statue-at-the-university-of-ghana-must-come-down, accessed 11 November 2019.

Dhoot, V. 2017. 'Africa our top priority in foreign policy matters: Modi', *The Hindu*, 23 May 2017, https://www.thehindu.com/news/national/narendra-modi-inaugurates-african-development-banks-agm/article18528915.ece, accessed 19 December 2019.

Faiti, O. 2019. 'India to proceed with Mahatma Gandhi statue but changes site', *Nyasa Times*, 16 September 2019, https://www.nyasatimes.com/india-to-proceed-with-mahatma-ghandi-statue-in-malawi-but-changes-site/, accessed 30 January 2020.

Financial Express. 2017. 'Mission Gujarat: PM spins charkha at Sabarmati Ashram; see rare images of Modi', 29 June 2017, https://www.financialexpress.com/photos/business-gallery/741004/narendra-modi-in-gujarat-pm-spins-charkha-at-sabarmati-ashram-see-pics/, accessed 19 December 2019.

Foster, R.J. (ed.). 1997. *Nation making. Emergent Identities in Postcolonial Melanesia* (Ann Arbor: The University of Michigan Press).

Geertz, C. 1985. 'Centres, kings, and charisma: Reflections on the symbolics of power', in S. Wilentz (ed.), *Rites of Power: Symbolism, Ritual and Politics since the Middle Ages* (Philadelphia: University of Pennsylvania Press), 13–38.

Golwalkar, M.S. 1996. *Bunch of Thoughts* (Bangalore: Sahitya Sindhu Prakashana, third edn.).

Hall, I. 2015. 'Is a `Modi doctrine´ emerging in Indian foreign policy?', *Australian Journal of International Affairs*, 69/3, 247–52.

——. 2017. 'Modi's vision for India as a normative power', *East Asia Forum*, 8 February 2017, https://www.eastasiaforum.org/2017/02/08/modis-vision-for-india-as-a-normative-power/, accessed 30 January 2020.

——. 2019. *Modi and the Reinvention of Indian Foreign Policy* (Bristol: Bristol University Press).

Hansen, T.B. 2004. 'Politics as permanent performance: the production of political authority in the locality', in J. Zavos, A. Wyatt and V. Hewitt (eds.), *The Politics of Cultural Mobilisation in India* (New Delhi: Oxford University Press), 19-36.

Harris, D. and Vittorini, S. 2018. 'Taking "development cooperation" and South-South discourse seriously: Indian claims and Ghanaian responses', *Commonwealth & Comparative Politics*, 56/3, 360–78.

Jaffrelot, C. 1996. *The Hindu Nationalist Movement and Indian politics, 1925 to the 1990s: Strategies of Identity-Building, Implantation and Mobilisation (with special reference to Central India)* (London: Hurst).

——. 2013. 'Gujarat election: The sub-text of Modi's "hattrick" – High tech populism and the "neo-middle class"', *Studies in Indian Politics*, 1/1: 79–95.

Jeffrey, R. 1980. 'What the statues tell: The politics of choosing symbols in Trivandrum', *Pacific Affairs*, 53/3: 484–502.

Jayal, N.G. 2019. *Re-forming India: The Nation Today* (Gurgaon: Penguin Random House India).

Kertzer. D.I. 1988. *Rituals, Politics and Power* (New Haven: Yale University Press).

——. 1996. *Politics and Symbols. The Italian Communist Party and the Fall of Communism* (New Haven: Yale University Press).

Khilnani, S. 2014. 'Nehru, year of death, 2014?', *Outlook India*, 17 November 2014, https://www.outlookindia.com/magazine/story/nehru-year-of-death-2014/292502, accessed 30 February 2020.

Lartey, N.L. 2019. 'Relocation of Gandhi's statue an end to misguided campaign – Indian High Commissioner', *Citi Newsroom*, 27 February 2019, https://citinewsroom.

com/2019/02/relocation-of-gandhis-statue-an-end-to-misguided-campaign-indian-high-commissioner/, accessed 20 October 2020.

McDonnel, D. and Cabrera, L. 2018. 'The right-wing populism of India's Bharatiya Janata Party (and why comparativists should care)', *Democratisation*, 26/3, 484–501.

MEA. 2015. 'India Africa Forum Summit', *GoI*, n.d., http://mea.gov.in/india-africa-forum-summit-2015/index.html###, accessed 30 January 2020.

——. 2018a. 'Prime Minister's address at Parliament of Uganda during his State Visit to Uganda', *GoI*, 25 July 2018, https://mea.gov.in/Speeches-Statements. htm?dtl/30152/prime+ministers+address+at+parliament+of+uganda+during+his+state+visit+to+uganda, accessed 19 December 2019.

——. 2018b. 'Re-energising India's engagement with Africa: Highlights of PM Narendra Modi's visit to three nations', *GoI*, n.d., http://mea.gov.in/flipbook/Re-energising-India-Engagement-With-Africa/, accessed 25 January 2020.

——. 2019a. 'Mahatma Gandhi Information Technology & Biotech Park inaugurated in Côte d'Ivoire', *GoI*, 29 June 2019, https://mea.gov.in/press-releases. htm?dtl/31518/Mahatma+Gandhi+Information+Technology+amp+Biotech+Park+Inaugurated+in+Cte+dIvoire, accessed 5 January 2020.

——. 2019b. 'Leadership matters: "Relevance of Mahatma Gandhi in the contemporary world", ECOSOC Chamber', *GoI*, 24 September 2019, https://www.mea.gov. in/press-releases.htm?dtl/31855/Leadership+Matters+Relevance+of+Mahatma+Gandhi+in+the+Contemporary+World+ECOSOC+Chamber, accessed 17 January 2020.

Ministry of Culture. 2019. '150 years of celebrating the Mahatma', *GoI*, n.d., https://gandhi.gov.in/, accessed 30 January 2020.

Mishra, P. 2018. 'Gandhi for the post-truth age', *New Yorker*, 15 October 2018, https://www.newyorker.com/magazine/2018/10/22/gandhi-for-the-post-truth-age?verso=true, accessed 23 February 2020.

Mitra, A. 2019. 'Modi reinvents Gandhi as "cool" twenty-first century icon', *IndiaInc*, 12 October 2019, https://indiaincgroup.com/modi-reinvents-gandhi-as-cool-21st-century-icon-india-global-business/, accessed 23 February 2020.

Mukhopadhyay, N. 2016. 'Modi's mid-term: Efforts to usurp Nehru's legacy and copy Indira', *The Quint*, 23 November 2013, https://www.thequint.com/voices/opinion/modis-mid-term-efforts-to-usurp-nehrus-legacy-and-copy-indira-1984-sikh-riots-post-2002-godhra-riots, accessed 2 January 2020.

Muraleedharan, S. 2017. 'Visualising Hindutva security: Modi and his gifts', Paper presented at *A shifting world: International relations from beyond the West*, June 2017 (Royal Holloway: Conference, Centre for Politics in Africa, Asia and the Middle East).

Nandy, A. 2008. 'Blame the middle class', *Times of India*, 8 January 2008, https://timesofindia.indiatimes.com/edit-page/LEADER-ARTICLE-Blame-The-Middle-Class/articleshow/2681517.cms, accessed 30 January 2020.

Narayan, L. 2014. '"Vasudhaiva Kutumbakam" is India's philosophy: Modi', *The Hindu*, 28 September 2014, https://www.thehindu.com/news/national/vasudhaiva-kutumbakam-is-indias-philosophy-modi/article6453203.ece, accessed 20 January 2019.

Payne, R. 1969. *The Life and Death of Mahatma Gandhi* (New York: E.P. Dutton and Company).

PIB. 2018. 'Cabinet approves opening of Missions in Africa to implement commitments of India Africa Forum Summit (IAFS-III)', *NIC*, 21 March 2018, http://pib.nic.in/newsite/PrintRelease.aspx?relid=177821, accessed 9 December 2019.

———. 2019. 'Parliament passes the Citizenship (Amendment) Bill 2019', *GoI*, 11 December 2019, https://pib.gov.in/PressReleseDetailm.aspx?PRID=1596059, accessed 19 December 2019.

Radio Univers. 2018. 'Mahatma Gandhi statue relocated to Kofi Annan Centre of Excellence', *Radio Univers*, 28 February 2019, https://www.universnewsroom.com/news/mahatma-gandhi-statue-relocated-to-kofi-annan-center-of-excellence/, accessed 30 January 2020.

Rajeshwari, A. 2016. 'South Africa transformed Mohandas into Mahatma: PM tells Indian community in Johannesburg', *Times of India*, 9 July 2016, https://timesofindia.indiatimes.com/india/South-Africa-transformed-Mohandas-into-Mahatma-PM-Modi-tells-Indian-community-in-Johannesburg/articleshow/53122998.cms, accessed 30 January 2020.

Rampal, N. 2018. 'Why some in Malawi believe Mahatma Gandhi was "racist"', *The Quint*, 10 November 2018, https://www.thequint.com/news/world/mahatma-gandhi-statue-protests-in-malawi, accessed 30 March 2020.

Rao, R. 2015. 'What do we mean when we talk about statues?', Tenth Africa Day Memorial Lecture, *University of the Free State*, May 2018, https://www.ufs.ac.za/docs/default-source/ufs-news-list/read-lectures-here.pdf?sfvrsn=8b96b821_0, accessed 10 March 2020.

———. 2016. 'On statues', *The Disorder of Things*, https://thedisorderofthings.com/2016/04/02/on-statues/, accessed 30 January 2020.

Roy Chaudhury, D. 2018. 'India takes convention centre route to Africa', *Economic Times*, 14 May 2018, https://economictimes.indiatimes.com/news/politics-and-nation/india-takes-convention-centre-route-to-africa/articleshow/64153493.cms, accessed 2 January 2020.

Sagar. 2019. 'Give us a statue of Ambedkar, not Gandhi: Ghana university professor Ọbádélé Kambon', *The Caravan*, 13 January 2019, https://caravanmagazine.in/caste/gandhi-must-fall-interview, accessed 20 January 2020.

Shah, R. 2018. 'Narendra Modi's shadow on Sabarmati Ashram and Gandhi Kutir', *National Herald*, 1 October 2018, https://www.nationalheraldindia.com/opinion/modis-shadow-on-sabarmati-ashram-and-gandhi-kutir, accessed 29 December 2019.

Sharma, A. 2016. 'PM Modi retraces Mahatma Gandhi's train journey in South Africa', *The Tribune*, 9 July 2016, https://www.tribuneindia.com/news/archive/pm-retraces-mahatma-gandhi-s-train-journey-in-south-africa-263512, accessed 30 January 2020.

Shringapure, B. 2015. 'Rage against the monuments', *Warscapes*, 20 July 2012, http://www.warscapes.com/opinion/rage-against-monuments#:~:text=The%20deliberate%20destruction%20of%20monuments,to%20build%20those%20 very%20monuments.&text=Recently%2C%20rebels%20in%20Mali%20 used,15th%20century%20mosque%20in%20Timbuktu, accessed 23 December 2019.

Thakur, V. and Davies, A. 2016. 'Why Modi's razzmatazz diplomacy isn't serving African interests', *The Conversation*, 20 July 2016, https://theconversation.com/ why-modis-razzmatazz-diplomacy-isnt-serving-african-interests-62577, accessed 30 January 2020.

Times of India. 2019. 'Ram Mandir-Babri Masjid case verdict as it happened: Highlights', 9 November 2019, https://timesofindia.indiatimes.com/india/ ayodhya-babri-masjid-ram-mandir-case-verdict-highlights-supreme-court-declared-verdict-on-ram-janmabhoomi-case/articleshow/71978918.cms, accessed 19 December 2019.

Tokale, V. 2018. 'Naidu launches "Jaipur Foot" camp in Malawi distributes India-made prosthetic limb to beneficiaries', *The Week*, 5 November 2018, https://www.theweek. in/wire-updates/international/2018/11/05/fgn41-naidu-malawi-jaipurfoot.html, accessed 30 January 2020.

Van der Veer, P. 1994. *Religious Nationalisms: Hindus and Muslims in India* (Berkeley: University of California Press).

Verderey, K. 1999. *The Political Lives of Dead Bodies: Reburial and Post-socialist Change* (New York: Columbia University Press).

Vice President of India. 2019. 'Vice President kick-starts his tour to Comoros and Sierra Leone', *NIC*, 10 October 2019, https://vicepresidentofindia.nic.in/ pressrelease/vice-president-kick-starts-his-tour-comoros-and-sierra-leone, accessed 10 January 2020.

Vittorini, S. 2009. *Rituals, Symbols and Politics of Indian Nationalism* (Torino: Trauben).

———. 2016. 'Africa day', *SOAS blogs*, 20 June 2016, https://blogs.soas.ac.uk/ssai-notes/2016/06/20/africa-day-by-simona-vittorini/, accessed 19 January 2020.

Viswanathan, H.H.S. and Mishra, A. 2019. 'The ten guiding principles for India-Africa engagement: Finding coherence in India's Africa policy', *ORF Online*, Occasional Paper No. 200, 25 June 2019, https://www.orfonline.org/research/ the-ten-guiding-principles-for-india-africa-engagement-finding-coherence-in-indias-africa-policy/, accessed 30 January 2020.

Whelan, J. 2002. 'The construction and destruction of colonial landscape: Monuments to British monarchs in Dublin before and after independence', *Journal of Historical Geography*, 28/4, 508–33.

PART 3

Capacity Building: Shifting Modalities and New Knowledgescapes

5

India's Changing Human Resource Diplomacy with Africa, and Africa's Responses

KENNETH KING

Introduction

Currently, India's engagements with Africa are much more visibly celebrated by India than by Africa. Or, rather, the Indian initiative behind the three India-Africa Forum Summits (IAFS) of 2008, 2011 and 2015 has produced a good deal of celebratory literature on the special relationship between India and Africa. Coffee table volumes have been associated with two of the IAFS events, and there have been several others (e.g. Arora and Chand 2015), but all deriving from the Indian side of the partnership (King 2019). There are, however, some African voices captured in these volumes, and none is more influential than Meles Zenawi, the former Prime Minister of Ethiopia, commenting on India supporting Africa while still dealing with large-scale poverty in India, and the former President of Malawi, Bingu Mutharika, a graduate of Indian higher education, attesting to the high quality of education available in India (King 2019; see McCann, this volume).

An illustration of this visibility of India–Africa, from the Indian side, is that, in 2019 alone, different Indian bodies organised no less than five high-level conferences on India–Africa. These include the Confederation of Indian Industry (CII) with EXIM Bank holding its fourteenth Conclave on India-Africa; the Indian Council of World Affairs (ICWA) reviewing India–Africa partnerships in a changing global order; the CII with the Ministry of Commerce and Industry (MCI) organising an India–Africa higher education and skill development summit; the CII-EXIM Bank holding a Regional Conclave on India and Southern Africa, and the Federation of Indian Chambers of Commerce and Industry (FICCI) with MCI arranging an India-East Africa Business Forum. Thus, India's private sector might appear more strategically interested in Africa than the Ministries of Education; Skill Development and Entrepreneurship; or External Affairs. This

commercial emphasis, however, was not present in a sixth high-level conference organised by the Indian International Centre (in February 2020) on
'Understanding Africa: Continuity and change'. Its focus was explicitly on
India–Africa interaction in the arts, history, culture and literature. Despite the
pandemic in 2020, the ICWA organised a further India–Africa conference,
online in November 2020, on contemporary realities and emerging prospects.

However, on the many different dimensions of capacity building and
human resource development (HRD) provided to Africa by India, this
chapter offers some commentary by several African beneficiaries. These will
include some of the many students who have gained qualifications in India.
There will also be reactions from a few of the tens of thousands who have
accessed the short-term professional courses offered through Indian Technical and Economic Cooperation (ITEC).

As far as sources on wider African angles on India are concerned, there
is still no India–Africa parallel to the survey carried out by Sautman and
Yan entitled 'African perspectives on China-Africa links' in nine countries of
Africa (Sautman and Yan 2009). The present analysis, however, is based on
a series of about 160 interviews in Ethiopia, India, Rwanda and Tanzania,
carried out over a period of five months between March 2017 and April
2019. Three months of this were spent in the Manohar Parrikar Institute
for Defence Studies and Analyses (MP-IDSA) in New Delhi in early 2018,
and the results of that fellowship are available as an MP-IDSA Occasional
Paper (King 2019). The chapter, therefore, draws more particularly on the
research visits to Tanzania, Rwanda and Ethiopia, between November 2018
and March 2019.

Its primary focus is on human resource development or capacity building,
since the latter has been 'the single most important fulcrum of our development cooperation with Africa' according to the Ministry of External Affairs
(MEA) (Tirumurti in MEA 2020a). In the series of statements by MEA
about its bilateral relations with individual African countries, there is always
a section on development assistance, and within that there is a discussion
of people-to-people contacts, cultural cooperation, cooperation in capacity
building, in education and training, and in science and technology (see MEA
2017b). On the African side, there is certainly enthusiasm for the take-up of
the scholarships offered by the Indian Council for Cultural Relations (ICCR)
and for the short-term awards of ITEC (King 2019; MEA 2017a). There
are also several major new schemes for offering Indian higher education to
Africa and beyond, discussed below. However, the Covid-19 pandemic has
suddenly and dramatically altered the basic assumptions about Africa–India
student mobility and India–Africa human resources cooperation; and it will

therefore be important to recognise, initially, how the capacity building side of development diplomacy is being affected in all the main schemes.

Scholarships and training awards have been one of the oldest, yet most sustained forms of development cooperation right back to the 1940s, 1950s and 1960s, both for OECD donors and for South–South Cooperation (SSC). Physical exposure to the host countries' institutions, staff and to their wider societal environments was assumed to be a critical dimension of such international student mobility. Quite suddenly, within the space of a few weeks in February–March 2020, universities and training institutes across the world had to make a rapid switch to online learning. How rapidly, once vaccines become universally available, they will return to the old modalities remains to be seen. But the shift from face-to-face has not only affected studying at a distance, from home, but it was recognised, at the same time, that working at home quite suddenly became the norm for huge swathes of employment outside construction, transport and manufacturing. Worldwide, the relationship between studying and working, and between doing both of these at home rather than in the office or in a school or college dramatically shifted.

Indian teachers in African schools

But there is one dimension of India's HRD cooperation with Africa that has been given a good deal less attention in most of these formal Indian documents about bilateral connections with Africa which is, nevertheless, high up on African accounts of India in Africa. That has been the presence in particular African countries of a very large number of Indian teachers, especially at school level. These were not present as part of a major government initiative such as the United States Peace Corps or the United Kingdom's Voluntary Service Overseas (VSO). Rather they were the result of thousands of individual Indians deciding on their own account to go abroad and teach in Africa. This was perhaps most evident in Ethiopia where, following the visit of Emperor Haile Selassie to India in 1956, there was a build-up of 'tens of thousands of Indian teachers in schools all over Ethiopia, even in the most remote parts' (MEA 2017b: 1). India's teachers in Africa remain largely unsung. But particularly in Ethiopia, there continue today to be stories about Indian teachers and their dedication. More importantly, in research terms, these thousands of teachers remain invisible. By contrast, in the case of the Peace Corps, VSO, and also Japan's volunteers, the experience of teaching in Africa often led on to post-graduate degrees in development, African studies, or into careers in non-government organisations (NGOs) and the foreign service. It would be intriguing to explore whether there was any parallel development with the tens of thousands of Indian teachers who served in African schools. If there was any such follow-on, it would have been determined by a whole set of different factors in India from elsewhere. But a serious study of their role within Africa and afterwards in India could be rewarding.

Indian university teachers in Africa

The large-scale presence of Indian teachers in African secondary schools has now passed. But Indian lecturers and professors have continued to be a key dimension of the expansion of African university systems in the last twenty years. This was particularly a feature of the dramatic expansion of the university system in Ethiopia in the early 2000s, and was very obvious in the rebuilding after 1994 of high-level capacity lost in the genocide in Rwanda.[1]

There, Indians were present in the initiatives such as Human Resources for Health, as well as in the major recruitment through EdCIL (a Government of India enterprise in educational consultancy) which brought many Indian staff to the different colleges of the University of Rwanda. Most of these were recruited through EdCIL though not paid by the Government of India, but by different funds from within Rwanda. These were far from being stop-gaps, and in several cases, they stayed in the University of Rwanda and in other institutions for a decade or more, and contributed to capacity building and research.

Indian university teachers were similarly sought out in the expansion of Addis Ababa University as well as in the staffing of a large number of other new Ethiopian universities in the first decade of the twenty-first century.

Like the school teachers before them, the numbers of Indian university teachers in Africa are rapidly declining from when there were hundreds, even thousands, just fifteen years ago. This raises a key point about the longer-term impact of such forms of academic capacity building. China for instance – which is often compared with India in Africa – has provided very few regular teaching staff to African universities. The exception is the spread of no less than sixty-one Confucius Institutes in forty-five different African universities, as of December 2020, a long-term institutional development that may have more lasting impact than India's contribution to higher education capacity building. Indeed, the total number of Chinese co-directors, teachers and volunteers in these sixty-one institutes will reach several hundred;

[1]   Kuruvilla Mathews to Kenneth King, personal communication, 16 April 2020, Addis Ababa.

and as each of the institutes provides an ongoing and well-funded link to a Chinese university, there is available a more substantial, institutional, academic partnership than those connected to the several hundred individual Indian scholars supporting African universities (King 2017).

African professional training in India

What is often called 'the flagship programme' of India's development diplomacy is ITEC, founded in 1964. The numbers of training awards which are annually offered to Africa would be several thousand out of the 2019–20 total of 11,645; Tanzania alone was offered over five hundred training slots in 2018–19. These offers of short-term professional training are for periods from two weeks to three months, and are for both civilian and defence training. There is a very wide range of over three hundred courses offered in thirty-eight sectoral specialisations. Satisfaction levels appear to be high though it is noticeable that more offers are made than are taken up for some countries. Careful selection seems to be absolutely critical to the effectiveness of the programmes, according to feedback from ITEC alumni (Mullen et al. 2015: 33). After an internal 2018 evaluation by the Ministry of External Affairs, there have been a series of new initiatives, including e-ITEC where the courses are offered by Indian institutions online in partner countries rather than India. With the benefit of hindsight, it was coincidental that this distance modality was developing, because suddenly during the Covid pandemic from March 2020, the only courses that were on offer were the e-ITEC ones. Only nine were on offer online at the time of writing in November 2020, compared with the hundreds that would usually have been accessed face-to-face. Interestingly, the length of most of these online courses is just a few days, and many are explicitly Covid-related (ITEC 2020a; ITEC 2020b). For the future, if there is a shift on a massive scale towards e-ITEC, then the current assumption, which is based on many participants coming together in a single institution from one country, may need to be rethought. If the important, international, cross-country dimension of regular ITEC is to be retained in e-ITEC, then individuals from multiple countries will need to access online a single host site in India.

Africans studying in India

Though the focus of this essay is primarily on Indian capacity building with Africa, it is worth recalling that the principal recipients of India's development assistance are in its immediate neighbourhood. Thus, as recently as MEA's

'Annual Report 2018–19', technical and economic cooperation for Bhutan was USD 350 million whilst for the whole of Africa it was USD 137 million (MEA 2019: 278).[2] Similarly in the realm of long-term scholarship support from ICCR, a single country in the neighbourhood, Afghanistan, received 1,000 awards in 2018–19 as compared to 908 for the whole of Africa. Though these awards for study in India's public universities and colleges were well regarded by those that took them up, it should be noted that only 498 of the 908 available slots were actually used in the most recent period (ICCR 2019: 129). This would suggest that a significant number of African applicants decided to go elsewhere rather than take up the offer in India. There may well be a trade-off between the low cost of studying in India and the international ranking of Indian universities (Altbach and Mathews 2019). In the present academic year, 2020–21, it can be noted that, due to Covid, none of the awards will have been taken up face-to-face. Indeed, the awardees for this year have all secured online access to their respective Indian host universities.

It has been possible, however, to discuss the experience, prior to Covid, of studying in India with a number of ICCR and self-funded graduates from Ethiopia, Rwanda, Tanzania and Uganda. For several of these, the experience of studying in India was life-changing and led to a deep identification with the subcontinent:

> My time in India was meaningful and gave me more positive attitudes in such a way that it opened my eyes! I got exposure. I have learnt many things beyond what I had expected to get. So, India is my second home.[3]

> I feel a unique connection to India; even now as I prepare to leave, I deeply feel that I am leaving a part of me behind – friends and food among others.[4]

In other cases, former students had been warned about the race issue, but they found nothing untoward:

> This was in the late 1980s. I was there for five plus years. And the experience was good. We were so glad. We got used to the ways they taught.

---

[2] The figure for 'African countries' in the Report was given as USD 27 million but this omitted Mauritius (USD 70 million) and Seychelles (USD 40 million); hence the total of USD 137 million (MEA 2019: 377-8).

[3] Jean Bosco Rusagara to Kenneth King, personal communication, 13 May 2019, Kigali

[4] John Patrick Omegere to Kenneth King, personal communication, 6 June 2019, New Delhi

Perhaps too much by rote in the BA degree but in the MA in JNU much more open with debates and discussions, and protests. All in all, friendly people and easy-going. Not a hard time. Nothing on the racism side. Nothing happened to me.[5]

Despite this individual experience, there have been concerns about 'The continuing challenge of social relations' for African students and trainees in India (King 2019: 15–17; see also McCann and Shangwe, this volume).

What about the key elements of the Indian student experience? Here is one positive listing of these by a Rwandan lecturer who had studied in India:

1) Simplicity. They use small cars even if they are professors. Humble.

2) My supervisor – inviting me along like a friend. We stay in touch. He may come to Rwanda.

3) When my mother died, my supervisor contributed to the air ticket Rw. fr. 250,000 and another colleague bought the return.

4) Old people are respected – e.g. seats for them on the metro.

5) Doing business is their speciality – always smiling.

6) They don't cheat.[6]

A number of African students had experienced both India and China, and one of these commented:

In India I had been happy to go there and everything was fine.
In China, I was already educated, but the facilities were better; and time-keeping was key; cleaning the roads at 5:00 am.[7]

Interestingly, no full account of African students' experience in India is available on the scale of African students in China (e.g. King 2013: 68–103).

Apart from these individual impressions, there were major initiatives taken by different African governments to secure training of their students in India. One of these took place a few years after the Rwandan genocide, and, through an agreement with EdCIL and the Government of Rwanda

---

[5] Tsegab Kebebew to Kenneth King, personal communication, 28 February 2019, Addis Ababa

[6] Jean Bosco Rusagara to Kenneth King, personal communication, 4 February 2019, Kigali

[7] Clement Nkurunziza to Kenneth King, personal communication, 8 February 2019, Kigali

in 1998, nearly five hundred Rwandan students joined Indian universities. Several of these were granted entry to the prestigious Indian Institutes of Technology (IITs). Parallel to this, the Ethiopian and Indian Ministers of Science and Technology agreed a science initiative (Science without Borders) in 2017, and as a result no less than 673 Ethiopian students were sent to five engineering institutions in India at the undergraduate, postgraduate and PhD levels (EoI, Ethiopia 2017). In a third illustration of the attractions of large-scale student/lecturer training in India, the Remote Engineering Postgraduate Programme, set up between IIT Delhi and the Addis Ababa University, led to almost five hundred Ethiopians, from the University and technical schools, gaining qualifications across four engineering disciplines (Genet 2018: 191–96).[8] Many went on to become lecturers and tutors in their fields. This last initiative was completely funded by the Government of Ethiopia.

Though there have been just three examples given of larger African student training schemes with India, it should be mentioned that the overall figure for African students in India has been over ten thousand (King 2019: 10–11). Three of the larger sending countries in Africa in 2017 would be Nigeria (2,086), Sudan (2,073) and Tanzania (1,026) (UIS 2017). But again, the neighbourhood contrast should be borne in mind; out of the total number of foreign students in India in 2016–17 (47,575), no less than 10,294 students came from a single country, Nepal. Certainly, all of these foreign student numbers will have been affected during 2020 by the pandemic.

Internationalising Indian higher education: virtual and face-to-face

India is clear that access to relatively low-cost, high-quality Indian higher education should be central to its development cooperation mission, and more generally to the internationalisation of its universities. This affirms the discourse about capacity building that runs through the declarations and frameworks for action of the three India-Africa Forum Summits. This is evident not just in 'Cooperation in education and skills development' but across all sub-sectors, from trade and industry, to agriculture and health. Rather than present 'capacity building' as something India is doing for Africa, the phrasing emphasises the shared acceptance of this objective:

---

[8]   At one time, more than 80 per cent of the teachers in technical schools in Ethiopia were trained by IIT Delhi according to Prof. Balakrishnan (M. Balakrishnan to Kenneth King, 9 June 2019, New Delhi).

6) This partnership encompasses human resource development through scholarships, training, capacity building, financial assistance through grants and concessional credit....

38) Both sides recognise the fundamental importance of educational cooperation and skills transfer in enhancing opportunities available to their youth in contributing to economic, scientific, technical and social development ...

39) Both sides emphasize the importance of the early introduction of ICT in educational institutions as a key enabler for capacity building, education, health, industry, poverty eradication and delivery of public services (MEA 2015);

There are therefore a whole series of schemes dedicated to offering educational cooperation. The follow-up to the earlier flagship Pan-African e-Network (PAN), which had offered access across Africa via satellite to degrees and medical consultation from Indian universities and hospitals,[9] was the launch in October 2019 of e-VidyaBharati and e-ArogyaBharati (e-Knowledge India and e-Health India) (e-VBAB). The website for this new, online scheme, launched by the Ministry of External Affairs, is iLearn. gov.in (MEA 2020a). It offers 15,000 scholarships 'for students and professionals in Africa to pursue courses by premier Indian institutions in emerging areas' (MEA 2020c). Unlike PAN, which was explicitly Africa-wide, just eighteen African countries have so far become partners in this initiative since the launch. Doubtless, it will seek to expand continent-wide. The choice of a Hindi title underlining India's special knowledge and health resources is a significant shift from the English (see Venkatachalam, this volume).

It may also be indicative of the desire to promote India's traditional knowledge resources that under the catalogue of course options for 'Education', four of the six courses on offer are related to yoga (MEA, 2020b). The options are hugely varied under other topics from Law, to Humanities, Engineering, Sciences and Management. But it is worth noting that at the moment almost all courses on offer are short-term – for just four, eight, twelve or twenty-four weeks. There do not yet seem to be any degree courses available, apart from a handful, though undergraduate and postgraduate availability is clearly stated on the portal: 'The initiative, announced as the e-VidyaBharati network project, will span over the next five years and offer certifications, diplomas, undergraduate and postgraduate degree courses' (MEA 2020c). Unlike the ITEC and ICCR training awards and scholarships which have had rapidly

---

[9]   For this Africa-wide scheme, see King 2019 and Duclos, this volume.

to explore how to offer online, distance options, the India-Africa Tele-education and Tele-medicine Network Project was designed to be offered digitally online. Hence, it is Covid-secure.

It appears to be designed for Africa and to be Africa-specific in its offerings. Yet it is noticeable that its partner institutions include a number of private universities such as Amity and Manipal. Thus, like PAN, iLearn is a public–private partnership. Another of its six partners is SWAYAM (Free online education), which is linked to the Ministry of Education in India, to which we now turn.

SWAYAM too has a portal through which there is access to a huge number of courses connected to nine major Indian coordinators, all in the public sector (Ministry of Education 2020a). Despite what is said on the site about there being opportunities to study at all levels, from secondary school to undergraduate and postgraduate, accessible 'by anyone, anywhere at any time', and to be 'free of cost to any learner', the courses currently on offer all appear to be short-term. Also, SWAYAM is explicitly and visually aimed at 'Indian learning communities' and 'all citizens of this country' – India (Ministry of Education 2020b); while there is no mention of access for learners beyond India, such as those in Africa, it has proved possible to register for SWAYAM in Uganda, for example.[10]

A second major programme promoted by the Ministry of Education is 'Study in India' (Ministry of Education 2020c). This not only has 'niche' courses linking to Ayurveda, Buddhism and yoga, but also some 2,600 courses across the range of one hundred of India's public and private universities, with fee waivers and offers of scholarships. Although Africa is said to be 'a major focus under this scheme' (CII 2019), it would appear that Africa is just one part of a wider Indian strategy to internationalise its higher education. Covid does not appear conspicuously on the home page of 'Study in India', whose website assumes study face-to-face in India. But under the blogs on the portal is a whole series of items on the importance of online learning, including 'transforming the conventional to online learning experiences' (Ministry of Education 2020d). Hence this programme is also seeking to become Covid-secure.

As discussed in the Introduction, it is clear that this initiative is perceived in soft power terms as drawing on the long traditions of India as an ancient knowledge hub: Sushma Swaraj, former Minister of External Affairs, in

---

[10]   John Patrick Omegere to Kenneth King, personal communication, 26 November 2020, Kampala.

launching 'Study in India, in 2018', said 'the quest for knowledge has always been fundamental to India's culture and civilisation. Throughout our history, India has made seminal contributions to human thought, philosophy and development. Our ancient philosophical concepts, such as *Vasudaiva Kutumbakam* (the world is one family) and *Sarva Dharma Sambhava* (all faiths are equal), remain eternal' (PIB 2018). The fact that all three of these major study initiatives were launched in the years 2017, 2018 and 2019 underlines Modi's aspiration for India to be viewed as *vishva guru* (the teacher of the world; see further Venkatachalam, this volume).

India's institutions in Africa

Particularly since the launch by India of the series of India-Africa Forum Summits (IAFS) in 2008, there have been ambitions to provide, via the African Union (AU), India–Africa specialist institutions across the continent. Many of these were meant to focus on areas of India's expertise and comparative advantage such as information technology. It is still not clear exactly how many of these ambitions have been fulfilled, but certainly the one nearest to this chapter's theme of HRD and capacity building – the India-Africa Institute of Educational Planning and Administration, offered through the AU to Burundi – is still nowhere to be seen more than twelve years after it was first offered by India. In contrast to China, which has taken full charge, bilaterally, of the implementation of its pledges to develop institutions, India has felt it more appropriate to go via the AU and secure buy-in from the recipient, in terms of providing land and buildings. However, the delays in getting institutions actually delivered have been very challenging. Even twelve years after the original pledge in 2008, there has been no concrete development in many cases. African ambassadors and high commissioners in New Delhi accordingly made sure that the IAFS *Framework for Action* in 2015 should include the following item:

> Agree to establish a regular formal monitoring mechanism to review the implementation of the agreed areas of cooperation and identified projects by the competent bodies of the partnership. Modalities of the monitoring mechanism and the detailed Plan of Action will be jointly developed within three months (MEA 2015: 11).

Four years later, there was finally a move forward on this monitoring modality in September 2019, with the MEA and AU brainstorming 'to fructify the promises made at the last summit in October 2015' (Chand 2019: 1). On the other hand, of the ten vocational training centres (VTCs) cum incubation centres promised in IAFS in 2008, no less than seven have been established in Africa. Interestingly, they were not delivered through India's Ministry of Skill Development and Entrepreneurship (MSDE) but through the National Small Industry Corporation (NSIC), which is under the Ministry of Micro, Small & Medium Enterprises of India. By mid-2018 the seven in place were in Ethiopia, Rwanda, Burundi, Egypt, Burkina Faso, Zimbabwe and Gambia, and a further was under execution in Mozambique. In the case of Rwanda, based on the claimed success of the first VTC, ten further VTCs have been promised along with four business incubation centres through an USD 81 million line of credit from India. This was a bilateral arrangement and not a deal brokered by the AU on behalf of India.

Thus, where India has taken a strong bilateral approach, institutions appear to have flourished, as is evident with the Advanced Information Technology Institute-Kofi Annan Centre of Excellence in ICT commissioned between the Prime Minister of India and the President of Ghana in 2003 (Arora and Chand 2015: 37–43). A similar bilateral arrangement led to the inauguration of the Rajiv Gandhi Science Centre in Mauritius in 2004, and also to its Mahatma Gandhi Institute in 1976. The latter's mandate was to promote the cultures of the two countries along with Chinese Studies, African Studies and the performing arts (Arora and Chand 2015: 45–51, 53–64).

More recent institutional developments include the Centre for Entrepreneurship and Leadership in Djibouti, focusing on micro- and small enterprise development, established in 2018, and a forthcoming entrepreneurship development centre in Kigali, Rwanda. In Kenya, there has been the USD 1 million refurbishment of the Gandhi Memorial Library in the University of Nairobi. There will also be a Mahatma Gandhi Convention/Heritage Centre in Jinja, Uganda (see further Vittorini, this volume).

India's private sector has also been active in proposing institutional development in Africa. For instance, India's National Institute for Information Technology (NIIT) has partnered with the CII to develop the latest information infrastructure in Africa. How far this has proceeded is not yet certain, but, on its own, NIIT has partnered with a South African communications network provider. Tata Communications has also been active in South Africa and more widely in Sub-Saharan Africa.

Summarising the state of play for India's institutional development in Africa, it would appear to be the case that India's bilateral agreements have come to pass much more rapidly than those entrusted to the AU to dispense through its eight regional economic communities.

African perceptions of India's soft power and cultural diplomacy

India faces a number of challenges in the promotion of its historical and cultural affinity with Africa, and not least in the 150th anniversary year of Mahatma Gandhi (Vittorini, this volume). There is an additional challenge when there is a large diasporic community in a particular African country, such as South Africa (1.5m), Mauritius (894k), Kenya (80k), Tanzania (60k) or Nigeria (40k). Is the diaspora part of the reason for the location of Indian Cultural Centres (ICCs) in Africa? Perhaps so, as there are two ICCs in South Africa, and one each in Mauritius and Tanzania, but then the fifth on the continent is in Egypt (3.7k).[11]

Cultural affinity between Africa and India is something of a contested area despite the rhetoric, and it has been argued that there is also a need for African cultural centres in India as there is so little known there about the particular countries of Africa. This is what lay behind the start of the Ethiopian Cultural Centre in New Delhi, on the initiative of the then-Ethiopian ambassador, Genet Zewide. There are, in addition, claims about similarities between particular countries such as Ethiopia and India, in respect of food, clothes and some Christian links. It is also noticeable that many African students have gravitated towards South India, which they found warm and welcoming. Indeed, some African students have found Indo-African relations warmer in India than with their 'Asian' diasporic communities in Africa.

Unlike China's sixty-one Confucius Institutes covering most countries on the continent, mentioned earlier, there are only seven countries in Africa represented in the community of seventy-four Chairs of Indian Studies worldwide: Mauritius (2), Morocco (2), Sudan, Ethiopia, Kenya, Tanzania and Egypt (ICCR 2017). It can be readily seen, therefore, that only three countries in the whole of Africa have both an Indian Cultural Centre and an Indian Studies Chair: Egypt, Mauritius and Tanzania. Of course, it can be argued that one lens on Indian culture (and soft power) is extremely well known and popular across the whole of Africa, through Indian cinema: Bollywood. Beyond this, and with a link to Indian films, there is one Indian group in Dar es Salaam, Varda Arts, that is very popular for its renditions of

---

[11] Founded in 1982 and called the Maulana Azad Centre for Indian Culture, it is the only cultural centre in the region, and is named because of the close links of the Indian scholar and first education minister, Maulana Azad Kalam, with the Arab world.

Bollywood songs in Kiswahili, and equally, in Addis Ababa there are Indian artists who sing popular songs in Amharic.

It is intriguing that across East Africa, most Indians, despite all their diversity of languages and groupings, are simply called Wahindi in Kiswahili or, in English, they are Kenyan, Tanzanian or Ugandan 'Asians'. The rich diversity of different Indian communities is not acknowledged, but in many cases these communities continue to have their own temples and language associations in Dar es Salaam, Nairobi, Kigali and Kampala. In Dar es Salaam, for instance, there are no less than twenty Indian associations, most of them linked to the 10,000 expatriate Indians. By contrast, 95 per cent of the local Indians are from Gujarat (MEA 2017c: 6).

Preliminary conclusions and further research

Beyond this short account of human resource diplomacy, there is still a story to be told about African reactions to Indian business, especially in the hundreds of thousands of Africans who have learnt their skills within Indian enterprises, large and small. Arguably, in several parts of Africa, the growth of the informal (*jua kali* in Kiswahili*)* sector has been based on the products and approaches of India's diasporic micro-enterprises in Africa. Indo-African skill transfer has not been a 'cooperation project' of India but something that has happened quietly over the decades (King 2013). In other words, many of the African 'graduates' of Indian enterprises are informally, not deliberately or formally trained (see Mgumia and Chachage, this volume). Equally, it will be worth examining whether the sub-continent's massive decade-long ambitions to 'Skill India' have had any implications for India's support to VTCs, IT centres or enterprise development in Africa. Thus far there has only been a single workshop on Skill India and Africa, organised by the World Bank and India's Ministry of Skill Development and Entrepreneurship (Skill Reporter 2017). In addition, as India's brand-name enterprises have spread across the continent, it will be worth researching whether their preference to learn on the job has been echoed in Africa's medium- and small-scale enterprises.

Apart from the HRD dimensions of Indian business, including in its corporate social responsibility, and thus far the relatively minor impact of Indian NGOs operating in Africa, what are some of the take-aways from African reactions to India's HRD engagement with Africa?

First, the large-scale involvement of Indians in the development phase of thousands of schools and universities in Africa has gone largely unresearched.

But it is increasingly an historical event, and it was undertaken largely on the initiative of thousands of individuals rather than by the Government of India.

Second, the search by Africa for further education and training in India also has an historical aspect, since some of it precedes the dramatic expansion of public and private universities in Africa. Better data are needed to clarify whether African student numbers in India are continuing to rise, or whether other quality destinations, including South Africa and China, are attracting more African students than India. Preliminary work suggests that there may be more self-funded students from Africa going to South Africa than are going to India (King and King 2019).

But India does continue as a scholarship destination for Africans, as can be seen in the multiplicity of schemes, examined above, for the inter-nationalisation of higher education in India. Covid has, however, rapidly and dramatically raised questions about the modalities associated with both the older schemes, ICCR and ITEC, as well as the new schemes of e-VBAB, SWAYAM and Study in India. The online modality of e-VBAB and SWAYAM may well commend itself to ICCR and to Study in India, and could become commonplace with ITEC. While only e-VBAB is explicitly connected to the Ministry of External Affairs and can be construed as devel-opment diplomacy for Africa, the pandemic may make it necessary to rethink the audiences for development diplomacy versus self-funded study, and to re-assess the comparative advantages of online versus face-to-face learning.

How will the 'new normal', influenced by Covid, impact on the fifty thousand scholarships, offered to Africa, over the five years from the third IAFS in 2015 (Modi 2015)? This pledge has not impacted on ICCR's scholarship numbers for Africa, which remain at around nine hundred for 2019–20. Nor has it apparently influenced the fifteen thousand scholarships offered online to Africa under e-VBAB, iLearn's virtual university. It is not clear over what time period these fifteen thousand awards are available. If the ten thousand annually pledged by IAFS include almost one thousand awards from ICCR, a few thousand from ITEC and, say, a proportion of e-VBAB's pro rata over a five-year period, then India is offering to Africa a maximum of ten thousand training awards and scholarships a year. Covid has, however, made quite unclear the numbers that are online and those that are face-to-face.

There is an urgent need for greater clarity amongst the different ministry-sponsored schemes touched upon here. However, as long as the impact of Covid-19 in India and of its 141,000 Covid-related deaths as of 9 December 2020, remains so stark compared with the relatively small number of deaths in Sub-Saharan Africa,[12] there will continue to be huge reverberations within both the long- and short-term scholarship and training environments offered by India.

Third, perspectives on India in Africa need to move on from celebratory accounts of Indian engagement with Africa, many of them associated with the India-Africa Forum Summits, to a review of the full range of what has been achieved by development diplomacy and trade, as well as by people-to-people contacts. This needs to happen in the particularity of different regions of Africa. It will be also relevant to do research on some of the largest Indian HRD projects such as the education side of the Pan-African e-Network (PAN), and especially as this has been relaunched as e-VBAB in 2019 with a very different delivery model and focus (for the medical side of PAN, see Duclos, this volume).

But cutting across all of what has been achieved in Africa by India, and by Africans studying and researching in India, is the big question of how actually Africa fits into the larger picture of India's development cooperation. What are the characteristics of its engagement? Despite the pageantry of the three India-Africa Forum Summits, what is the real story of how Africa fares in the scale of Indian support versus some of the key countries of India's immediate neighbourhood such as Bhutan, Nepal, Mauritius and Afghanistan?

Finally, it would be valuable to review the delivery of the ten principles of India's engagement with Africa, as elaborated by Prime Minister Modi in Kampala in July 2018. The second of these ten principles is central to human development in Africa, based on Africa's priorities. It could be valuable to have a coordinated, critical African reaction to this, and to the whole ten-point agenda, before the next India-Africa Forum Summit in 2024:

> Our development partnership will be guided by your priorities. It will be on terms that will be comfortable for you, that will liberate your potential and not constrain your future. We will rely on African talent and skills. We will build as much local capacity and create as many local opportunities as possible (MEA 2018).

Only then will it be possible to put into perspective India's ambition to be the *vishva guru* (the teacher of the world) – and of Africa – but for Africa also to

---

[12] On 9 December 2020, Johns Hopkins University's Covid map reported just twenty-one deaths in Tanzania and fifty-one in Rwanda. Several countries, such as Kenya, Ethiopia, and Nigeria had over a thousand deaths, and only South Africa had a high total of 22,000 (Johns Hopkins University 2020).

be the teacher of India, as Nehru hoped for in a speech on the day of Ghana's independence in 1957:

> We shall welcome here ever more students from Africa who will learn something about India, but who, more specially, will teach us something about their own country, because we shall inevitably be thrown more together (Nehru 1958: 341).

Bibliography

Altbach, P. and Mathews, E. 2019. 'Why India is still not able to attract global faculty', *University World News*, 5 October 2019, https://www.universityworldnews.com/post.php?story=20191001114117234, accessed 10 December 2019.

Arora, M. and Chand, M. 2015. *India-Africa Partnership Towards Sustainable Development* (New Delhi: FIDC/RIS).

Chand, M. 2019. 'India, Africa to hold review meet, raise the bar for 2020 summit', *India Writes*, 12 September 2019, https://www.indiawrites.org/india-and-the-world/india-africa-to-hold-review-meet-raise-the-bar-for-2020-summit/, accessed 4 December 2019.

CII. 2019. 'India Africa: Higher Education & Skill Development Summit, 27–29 August 2019', *HCI Kampala*, n.d., https://hci.gov.in/kampala./?pdf8278, accessed 7 December 2017

EoI (Embassy of India) Ethiopia. 2017. 'India and Ethiopia to further enhance science & technology cooperation', 7 December 2017, http://indembassyeth.in/wp-content/uploads/2017/12/press-ethopia-2017.pdf, accessed 9 June 2019.

Genet, Z. 2018. *No One Left Behind: Redesigning the Ethiopian Education System* (Addis Ababa: Mega Publishing and Distribution).

ICCR. 2017. *Annual Report April 2016–March 2017*, n.d., https://www.iccr.gov.in/sites/default/files/Annual%20reports/Annual_Report_2016-17_English.pdf, accessed 7 December 2019.

——. 2019. *Annual Report 2019–20*, n.d., https://www.iccr.gov.in/sites/default/files/Annual%20reports/Annual_Report_Final_12-11-2020.pdf, accessed 21 November 2020.

ITEC. 2020a. https://www.itecgoi.in/e-itec, *GoI*, n.d., accessed 20 November 2020.

——. 2020b. https://www.itecgoi.in/about_e-ITEC.php#, *GoI*, n.d., accessed 2 June 2020.

Johns Hopkins University. 2020. 'Global Map', *Coronavirus Resource Centre*, n.d., https://coronavirus.jhu.edu/map.html, accessed 9 December 2020.

King, K. 2013. *China's Aid and Soft Power in Africa: The Case of Education and Training* (Woodbridge: James Currey).

——. 2017. 'Confucius Institutes in Africa: Culture and language without controversy?', in K. Batchelor and X. Zhang (eds.), *China-Africa Relations: Building Images through Cultural Cooperation, Media Representation and on the Ground Activities* (London: Taylor and Francis), 98–112.

———. 2019. 'India-Africa cooperation in human resource development: Education, training skills', *MP-IDSA*, Occasional paper no. 51, April 2019, https://idsa.in/system/files/opaper/ind-africa-cooperation-op-51.pdf, accessed 20 October 2019

King, K. and King, P. 2019. 'India's South-South cooperation in human resource development', *Round Table*, Special Issue: Education & the Commonwealth, 108/4, 399–409.

Ministry of Education. 2020a. SWAYAM. https://swayam.gov.in/, *GoI*, n.d., accessed 23 November 2020.

———. 2020b. SWAYAM., *GoI*, n.d., https://www.youtube.com/watch?v=6WpBA-sIqr9M&feature=emb_logo, accessed 9 December 2020.

———. 2020c. 'Study in India', *GoI*, n.d., https://www.studyinindia.gov.in/whyindia, accessed 2 June 2020.

———. 2020d. 'Study in India', *GoI*, n.d., https://www.studyinindia.gov.in/Blogs/Page/transforming-the-conventional-to-online-learning-experiences-?category=TrendingNow, accessed 27 November 2020.

MEA. 2015. 'Third India-Africa Forum Summit: India-Africa Framework for Strategic Cooperation', *GoI*, 29 October 2015, http://www.mea.gov.in/Uploads/PublicationDocs/25981_framework.pdf, accessed 11 December 2019.

———. 2017a. 'India-Kenya bilateral relations', *GoI*, July 2017, http://www.mea.gov.in/Portal/ForeignRelation/Kenya_June_2017.pdf, accessed 7 June 2019.

———. 2017b. 'India-Ethiopia relations', *GoI*, September 2017, https://mea.gov.in/Portal/ForeignRelation/Ethiopia_Sept_2017.pdf, accessed 7 June 2019.

———. 2017c. 'India-Tanzania relations', *GoI*, August 2017, http://www.mea.gov.in/Portal/ForeignRelation/Tanzania_August__2017.pdf, accessed 8 June 2019.

———. 2018. 'Prime Minister's address at Parliament of Uganda during his state visit to Uganda', *GoI*, 25 July 2018, https://mea.gov.in/Speeches-Statements.htm?dtl/30152/Prime_Ministers_address_at_Parliament_of_Uganda_during_his_State_Visit_to_Uganda, accessed 9 June 2019.

———. 2019. *Annual Report 2018-2019*, *GoI*, 6 April 2019, http://mea.gov.in/Uploads/PublicationDocs/31719_MEA_AR18_19.pdf, accessed 21 November 2019.

———. 2020a. 'About iLearn', *GoI*, n.d., https://www.ilearn.gov.in, accessed 20 November 2020.

———. 2020b. Course Catalogue: Education, *GoI*, n.d., https://ilearn.gov.in/explorer?category=Education, accessed 9 December 2020.

———. 2020c. iLearn about, *GoI*, n.d., https://ilearn.gov.in/about, accessed 9 December 2020.

Modi, N. 2015. 'India-Africa Summit: Full text of Narendra Modi's speech', *Times of India*, 29 October 2015, https://timesofindia.indiatimes.com/india/India-Africa-summit-Read-full-text-of-PM-Narendra-Modis-speech/articleshow/49577890.cms, accessed 10 June 2019.

Mullen, R.D., Prasad, K., Shivakumar, H., and Singh, K. 2015. 'Fifty Years of Indian Technical and Economic Cooperation. Indian Development Cooperation Research', *Centre for Policy Research*, 10 February 2015, https://www.cprindia.org/system/tdf/policy-briefs/IDCR%20Report%20-%2050%20years%20of%20ITEC.pdf?file=1&type=node&id=3853&force=1, accessed 6 December 2019.

Nehru, J. 1958. *Jawaharlal Nehru's Speeches: Volume Three: 1953–1957* (New Delhi: Ministry of Information and Broadcasting).

PIB. 2018. 'Study in India programme of HRD Ministry launched with the launch of "Study in India Portal" by Smt. Sushma Swaraj and Dr Satya Pal Singh in New Delhi today', *GoI*, 18 April 2018, https://pib.gov.in/PressReleaseIframePage.aspx?PRID=1529560, accessed 23 December 2019.

Sautman, B. and Yan, H. 2009. 'African perspectives on China-Africa links', *China Quarterly*, 199, 728–59.

Skill Reporter. 2017. 'Skill India and World Bank organise a "knowledge sharing workshop" for African delegates', *Skill Reporter*, 31 October 2017, https://www.skillreporter.com/2017/10/news/msde/msde-skill-india-world-bank-africa-knowledge-sharing-workshop/, accessed 9 December 2020.

UIS. 2017. 'Student flows to India', *UIS*, n.d., http://uis.unesco.org/en/topic/higher-education, accessed 18 January 2018.

6

A Shining Example: Modelling Growth in India's Pan-African e-Network

VINCENT DUCLOS

'We're a nation of a billion people and our thought is: "What can I give to the world?"' explained Dr Abdul Kalam when we met in his Rajaji Marg residence in New Delhi, in March 2011. 'We can give knowledge. We can remove the pain of the people. That is that type of culture we have,' continued Kalam. The former president of India then recalled how it all began. It started with his presidential visit to South Africa, in September 2004, when he was attending a session of the Pan-African parliament in Johannesburg. All of the African nations were represented, Kalam remembered. In his inaugural address, he engaged the audience with what he described as a vision: 'Then the idea came in. How to connect them. Our hospitals and the African hospitals, our universities and the African universities, how we can connect? And when I presented, they cheered.'[1]

Five years after Kalam's visit to South Africa, the Pan-African e-Network was launched. The Pan-African e-Network (which I will now refer to as 'PAN') provided tele-education and telemedicine services between 2009 and 2017. This chapter focuses on the telemedicine component of the network, which connected hospitals in over forty African countries with twelve tertiary care hospitals located in Indian metropolises. To do so, I draw upon field research carried over the past decade, and most intensively in 2010–12, when I conducted interviews and field observations in India, as well as in Dakar (Senegal) and Addis Ababa (Ethiopia).[2]

Right from the design stage, PAN was an exceptionally ambitious project, relying on a large network infrastructure. Its implementation involved laying out a transnational network, composed of a fibre-optic section (connecting sites in India), undersea cables (connecting India and Africa) and satellite

[1]   Abdul Kalam to Vincent Duclos, personal communication, March 2011, New Delhi.

[2]   I have spent some time in eight of the twelve participating Indian hospitals, including a prolonged stay at the Apollo Hospital in Chennai.

technology (connecting sites in Africa). PAN's telemedicine operations depended on dozens of doctors, and also on engineers, mostly of Indian origin, dispatched to the connected sites – including all participating hospitals, a data centre (New Delhi) and a satellite hub station (Dakar, Senegal). It also involved the importation, set up and maintenance of medical and computer equipment that was provided as part of the project. PAN was funded by the Indian government under the budget of the Ministry of External Affairs (MEA), with substantial annual operating costs.[3] The network was implemented and operated by Telecommunications India Limited (TCIL), an Indian public sector company which is very active in Africa. The African Union (AU) Commission assisted in laying out PAN, while participating countries facilitated (or not) the circulation of equipment, identified the sites to be connected, and provided physical infrastructure within those sites.

PAN was a thoroughly commercial enterprise which aimed to accelerate flows of medical knowledge, of patients and investments between African and Indian hospitals. The project was designed as a public–private partnership. Equipment and medical services were provided by private hospital chains, technology vendors and telecommunication companies. Remote medical services were offered free of charge, but participating Indian hospitals were compensated to do so. According to some of its actors, PAN was initially expected to become a private entity in the long term, when African medical teams would get habituated to the services it provided. This never materialised, most likely because issues of poor utilisation lowered expectations of future commercial profitability. The network nevertheless did come with some impact on clinical practice, including on patients. It established new referrals pathways, by which clinical work was being outsourced to Indian tertiary care hospitals – either via remote care or with patients travelling to India to receive treatment. After having seen its operations discontinued in 2017, the network was officially relaunched in 2018. In this new phase, the technical infrastructure of the network has been redesigned.[4] But the most visible change lies in the network's new Sanskrit designation:

---

[3]   In the course of this research, I have come across or heard about a whole range of estimated costs. USD 200 million is the official figure published by the African Union in the *First Progress Report of the Chairperson of the Commission on the Pan African E-Network on Tele-Education and Tele-Medicine* (African Union 2018).

[4]   In a nutshell, in this upgraded version, web-based portals are expected to replace PAN's massive – but costly – network infrastructure. This change will also affect the identity of participating African hospitals, given that many hospitals still do not have proper internet access.

e-VidyaBharati and e-ArogyaBharati, which may be respectively translated as e-Knowledge India, and e-Health India.

As its slogan suggested, the Pan-African e-Network was designed to stand as a 'shining example of South-South cooperation'. This chapter takes the slogan seriously by approaching PAN as an aesthetic vehicle, oriented to addressees, and producing commercial, political and moral value (Larkin 2013). PAN cannot be reduced to its economic, medical or technical function. The network, President Kalam suggested to me, came as a vision in response to a question: what can India give to the world? Slightly complicating that story, this chapter examines some recent historical developments which have contributed to making PAN into a model of what 'India has to give to the world'. But beyond historical accounts, the chapter examines how PAN aimed to model the future of cooperation between India and Africa, thereby reshaping the identity of the partners involved.

The chapter is divided into four parts. The first section traces the short history of PAN to the watershed moment in Indian foreign policy when the project was announced, insisting on how it aimed to model what a uniquely Indian approach to development cooperation might look like. The second part of the chapter shows how, in contrast with imaginations of a seamless South–South circulation of medical expertise, the network mediates between embedded and largely unequal clinical worlds – with all sorts of effects. A third section suggests that PAN adopts a model of healthcare provision developed in India in the years preceding its launch, when information technology came to be seen as the proper tool to fix a fragmented health system, and to create new markets for a booming hospital industry. This model facilitates the outsourcing of medical expertise to tertiary hospitals in India. Fourth, I suggest that PAN discursively claimed the 'South' as a series of future relations through which the Indian nation would come to imagine and project itself on the global stage. The architecture of the network provides indications of how such relations might be ordered.

A turning point

The Pan-African e-Network was announced at a turning point in India's approach to foreign aid and development cooperation. In February 2003, the Indian Minister of Finance, Jaswant Singh, announced that, with the exception of five countries – the United States, United Kingdom, Russia, Germany and Japan – India would no longer accept bilateral aid. India would also no longer accept any tied aid. The decision came just a few months after the Government of India had decided to prepay USD 3 billion of its external loan, and repay its bilateral debt to all but four of its creditor states. In his budget speech, Minister Singh justified this change in policy by insisting that India had reached a new 'stage' of development which entailed reviewing its dependence on external donors (Ministry of Finance 2003). Singh further announced India's intention to cancel the debt of seven Heavily Indebted Poor Countries (HIPCs). Besides refusing aid and writing off debt, India would also establish the India Development Initiative (IDI) with the dual purpose of providing grants and project assistance to developing countries and of promoting India's 'strategic economic interests abroad' (Ministry of Finance 2003: 20).

As a result of the shift in policy, India would soon become a benefactor in the geopolitics of aid: moving from being the world's largest recipient in foreign aid, to being a net donor – the country's annual financial volume for cooperation is currently estimated at somewhere between USD 0.5 billion and 1 billion (Katti et al 2009). While neighbouring countries such as Afghanistan, Nepal and Bhutan remained key beneficiaries, Africa soon became a prime destination for Indian cooperation (Chanana 2009). The factors underlying such a 'declaration of independence' have been examined at length in media coverage, institutional reports and academic literature (Price 2004; Six 2009; Bijoy 2010; Sinha 2010). But beyond individual factors, observers tend to agree that it did not only set the conditions for the expansion of India's development cooperation, but also aimed at conveying a sense of maturity and self-realisation. Retrospectively, 2003–04 appears as a key moment in the imagination of the nation as a global economic force in the making.

The question raised by President Kalam when we met, recalling the 'vision' he had of PAN, was already a topic of concern when he announced the project in 2004: what might India's unique contribution to the world be? In fact, this is a question which has been the object of a great deal of attention over the past decades. This is a conversation in which past, present and future, but also claims of difference and universality, are deeply entangled. The ancient rootedness of India's civilisational identity is, for instance, often expected to provide a model for the nation's unique approach to world affairs (Abraham 2007; Thussu 2013; Singh 2019). But the uniqueness of India's contribution is also crafted in relation to the globally dominant languages of economic growth and technological innovation. President Kalam's own speeches and writings are exemplary in that regard. For the 'People's President,' ancient-rooted civilisational wisdom legitimises the promise of a renaissance in which India at long last rediscovers itself as a knowledge and technology superpower (Kalam 2003).

Claims of exceptionality were also central in the numerous discussions I had as part of this research with Indian foreign affairs officers, project designers and entrepreneurs involved in the early days' design and implementation of PAN. The narrative was rather consistent: PAN was unique because it was not the type of project Western stakeholders would have designed and implemented. My interlocutors seldom referred to donor institutions such as the Global Fund, the Bill and Melinda Gates Foundation or the World Bank, to name just a few. Neither would they speak the language of aid or assistance – at times clearly distancing themselves from such paternalistic approaches. Western-centric agenda, institutions and moral economies were simply not key points of reference: PAN was to be modern, but not Western (Subramaniam 2019). But being 'non-Western' was also not going to be enough. In fact, my interlocutors insisted, PAN most crucially had to differentiate an 'Indian model' from what is perceived as China's approach in Africa. Whereas Chinese cooperation was portrayed as self-interested, and revolving around resource extraction and basic infrastructure projects, India would rather propose a model of inclusive growth. The director of the Africa section at the Confederation of Indian Industry (CII), explained the difference to me in these terms:

> The difference between the Chinese model and the Indian model is that the Indian model is more sustainable, developing local capacities. India has been a colony. So we understand those sensitive things better than some other countries. We want an inclusive growth, not an exploitative growth.[5]

This is where the 'South' gets mobilised as a discursive category. PAN's cooperation narrative is replete with references to a quasi-mythological 'South', and to past solidarity between India and Africa in particular. In promotional materials, press coverage and institutional documents, past figures such as Jawaharlal Nehru and Mohandas Gandhi, events like the Bandung Conference, and partnerships such as the Non-Alignment Movement (NAM) are continuously evoked.[6] PAN's slogan itself makes the 'South' into the key aesthetic and discursive category. Supplementing this framing of

---

[5] CII Director (Africa) to Vincent Duclos, personal communication, 10 December 2010, New Delhi

[6] This is not unique to PAN. As was noted by Gerard McCann, the 'continuities of Afro-Indian historical brotherhood have become the apparent *sine qua non* for descriptions of renewed neoliberal India-Africa relations'. This is a story, McCann notes, which does not 'tell the whole tale' (McCann 2013: 260) (see also Cheru and Obi 2010; Mawdsley and McCann 2011).

India–Africa solidarity lies the teleological – and dubious in many ways – claim according to which India has been, in the recent past, where Africa apparently is now in terms of development stages. Indian doctors and hospitals, it was, for instance, explained to me many times, were well suited to respond to the needs of the 'sister continent'. Stories of the past are thus mobilised as evidence of seamless, and mutually beneficial relations to come – in the clinic and beyond.

In-between clinical worlds

PAN delivered two forms of medical services: teleconsultations and continuing medical education. Both were provided by Indian tertiary care hospitals and covered a host of medical sub-specialities. Broadcast live in participating hospitals, continuing medical education (CME) sessions consisted of daily programmes of live medical training. Each of the twelve participating Indian hospitals offered six sessions per month, covering a broad range of topics and specialties. As many as seventy-two sessions were thus broadcast every month in connected African hospitals. During the time I conducted field research in Africa, CME sessions were more often than not poorly attended. Taking place in studios that were designed and equipped for this purpose, teleconsultations consist of videoconference sessions between Indian specialists and their African colleagues in which they discussed patient cases, clinical impressions, probable diagnoses and advisable treatments. Usually requested by medical teams in participants' African hospitals to address challenging patient cases, teleconsultations could be used to obtain a second opinion when a diagnosis was uncertain. They could also provide support in the therapeutic management of patients and in assisting doctors who were inexperienced with performing certain procedures. When compared with the capacity of the network and the availability of participating Indian hospitals, teleconsultations suffered from low utilisation – a situation which has been acknowledged by PAN's actors (Duclos 2016). But many teleconsultations did take place, with all sorts of effects.

At the Centre Hospitalier National Universitaire (CHNU) in Fann, a university hospital located in Dakar, where I have conducted research, teleconsultations have become integrated into everyday clinical work. In some units, including neurology and paediatric cardiology, treating teams knew that they could use the network if need be. A good example is the case of Omar, a four-year-old Senegalese boy who was hospitalised at Fann.[7] Omar suf-

---

[7]   The names of patients and doctors have been changed for confidentiality purposes.

fered from a chronic heart condition, and the treating team at Fann believed that he needed a pacemaker. However, having never seen a similar case, the cardiologists at Fann were unsure about the sort of pacemaker they should install in such a young child. Paediatric cardiology was relatively new at Fann hospital. Until recently, similar cases had been transferred abroad, including to Morocco or France. After discussing Omar's case during a staff meeting, the treating team decided to ask their Indian colleagues for advice. The next day, a teleconsultation took place between Omar's treating doctor, Dr Faye, and Dr Khan, a paediatric cardiologist from Fortis Hospital in Delhi. During the session, Dr Khan and Dr Faye reviewed Omar's medical record, scrolling through and commenting on scan images. Dr Khan insisted that Omar needed to have the pacemaker installed as soon as possible. Then, for almost an hour, he guided Dr Faye through the surgical procedure. One week later, Omar underwent a successful surgery. Dr Faye later commented: 'A chef always has a special recipe, which is not in any cookbook. In this particular case, experience was the key.'

At first glance, this seemed to confirm one of the main expectations associated with PAN, namely to provide access to medical expertise and care through established South–South referral pathways. The network indeed opened up the clinic and generated new spaces of care. However, in contrast with images of seamless communication, the work of care in PAN entailed mediating between embedded, heterogeneous clinical worlds. As it circulated on the network, medical expertise was inevitably altered. This produced all sorts of effects, intended or not. For instance, participating African doctors often had to adapt courses of treatment according to the local availability of diagnostic testing or medicines. In other cases, patients could learn about the condition from which they were suffering, without having access to treatment locally. Such knowledge at times engendered a sense of frustration among the members of Senegalese treating teams. A neurologist at Fann Hospital explained: 'Sometimes we have already thought about the things they are asking us to do. However, we can't! We do not have the means! We have to improvise. It becomes very frustrating!'

Statements like this show how the work of care in PAN took place between largely unequal clinical worlds – each with their infrastructural constraints, therapeutic practices and established referral pathways. On other occasions, flows were interrupted in abrupt, potentially harmful ways. This is illustrated by the case of Aasiya. A woman in her thirties, Aasiya was experiencing symptoms of generalised itching, abdominal pain, dark urine and fever. At the time of the teleconsultation, she was hospitalised in a public hospital in Bosaso, Northern Somalia. The consultation involved her treating doctor and a gastroenterologist from Apollo Hospital in Chennai. After about fifteen minutes of discussion, the doctors agreed on a probable diagnosis of a dilated bile duct. However, the Indian gastroenterologist insisted that an abdominal CT scan was required before any surgical procedure was performed. This was not an option, explained Aasiya's attending doctor, since the hospital did not have a CT scanner. His Indian colleague then enquired about the possibility of Aasiya travelling to India to receive proper treatment. Getting a visa, he explained, would not be a problem. But Aasiya explained that she could not afford to pay for treatment abroad. Since PAN did not cover medical travels, and in the absence of better options, both doctors finally agreed to go ahead with the surgery, without a CT scan. Disheartened by the situation, the gastroenterologist at Apollo Hospital confided to me that he would never do that with his own patients.

A case like that of Aasiya shows the limits of PAN's capacity to remotely take care of patients. It makes visible a series of conditions, factors and situations which were critical to PAN's efficacy but upon which the network itself had little to no influence. More importantly, it suggests that PAN may sometimes have aggravated existing inequalities in the global distribution of biomedicine. It may have contributed to the production of connected enclaves of knowledge and care.

Ordering connections

The 'vision' that President Kalam had of the Pan-African e-Network, in 2004, was not only to 'connect India with Africa': it was also to model such a connection according to a specific technological form. PAN was launched at a particular moment in India's recent history, in which information and communication technology (ICT) came to be seen as *the* proper medium for development, growth and nation building. As the narrative went in a myriad of bestselling accounts published in the years preceding PAN, electronic media were to unleash long-suppressed entrepreneurial and technoscientific energies (Nilekani 2009). Indian entrepreneurs and technological 'geeks' were to act as the material engine that would 'catapult the nation to the forefront of emerging economies in the new millennium' (Philip 2016: 278). For President Kalam and many others, ICT appeared as the proper device for shaping an 'Indian model' of development cooperation. The 'Africa-India Framework for Enhanced Cooperation', adopted as an outcome of the Second Africa-India Summit in 2011, thus insisted on 'Africa's immense regard and admiration for the strides made by India in the development of its information and communications technology' (IAFS II 2011: 5). The contribution made by ICTs to the accelerated growth of GDP in India, the document suggests, is recognised by African partners as a model for future shared prosperity.[8]

PAN embodied and extended such imaginations of the future. A promotional film made about the network, for instance, informs us that: 'Technology has helped India script its growth story in the twenty-first century. Satellite information and communication technologies have fuelled a digital revolution that spans not just its own borders but aims to share its vision with Africa.'[9] The reference to satellite technology, whose enchanting power is also central to the aesthetics of the film, is not trivial. Himself a celebrated space scientist, President Kalam was well aware when he 'envisioned' PAN that India had recently become the theatre of significant telemedicine experiments using satellite technology. The early years of the 2000s have indeed witnessed the growth of telemedicine networks connecting tertiary care hospitals in the country's metropolises with dozens of hospitals located in rural or remote areas. These developments were supported by the Indian Space Research Organisation (ISRO), which provided satellite infrastructure as part of its 'social mission' (Bhaskaranarayana et al. 2009). As a result, telemedicine emerged as a technological solution to India's increasingly inequitable healthcare landscape in the early 2000s. In the tenth Five Year Plan of the Planning Commission of India, published in 2002, ICT features as the proper channel to better integrate a fragmented health system, by developing referral linkages between primary, secondary and tertiary care levels (Planning Commission 2002).

The expansion of telemedicine in India was primarily driven by private hospital chains, who were looking to build a presence in semi-urban, rural and remote areas. By means of telemedicine, 'we will vertically integrate the medical facility of our country,' explained Dr Prathap C. Reddy, Chairman of Apollo Hospitals, a leader in the field (Business Line 2001). Satellite technology was not so much anticipated to repair a broken public health care system, as it promised to circumvent – or 'leapfrog' – some of the most blatant challenges it faced. In the years leading to PAN, satellite technology was effectively transformed into new markets in India, producing remote patient populations. It operated, in a way similar to what Lisa Cartwright (2000)

[8]   The notion of India becoming a 'role model' for 'other developing nations' in terms of economic development is not new. As was suggested by Pankaj Mishra, it plays a key role in the self-fashioning of an Indian elite which has been increasingly expanding and entrenching itself in recent years (see Mishra 2013).

[9]   The film, called *Connecting Hearts: India's Pan African e-Network*, is available on YouTube (see Indian Diplomacy 2011).

noted in her study of early telemedicine networks in the United States, as a style of health and resource management which assembled pools of clients in profitable enclaves or catchment 'regions' (see Cartwright 2000). Space technology was not only expected to provide healthcare: it modelled how health systems were to be managed and how care was to be distributed.

From the beginning, this model has been incorporated into PAN. During the course of this research, I was repeatedly reminded that PAN is to be delivered as a turnkey solution. PAN came in a one-size-fits-all format, capable of operating in highly variable conditions. To do so, it relied on a few different strategies. Two engineers worked full-time on the project at all participating hospitals. They executed a range of tasks such as scheduling teleconsultations, managing bandwidth and perfecting image and sound quality. Providing a turnkey network also involved partially isolating it from the everyday operations of participating hospitals – by definition too diverse to be integrated into such a large project.

Most importantly, PAN's capacity to provide a turnkey solution primarily depended on satellite technology. As mentioned earlier, to connect African hospitals PAN leased bandwidth from RascomStar-QAF, a private company in which the primary investor is the Regional African Satellite Communication Organisation (RASCOM).[10] For the network designers, satellite was chosen as a viable alternative to the cost, time and energy-intensive practice of laying thousands of miles of fibre-optic cable across the continent. A TCIL project manager explained: 'Satellite was the only means which could connect all the countries on the network. Landline was unavailable and it was not possible also.' Rascom QAF-1R's footprint was unique in its capacity to cover the whole African continent. But beyond technical issues, satellite technology promised to integrate remote sites into new patterns of commerce and communication. It pointed towards a future in which patients, doctors and hospitals would be interconnected in a common market formation, organised around the knowledge and care emanating from remote Indian hospitals.

Growing south

Over the past few years, significant attention has been given to how new forms of South–South solidarities may challenge the established economic order (Hofmeyr 2018; Menon 2018). PAN did no such thing. It did not claim the South as a site of resistance to Western hegemony. Cooperation in PAN did not carry to kind the redemptive hopes found in early forms of

[10]   For a short history of Rascom QAF-1R, see Parks 2012.

Afro-Asian solidarity. It did not promise redemption from the kind of market commodification that has been shaping global health spheres for some time. By contrast, in PAN, the South provides moral legitimacy for the emergence of new market formations that challenge tenacious North–South binaries.

As is the case with much of South–South cooperation discourse, PAN was discursively framed as a 'win-win scenario,' insisting on reciprocal benefit (Duclos 2012; Mawdsley 2012). African hospitals, doctors and patients would have access to medical expertise while Indian corporate hospitals could access new pools of patients. But although some patients did travel to India after being referred via the network, PAN was not designed for short-term profit. It did not in itself generate a sustainable stream of revenue. Nevertheless, hospital managers involved in the project were pretty straightforward about their motivations in opting in: telemedicine would help them build a presence into new markets.[11] The network opened up new referral pathways, in which medical expertise and treatment were outsourced to private Indian hospitals. PAN created value by building trust in relations to come. A manager at the Narayana Hrudyalaya hospital in Bengaluru (formerly Bangalore) explained his motivation in joining the network: 'We are building a presence. This is what growth is all about.'[12]

How exactly would such growth be channelled, and organised? The very design of the network, again, provides indications. PAN was a private and centralised infrastructure. This reflected the ambition to rapidly connect dozens of hospitals spread across two continents, as well as concerns with the protection of medical data. But there is more to it. As a recent AU report noted, although in theory the network could have been integrated with other local networks, it remained a Closed User Group which primarily delivered services 'from Indian institutions to the Member States' (AU 2018). Only a defined set of sites had access to the network's services. Furthermore, PAN's star network topology channelled all communications through the satellite hub hosted near Dakar – operated and staffed by TCIL, preventing direct exchange between African sites. This choice of topology facilitated a centre–periphery model for the circulation of knowledge, care and patients. Growth, in PAN, was thus shaped by heavily patterned connections. In spite of some efforts to make it more adaptable, PAN remained a rigid, primarily unidirectional network.

---

[11] On the recent history and promise of India–Africa healthcare trade, see Modi 2011; CII 2016.

[12] Manager, Narayana Hrudyalaya hospital, to Vincent Duclos, 20 December 2010, Bengaluru.

At both political and technical levels, PAN remade the identity of both donor and receiver. PAN should be understood in relation to what Kaur and Blom Hansen (2016) refer to as an 'aesthetics of arrival': performing 'India's arrival on the global stage as a spectacle' in which the nation is being celebrated for a worldwide audience. In PAN, the aesthetic aggrandisement of the nation and the global expansion of medicine and technology are feeding into one another (Kamat 2004). In PAN, nationalist desires and promises of global economic growth do not merely co-exist but effectively reinforce and sustain each other. PAN fed the imagination of a South to come, and in whose future India would be called to play a central role. The 'uniqueness' of what India has to offer the world, to borrow President Kalam's phrase, lies in the performance of the nation itself. The network acted as a medium through which the nation would come to imagine itself in relation to a South it conjured and intervened in. But while in President Kalam's vision, India clearly was the name of the nation to imagine, the network's new denomination suggests this vision is now at least partially a thing of the past. What futures e-ArogyaBharati might have us imagine remain uncertain, but they are nevertheless a good deal worrisome.

Bibliography

Abraham, I. 2007. 'The future of Indian foreign policy', *Economic and Political Weekly*, 4209–212.

AU. 2018. 'First progress report of the chairperson of the commission on the Pan African e-network on tele-education and tele-medicine', *African Union*, 29 March 2018, https://au.int/en/documents/20180329/first-progress-report-chairperson-commission-pan-african-e-network-tele-education, accessed 5 December 2019.

Bhaskaranarayana, A., Satyamurthy, L.S. and Remilla, M. 2009. 'Indian Space Research Organisation and telemedicine in India', *Telemedicine and e-Health*, 15, 586–91.

Bijoy, C.R. 2010. 'India: Transiting to a global donor', in The Reality of Aid (ed.) *South–South Cooperation: A Challenge to the Aid System?* (Quezon City: IBON Books), 65–76.

Business Line. 2001. 'Apollo hospitals to focus on telemedicine', *The Hindu Business Line*, 19 June 2001, url unavailable, accessed 15 August 2001.

Cartwright, L. 2000. 'Reach out and heal someone: Telemedicine and the globalisation of health care', *Health*, 4, 347–77.

Chanana, D. 2009. 'India as an emerging donor', *Economic and Political Weekly*, 34, 11–14.

Cheru, F. and Obi, C. 2010. 'Introduction – Africa in the twenty-first century: Strategic and development challenges', in F. Cheru and C. Obi (eds.) *The Rise of China & India in Africa* (London and New York: Zed Books), 1–12.

CII. 2016. 'India-Africa Health Forum: Post-Event Report', *Embassy of India in Kinshasa (GoI)*, 21 April 2016, https://eoi.gov.in/kinshasa/?pdf5906, accessed 4 December 2019.

Duclos, V. 2012. 'Building capacities: The resurgence of Indo-African technoeconomic cooperation, *India Review*, 11, 209–25.

———. 2016. 'The map and the territory: An ethnographic study of the low utilisation of a global eHealth network', *Journal of Information Technology*, 31/4, 329–33.

Hofmeyr, I. (ed.). 2018. *Against the Global South* (Cambridge: Cambridge University Press).

IAFS II. 2011. 'Second India-Africa Forum Summit 2011, Addis Ababa: Plan of Action of the Framework for Cooperation on the India-Africa Forum Summit', *IAFS II*, 25 May 2011, http://www.iafs.in/documents-detail.php?archive_id=5, accessed 5 May 2016.

Indian Diplomacy. 2011. 'Connecting Hearts: India's Pan African e-Network', *GoI*, n.d., https://www.youtube.com/watch?v=73LMVBnPacg, accessed 4 December 2019.

Kalam, A. 2003. *Ignited Minds: Unleashing the Power within India* (New Delhi: Penguin Global).

Kamat, S. 2004. 'Postcolonial aporias, or what does fundamentalism have to do with globalisation? The contradictory consequences of education reform in India', *Comparative Education*, 40, 267–87.

Katti, V., Chahoud, T. and Kaushik, A. 2009. *India's Development Cooperation – Opportunities and Challenges for International Development Cooperation* (Bonn: German Development Institute).

Kaur, R. and Blom Hansen, T. 2016. 'Aesthetics of arrival: Spectacle, capital, novelty in post-reform India', *Identities*, 23, 265–75.

Larkin, B. 2013. 'The politics and poetics of infrastructure', *Annual Review of Anthropology*, 42, 327–43.

Mawdsley, E. 2012. *From Recipients to Donors: Emerging Powers and the Changing Development Landscape* (New York: Zed Books).

Mawdsley, E. and McCann, G. 2011. 'Introduction: Towards a re-evaluation of contemporary India-Africa relations', in E. Mawdsley and G. McCann (eds.) *India in Africa: Changing Geographies of Power* (Oxford: Pambazuka Press), 1–10.

McCann, G. 2013. 'From diaspora to third worldism and the United Nations: India and the politics of decolonising Africa', *Past and Present*, 218, 258–80.

Menon, D.M. 2018. 'Thinking about the Global South', in R. West-Pavlov (ed.) *The Global South and Literature* (Cambridge: Cambridge University Press), 34–44.

Ministry of Finance. 2003. 'Budget 2003-2004. Speech of Jaswant Singh, Minister of Finance and Company Affairs', *GoI*, 28 February 2003 https://www.indiabudget.gov.in/doc/bspeech/bs200304.pdf, accessed 4 December 2019.

Mishra, P. 2013. 'Which India Matters?', *The New York Review of Books*, 21 November 2013, https://www.nybooks.com/articles/2013/11/21/which-india-matters/, accessed 5 December 2019.

Modi, R. 2011. 'Offshore healthcare management: Medical tourism between Kenya, Tanzania and India', in E. Mawdsley and G. McCann (eds.) *India in Africa. Changing Geographies of Power* (Oxford: Pambazuka Press), 125–39.

Nilekani, N. 2009. *Imagining India: The Idea of a Renewed Nation* (New Delhi: Penguin Press).

Parks, L. 2012. 'Footprints of the global south', in Volkmer, I (ed.) *The Handbook of Global Media Research* (Malden: Wiley Blackwell), 123–42.

Philip, K. 2016. 'Telling histories of the future: The imaginaries of Indian technoscience', *Identities*, 23, 276–93.

Planning Commission. 2002. 'Tenth Five Year Plan 2002–07', *Volume II: Sectoral Policies and Programmes* (New Delhi: Government of India).

Price, G. 2004. 'India's aid dynamics: From recipient to donor?', *Asia Programme Working Paper* (London: Chatham House).

Singh, Z. D. 2019. 'India's civilisational identity and the world order', *Economic & Political Weekly*, 54, 10–12.

Sinha, P. K. 2010. 'Indian development cooperation with Africa', in F. Cheru and C. Obi (eds.) *The Rise of China & India in Africa* (London and New York: Zed Books), 77–93.

Six, C. 2009. 'The rise of postcolonial states as donors: A challenge to the development paradigm?', *Third World Quarterly*, 30, 1103–21.

Subramaniam, B. 2019. *Holy Science: The Biopolitics of Hindu Nationalism* (Seattle: University of Washington Press).

Thussu, D. 2013. *Communicating India's Soft Power: Buddha to Bollywood* (New York: Palgrave Macmillan).

7

Partnership in Times of Pandemic: India's Covid Diplomacy in Africa

SUPRIYA ROYCHOUDHURY AND EMMA MAWDSLEY

In 2020, India's 'Covid diplomacy' drew considerable attention and praise from foreign policy observers and analysts. This was hardly surprising, given its energy, velocity and ambition. This chapter builds on existing analyses and commentaries to advance our understanding of India's Covid diplomacy, focusing on its engagements in the African continent in particular, while also drawing attention to how its Covid diplomacy became so deeply mired in criticism and controversy almost one year after it first launched.

India's global health diplomacy

Although the concept of 'global health diplomacy' was institutionalised by the United Nations only in 2009, it has existed as a practice for much longer (Kickbusch 2013). Indian state and non-state actors have been involved in global health diplomacy since India's independence. For example, in 1963, the Indian community in Addis Ababa, with support from the Indian mission, set up the Gandhi Memorial Hospital for gynaecology and obstetrics to commemorate the twenty-fifth anniversary of the then Emperor Haile Selassie I (Embassy of the Federal Republic of Ethiopia n.d.).

In academic literatures, global public health diplomacy has variously been defined as a framework that encourages multilateral cooperation and investment in global health (Reid et al. 2019), an assemblage of negotiation processes involving multiple actors across multiple levels to manage the global policy environment (Kickbusch et al. 2007; Kickbusch and Behrendt 2017) and an educational tool that improves both global health and international relations (Adams et al. 2008; Katz et al. 2011). Common to these definitions is an understanding of the interdependent nature of public health and the need to develop transnational strategies to respond to public health risks.

An analytical review of the academic and grey literatures suggests that India's global health diplomacy has, to date, broadly taken place along four main axes: social, economic, political and humanitarian.

The social dimension of India's global health diplomacy has involved efforts to widen global access to medicines and vaccines and improve healthcare infrastructures in partner countries. This includes the provision of antiretroviral and antimalarial medicines to the Global Fund to Fight AIDS, TB and Malaria by Indian pharmaceutical companies such as Ranbaxy, Strides and Cipla (Horner 2020). Indian companies currently manufacture between 60 to 80 per cent of all vaccines procured by United Nations agencies (Chaturvedi 2016), although as the pandemic has acutely revealed, it relies on imports from China and elsewhere for some of their component parts and raw materials. India has also contributed to global health initiatives such as Gavi,[1] extended financial support to build and maintain hospitals and specialised clinics in Afghanistan and Nepal, and donated ambulances to Nepal and Mozambique (Chaturvedi 2016).

The economic dimension of India's global health diplomacy has involved the provision of medical goods and services. As noted by the Minister of External Affairs of India, Dr Jaishankar, 'Respect for Indian medical professionals and Indian medical expertise is not restricted to the United States. We have worldwide brand recognition in the healthcare industry' (MEA 2020d). In recent years, there has been increasing governmental interest in promoting India as a preferred destination for the treatment of patients from overseas. As well as high quality allopathic medical services, India has sought to cultivate and expand the global market for Indian traditional systems of medicine such as Ayurveda, Yoga, Unani, Siddha and Homeopathy (AYUSH). To that end, India has set up a cross-departmental institutional platform to promote medical and wellness tourism in India.[2]

At a political level, India's global health diplomacy has helped to democratise systems of global health governance. At the World Trade Organisation (WTO), India has consistently championed members' rights to safeguard public health goals against the trade interests of pharmaceutical companies. India has defended its right to issue compulsory licences[3] for the production

---

[1]   In 2018, India doubled its contribution to the Gavi Alliance, committing USD 8 million for the 2018–22 period (Gavi 2020).

[2]   The National Medical and Wellness Tourism Board, established under the Chairmanship of the Minister of Tourism, comprising representation from the Ministries of Health, Commerce, External Affairs, AYUSH and Home Affairs, offers one such institutional platform (PIB 2018).

[3]   When a government allows someone else to produce a patented product or process without the consent of the patent owner. It is one of the flexibilities permitted by the Trade-Related aspects of Intellectual Property Rights TRIPS Agreement (WTO, n.d.).

of generic versions of patented medicines, and has withstood pressure from the United States to dilute these provisions in its domestic intellectual property laws (Sen 2018). At their Health Ministers Meeting in 2019, BRICS leaders reaffirmed their political commitment to 'promote access to safe, quality, effective and affordable, essential medicines, vaccines, diagnostics and other medical products' and make 'full use of TRIPS [Trade Related Aspects of Intellectual Property Rights] flexibilities', to protect '[their] policy space against TRIPS plus provisions and other measures that impede or restrict such access' (BRICS 2019). Actions such as these have allowed India to successfully project itself as the 'pharmacy of the world'.

And finally, India's health diplomacy has extended to geographies well beyond parts of the Global South. In response to Hurricane Noel in Haiti in 2007, India donated medicines valued at USD 50,000 (MEA 2013). Similarly, India offered to supply essential medicines as well as fly in a medical team from the Indian Army Medical Corps to New Orleans when Hurricane Katrina struck in 2005 (MEA 2005).

These achievements have to be read against India's notoriously low domestic health budget. In 2015, India spent about 1 per cent of its GDP on public health expenditure (WHO 2021). This put it well below many developed as well as developing countries, such as the United States (8.5 per cent), Brazil (3.8 per cent) and China (3.2 per cent). While India's wealthy have access to its world class medical facilities, the policy direction for the masses has been 'cheap' private provision, accessed by the very poor through complex and problematic voucher schemes (Hunter et al. 2020). India has among the highest levels of out-of-pocket expenditure in the world. The weaknesses of India's health provision were already apparent to many, and brutally revealed in the Covid-19 resurgence of April/May 2021.

India's health diplomacy in Africa

India's health partnership with Africa is multi-faceted. Perhaps most importantly, India is one of Africa's largest suppliers of generic drugs. For example, Indian-manufactured antiretroviral (ARV) drugs constitute 80 per cent of Africa's total consumption (Ngangom and Aneja 2016). India also offers its medical expertise to African medical practitioners and doctors. Established in 2009, the digitally enabled Pan-African e-Network (PAN) project connected twelve Indian super-specialty hospitals to forty-nine Patient-End (PE) African hospitals, enabling African medical practitioners to remotely consult with their Indian counterparts for medical advice (Ngangom and Aneja 2016; Duclos this volume). India has also responded to the outbreak of epidemics in Africa. When Ebola broke out in 2014 in West Africa, India contributed USD 10 million to the UN Ebola Trust Fund and USD 500,000 to the WHO to amplify the global response. It also coordinated with its Missions in affected countries to ensure that Indian citizens had easy and timely access to medical treatment (MEA 2015).

With the creation of the India-Africa Forum Summit (IAFS) in 2008, the India–Africa partnership was formally institutionalised. At the 2015 session of IAFS, Prime Minister Modi announced a USD 10 million India-Africa Health Fund – although specific details of where and how this fund has been utilised to date remain unclear.

And finally, India has supported health initiatives of direct benefit to African countries in and through various multilateral institutions and mechanisms. The India-Brazil-South Africa (IBSA) fund, for example, has helped to strengthen Burundi's infrastructural capacity to tackle HIV/AIDS (IBSA n.d). Under the Asia-Africa Growth Corridor (AAGC) framework, India plans to partner with Japan to undertake various developmental initiatives in Africa, including in the field of public health (RIS 2017). We note, however, that as with all development partnerships, below the headline statements and initiatives lie a more complex and sometimes controversial set of outcomes, some of which are raised in this volume (see also Modi 2011; Duclos 2016; Duclos, this volume).

India's COVID diplomacy: A framework

In many ways, India's diplomatic response to Covid-19 reproduces existing patterns in its global health diplomacy. However, the peculiarity of this virus, the magnitude of its geographical reach and the multidimensional nature of its impacts and implications (not only social, economic and humanitarian, but also short, medium and long term), have prompted a departure from previous diplomatic strategies.

In this section, we present the scope and range of India's Covid diplomatic actions to date. We develop an analytical framework that organises India's Covid diplomacy into three main clusters of activity: the transmission of ideas (normative contributions); the flow of resources and services (material contributions); and the sharing of expertise (knowledge contributions). As this book was being finalised, in May 2021, India was experiencing a massive Covid-19 resurgence, and we were just able to include preliminary views on the implications for its Covid diplomacy with Africa.

Normative contributions

Normative contributions include the transmission of ideas, values and norms aimed at amplifying India's soft power. Covid-19 has provided India with a strategic opportunity to socialise into the international community norms and values which it has long championed in its health diplomacy, as well as its diplomacy, more broadly (see Duclos 2020).

Cooperation and reformed multilateralism

From the very outset, India's response to the pandemic has been to emphasise cooperation and multilateralism as key guiding principles. In response to former President Trump's decision to cut the budget of the World Health Organisation (WHO), India reinforced its own resolve to stay focused on the global pandemic response (Laskar 2020). India has, to date, refrained from publicly holding China directly responsible for the spread of the virus,[4] unlike the former United States presidency which, in addition to blaming China, invoked racially encoded discourses to do so (see Trump 2020). In fact, in the initial days of the pandemic, India's official response was to express solidarity with China (Jaishankar 2020). While India continues to champion cooperation and multilateralism as principal modes of engagement on issues of global health governance, it has also used Covid-19 as an opportunity to push for its reform. At the G20 Virtual Summit on 26 March 2020, Prime Minister Modi advocated for the reform of the WHO, recommending that it invest more in early warning capacities (MEA 2020b). India has also declared multilateral reform to be a key priority for its own candidacy at the United Nations Security Council.

Health as a global public good

India used COVID-19 as an opportunity to advocate for universal and affordable access to medicines and vaccines. To that end, it co-sponsored two resolutions at the UN General Assembly (PTI 2020b), on 2 April 2020 and subsequently on 20 April 2020, calling for fair, transparent and equitable access to essential medical supplies and potential vaccines for Covid-19 (see UN General Assembly 2020a; UN General Assembly 2020b). Similarly, at the General Council Meeting of the WTO held in early 2020, India appealed for flexibility in global Intellectual Property Rights (IPR) agreements to ensure affordable access to essential medicines and vaccines (Mohanty 2020).

---

[4]   Although this is a widely held and circulated view amongst the Indian public (see Serhan 2020).

It also co-sponsored a resolution at the World Health Assembly calling for a relaxation in intellectual property issues (WHO 2020). India's aspiration to reinforce its identity as a global supplier of affordable pharmaceutical drugs has manifested in and through gestures such as its export of hydroxychloroquine (HCQ) (MEA 2020f),[5] its decision to act as the global mass manufacturer for a future Covid-19 vaccine and its repeated self-identification as the 'pharmacy of the world'.

Material contributions

Resources

Material contributions include the flow of resources and services to governments, multi-stakeholder initiatives, multilateral bodies and local communities. Specific activities include providing funding support to partner country governments, supplying qualified medical professionals and healthcare workers to overburdened healthcare systems overseas, and facilitating the repatriation and evacuation of Indian citizens (and citizens of other countries) from affected countries.

Medicines and food. Both Indian state and non-state actors have supplied medicines and medical equipment to governments and communities in partner countries. At the time of writing, India had supplied HCQ to a total of 133 countries.[6] India also delivered medicines to partners through various naval missions. The Indian Naval Ship (INS) Kesari delivered essential medicines to the African littoral island states of Mauritius, Madagascar, Comoros and Seychelles, under the maritime initiative Mission SAGAR (Security and Growth for All in the Region). In the case of Mauritius, the consignment was India's second, containing both essential and ayurvedic medicines (MEA 2020c). Mission SAGAR also delivered 580 tonnes of food to Maldives.

Medical personnel. Indian healthcare professionals, including doctors, nurses and medical experts, were at the frontlines of the pandemic response all over the world. India dispatched military doctors to the Maldives and Kuwait to help these countries manage the pandemic; fifteen doctors and

[5]   On 25 March 2020, India's Directorate General of Foreign Trade placed hydroxychloroquine (HCQ) on a restricted items' list. On 4 April 2020, it issued a blanket ban on the export of HCQ. It revoked the ban on 6 April 2020.

[6]   As of April 2020, India had supplied the HCQ drug to fifty-five countries: twenty-one of these countries received HCQ in the form of a grant; the remaining thirty-four countries received it on a commercial basis. As of June 2020, India had supplied medicines to 133 countries (446 million HCQ tablets and 1.54 billion Paracetamol tablets), also via grants and commercial sales (MEA 2020e).

paramedics to Kuwait; and an Indian Army team of six military doctors and eight paramedical personnel to set up quarantine and testing facilities in the Maldives. It also dispatched a delegation of eighty-eight nurses, affiliated with the Aster DM Healthcare group of private hospitals in Kerala, Karnataka and Maharashtra, to offer additional human resource capacity to the United Arab Emirates' already overstretched healthcare system (PTI 2020c).

Financial assistance. Indian investments in multi-stakeholder and multilateral initiatives unlocked new resources and funding streams to support efforts to address both the immediate and longer-term consequences of the pandemic. At the 2020 Global Vaccine Summit, India pledged USD 15 million to Gavi (MEA 2020f). India also initiated efforts to set up a South Asian Association for Regional Cooperation (SAARC) Emergency Fund, and contributed USD 10 million – the largest of all member states (MEA 2020a). The New Development Bank (NDB) of the BRICS, of which India is a founding member, established an Emergency Assistance Facility to help its members meet both their emergency and longer-term economic recovery needs (NDB 2020). Under this programme, India issued a USD 1 billion Covid-19 Emergency Loan to South Africa. The NDB also issued a USD 1.5 billion three-year Covid-19 Response Bond in the international capital markets.[7] And finally, India recently announced a USD 2 million contribution to 'ISA-CARE' to support the deployment of solar power in health centres in forty-six Small Island Developing States (SIDS) and Least Developed Countries (LDC) member states (Jayakumar 2020).

Services

Vaccine manufacture. AstraZeneca, the manufacturing partner for the vaccine developed by the University of Oxford, finalised a licensing agreement with the Serum Institute of India (SII) to supply one billion doses of the vaccine to low-and-middle-income countries (AstraZeneca 2020).

Repatriations and evacuations. Perhaps one of the most significant components of India's Covid diplomacy was its role in facilitating the safe return of stranded Indian citizens, and at times, citizens of other nationalities as well, from overseas. The repatriation mission, named the Vande Bharat Mission, took place across multiple phases, with each phase extending the mission to a different geographical region.[8] While India initiated the mission in early

---

[7]   Its proceeds will be used to finance emergency assistance loans to the Bank's member countries and sustainable development activities more broadly.

[8]   Vande Bharat has facilitated the return of 687,000 Indians from overseas since its launch in early May 2020 (PTI 2020e).

May 2020, calls for the repatriation of Indian citizens from overseas emerged much earlier, most notably from Kerala (see Vijayan 2020), a state that is home to approximately 1.89 million emigrants currently residing in the Gulf (Rajan and Zachariah 2019). Under the Vande Bharat Mission, India facilitated the repatriation of Indian citizens via flights operated by the national carrier, Air India, and through naval missions led by the Indian Navy under Operation Samudra Setu. A number of repatriation flights brought back Indians from various African nations, namely Mauritius, Nigeria, Egypt, Kenya, South Africa and Seychelles. While India did not make data available on the number of Indian repatriates returning from West Africa during the Ebola outbreak in 2014 (MEA 2015), it was relatively more transparent during Covid-19. The Vande Bharat webpage of the Ministry of External Affairs, for instance, contains details of all repatriation flights from Africa.

Debt relief. India provided financial relief to help partners cope with fiscal pressures triggered by Covid-19. In one case, for example, it provided debt relief to the Government of Mozambique by suspending repayment on concessional loans worth USD 700 million.

Knowledge contributions

Knowledge contributions include the dissemination of technical expertise and knowledge through online and on-site training, public information campaigns and collaborative research initiatives.

Sharing expertise

Various institutions were involved in the dissemination of Indian knowledge and expertise to partners. The Ministry of External Affairs offered e-ITEC courses on pandemic prevention and management to health care workers from SAARC countries, and several African countries, including Nigeria, Kenya, Mauritius and Namibia (Pant and Mishra 2020), for which it has been praised (ITEC 2020). It also offered an e-ITEC course on good governance for international civil servants from eighteen countries, including several African ones (Morocco, Nigeria, Somalia and Zambia) (see Department of Administrative Reforms and Public Grievances (DARPG), GoI 2020; MEA 2020g). Additionally, in Mauritius and Comoros, two fourteen-member Indian Navy medical teams toured local hospitals, provided training to medical personnel and shared Covid-19 management techniques, as part of Mission SAGAR.

Undertaking joint research

India activated existing bilateral research mechanisms to support and advance new collaborative research on Covid-19. For example, the Indo-US Science and Technology Forum (IUSSTF) issued a call for proposals to advance Covid-19 related research (PTI 2020a). These collaborations included plans to advance research on preventive technologies, data analytics, AI applications and Indian plant-based systems of medicines (PTI 2020d). This is a significant departure from India's response to the Ebola outbreak in 2014, when India publicly confirmed it would not be getting involved in the development of a drug or vaccine to treat the Ebola virus (MEA 2017). Finally, in line with a growing official commitment to alternative health approaches, Mauritius is currently looking to partner with India in the field of traditional medicines (Pant and Mishra 2020).

Managing information flows

India was one of thirteen countries leading a United Nations-supported global communications campaign, 'Verified', to prevent the spread of misinformation and fake news in relation to Covid-19 (see Department of Global Communications 2020). It co-authored a cross-regional statement endorsed by over 130 states, urging people across the world to spread fact-based advice and reliable information to counter the 'infodemic' that persisted in parallel to the pandemic. India's decision to join this campaign took place in a context where many members of the Indian public, the mainstream media and members of the ruling party, wrongly accused the Muslim community in India of wilfully spreading the virus (Ellis-Petersen and Rahman 2020). Meanwhile, the Kumbh Mela – a Hindu festival that draws hundreds of thousands of devotees to the Ganges once every twelve years – was allowed to proceed in Uttarakhand in mid-April 2021 despite escalating number of cases across the country, with several senior leaders of the ruling party openly downplaying its public health risks. These are examples of the deepening tensions and, indeed, contradictions between some elements of India's foreign policy claims and identity projection, and the BJP government's authoritarian and majoritarian tendencies.

Observations

Before its urgent suspension in April 2021, India's Covid diplomacy had been both multidimensional and multilayered. From the start of the outbreak until that point, it took place across the three planes: the normative, material and technical; and attempted to address both the immediate, health-related implications of the pandemic, as well as its longer-term, socio-economic consequences. As illustrated above, India's Covid diplomacy included a number of African nations in a variety of ways, from supplying medicines, to facilitating repatriations of Indians based overseas, to training African health care professionals in pandemic management.

While India's initial Covid diplomacy certainly reinforced Africa's ongoing significance to India's global health diplomacy overall, it also unsettled several established patterns in the India–Africa health partnership. For instance, whereas India traditionally mobilised the breadth of its foreign policy apparatus to support various elements of Africa's public health agenda, Covid-19 made visible an underlying interest in mobilising the global public health agenda to advance certain geopolitical and economic objectives. In other words, the first year of India's health diplomacy in Africa took on a distinctly geopolitical dimension. An interest in countering China emerged as a strong foreign policy priority (Baruah 2020; Brewster 2020; Chaudhury 2020; Pandalai 2020). India's Covid assistance to the African littoral island states of the Indian Ocean, under the securitised framework of SAGAR, reflected an attempt to counter China's expanding presence in the Indo-Pacific region. It allowed India to promote its image as a 'first responder' in the Indian Ocean region (Chaudhury 2020; Pandalai 2020).

India's Covid diplomacy also emerged as a vehicle for India to legitimise its identity as a 'natural' partner for Africa. Such exercises in self-fashioning are quite often predicated upon the projection of China as India's inferior 'other'. Indian commentators frequently portrayed China's Covid diplomacy in Africa as imperialistic and unfairly commercially minded by design, in contrast to what they claimed was India's naturally virtuous and people-centred approach.

And finally, Covid-19 allowed India to promote and make visible Indian medicines and treatments, such as yoga and Ayurveda, as natural, immunity-boosting alternatives to Western medicine. While the commodification of Indian indigenous knowledge systems has so far served India's soft power interests quite well (Venkatachalam, this volume), it remains to be seen whether its global advocacy of 'Hindu Science' under the garb of 'traditional' knowledge, will stand up to universal standards of scientific rigour, as India – and in particular, members of the ruling dispensation – increasingly begin to use this knowledge to make untested, and sometimes extraordinary, medical claims at home.[9] Some of its harshest domestic critics have gone so far as to label such practices as faith-based pseudoscience.

---

[9]   The Ministry of AYUSH earlier in 2021 issued a health advisory recommending the homeopathic medicine Arsenicum Album 30 as a prophylactic to prevent contracting the virus, even though reports claimed that there were no data to corroborate this. In more extreme cases, some BJP activists have suggested that

At the start of the first wave of the pandemic in March 2020 India held the world's longest – and strictest – lockdown, which disproportionately impacted India's migrant labour. The extremity of these circumstances notwithstanding, the number of deaths resulting from Covid-19 remained relatively low in 2020, by most estimates. In January 2021, only a few months before the second and more deadly wave of the pandemic was about to strike, India launched an ambitious new diplomatic initiative – Vaccine Maitri – in continuation of earlier efforts to support the global response to the pandemic. Under Vaccine Maitri, India supplied vaccines – both the AstraZeneca produced Covishield and the indigenously made Covaxin – on a commercial and grant basis at the request of over eighty countries (Prabhu 2021). In 2020, alongside South Africa, India tabled a WTO proposal to temporarily suspend intellectual property rights to enable access to COVID-19 vaccines and other new technologies by poor countries.[10] Throughout the first year of the novel coronavirus outbreak, India thus proactively engaged in health (and then eventually vaccine) diplomacy, which although arguably not on the scale of China's capacities, was still testament to its outward looking foreign policy and vaccine generosity – certainly vis-à-vis Western states.

India's own supposedly successful track record in containing the pandemic domestically added further moral weight and credibility to these diplomatic overtures and was reinforced in government discourse: 'Today, India is among countries that have succeeded in saving the maximum lives. The country, which comprises of 18 per cent of the world's population, has saved the world from disaster by bringing the situation under control', Modi famously pronounced at the virtual meeting of the World Economic Forum in January 2021 (PMINDIA 2021).

By April 2021, the domestic situation had dramatically turned as a rapid, deadly and deepening wave of Covid infections laid bare the inadequacies of India's domestic healthcare provision. One particularly damning report revealed that of the 162 oxygen plants for which tenders had been contracted in 2020, only thirty-three had been set up as of April 2021 (Lalwani and Saikia 2021). On 30 April, India became the first country in the world to

---

drinking cow urine can be used to cure Covid-19. Still more recently, in May 2021, it was reported that the Department of Science and Technology had funded a clinical trial at the All India Institute of Medical Sciences (AIIMS) Rishikesh to assess whether the chanting of the Gayatri Mantra (a sacred Hindu chant) and performing yoga could help in the recovery and cure of Covid-19.

[10] In May 2021, the United States under President Biden, agreed to support the proposal in what has been described as an extraordinary move (see BBC 2021).

report over 400,000 new cases in single day. The death count is almost certainly much higher than what is being officially recorded – in some cases up to twenty times more (Krishnan 2021).

Amid these dire circumstances and mounting pressure to vaccinate its own population, India suspended the Vaccine Maitri programme, causing concerned and vaccine-aid dependent partners in the neighbourhood – such as Bangladesh and Nepal – to turn instead to India's regional competitor: China. Some observers have argued that all is not lost, and Vaccine Maitri's geopolitical success is revealed in goodwill now converted into meaningful acts of mutual reciprocity (see Gupta 2021). US President Biden's reversal of the US embargo on the export of vaccine raw materials, for instance, was perceived in some part to be a response to India's assistance to the United States during the early months of the pandemic in 2020 (by way of hydroxychloroquine exports). Nonetheless, with huge numbers of the Indian population to vaccinate as of May 2021, other commentators highlighted India's short-sightedness in failing to roll out a comprehensive domestic vaccination plan *before* embarking on an ambitious international distribution strategy (Prabhu 2021). Government representatives, meanwhile, maintained that Vaccine Maitri was executed while keeping in mind in India's domestic need.

At the same time that India was forced to suspend Vaccine Maitri, offers of international aid started to pour in from other countries to help the domestic response in India: the United States, the United Kingdom, Singapore and Germany, to name just a few. At the time of writing, supplies received by the Indian Red Cross Society on behalf of the Indian government were in the process of being redistributed to state governments.

Covid-19 has shown the strength, breadth and depth of India's long-standing health diplomacy with many African partners, amongst others. It has also revealed the tensions inherent in such development partnerships when they are, or are perceived to be, at the cost of India's poor and needy. India's health competition with China may work well for African partners, but the wider consequences are unlikely to be positive regionally or globally. It is too early to tell whether India's external reputation will be damaged by the evident inadequacies of its domestic health provision, or the arrogance and monumental errors made by the Modi government in handling the pandemic.

Bibliography

Adams, V., Novotny, T.E. and Leslie, H. 2008. 'Global health diplomacy', *Medical Anthropology*, 27/4, 315–23.
AstraZeneca. 2020. 'Agreements with CEPI and Gavi and the Serum Institute of India will bring vaccine to low-and-middle income countries and beyond', 4 June

2020, https://www.astrazeneca.com/media-centre/articles/2020/astrazeneca-takes-next-steps-towards-broad-and-equitable-access-to-oxford-universitys-potential-covid-19-vaccine.html, accessed 10 July 2020.

Baruah, D. 2020. 'India in the Indo-Pacific: New Delhi's theatre of opportunity', *Carnegie Endowment for International Peace*, 30 June 2020, https://carnegieendowment.org/2020/06/30/india-in-indo-pacific-new-delhi-s-theater-of-opportunity-pub-82205, accessed 11 July 2020.

BBC. 2021. 'US backs waiver on vaccine patents to boost supply', 6 May 2021, https://www.bbc.com/news/world-us-canada-57004302, accessed 9 May 2021.

Brewster, D. 2020. 'Covid contest in Indian Ocean region: India, China jostle for top spot', *Interpreter*, 15 May 2020, https://www.lowyinstitute.org/the-interpreter/covid-contest-indian-ocean-region-india-china-jostle-top-spot, accessed 11 July 2020.

BRICS. 2019. 'Declaration of the IX BRICS Health Ministers Meeting', *University of Toronto*, 25 October 2019, http://www.brics.utoronto.ca/docs/191025-health.html, accessed 17 February 2020.

Chaturvedi, S. 2016. 'Towards health diplomacy: Emerging trends in India's South-South health cooperation', in S. Chaturvedi and A. Mulakala (eds.) *India's Approach to Development Cooperation* (New York: Routledge), 46–60.

Chaudhury, D.R. 2020. 'India steps up engagement in Indo-Pacific region amid China's Health Silk Road initiative', *Economic Times*, 10 May 2020, https://economictimes.indiatimes.com/news/defence/india-steps-up-engagement-in-indo-pacific-region-amid-chinas-health-silk-road-initiative/articleshow/75664015.cms, accessed 13 June 2020.

DARPG, GoI. 2020. *Secretary DARPG Dr K Shivaji addressed the valedictory session of the 2-day @ITECnetwork-NCGG workshop on 'Good Governance Practices in a Pandemic' for International Civil Servants from 18 countries on 19.06.2020*, Twitter, 19 June 2020, https://twitter.com/DARPG_GoI/status/1273982272098545664, accessed 25 May 2020.

Department of Global Communications. 2020. ''Verified' initiative aims to flood digital space with facts amid COVID-19 crisis', *United Nations*, 28 May 2020, https://www.un.org/en/coronavirus/%E2%80%98verified%E2%80%99-initiative-aims-flood-digital-space-facts-amid-covid-19-crisis, accessed 13 June 2020.

Duclos, V. 2016. The map and the territory: an ethnographic study of the low utilisation of a global eHealth network. *Journal of Information Technology*, 31/4, 334–46.

——. 2020. 'The empire of speculation: Medicine, markets, and nation in India's Pan-African e-Network', 24 August 2020, *BioSocieties*, https://link.springer.com/article/10.1057%2Fs41292-020-00198-1, accessed 14 October 2020.

Ellis-Petersen, H. and Rahman, S.A. 2020. 'Coronavirus conspiracy theories targeting Muslims spread in India', *Guardian*, 13 April 2020, https://www.theguardian.com/world/2020/apr/13/coronavirus-conspiracy-theories-targeting-muslims-spread-in-india, accessed 7 May 2020.

Embassy of the Federal Republic of Ethiopia. n.d. 'Ethiopia India relationship', n.d., http://www.ethiopianembassy.org.in/EthiopiaIndia.htm, accessed 10 March 2020.

Gavi. 2020. 'Donor profile: India', n.d., https://www.gavi.org/investing-gavi/funding/donor-profiles/india, accessed 10 March 2020.

Gupta, S. 2021. 'Vaccine Maitri pays off, US medical supplies on way to India', *Hindustan Times*, 26 April 2021, https://www.hindustantimes.com/india-news/vaccine-maitri-pays-off-us-medical-supplies-on-way-to-india-101619410041293.html, accessed 8 May 2021.

Horner, R. 2020. 'The world needs pharmaceuticals from China and India to beat coronavirus', *The Conversation*, 25 May 2020, https://theconversation.com/the-world-needs-pharmaceuticals-from-china-and-india-to-beat-coronavirus-138388, accessed 22 August 2020.

Hunter, B., Bisht, R., and Murray, S.F. (2020) Neoliberalisation enacted through development aid: the case of health vouchers in India. *Critical Public Health*, published online.

IBSA. n.d. 'IBSA Fund', n.d., http://www.ibsa-trilateral.org/ibsa_fund.html, accessed 20 March 2020.

ITEC. 2020. *Down But Not Out: Lock-downs have not restricted the learning and sharing. 150 Healthcare professionals of @SAARCsec countries participating in the first session of e-ITEC Training programme on #COVID19 Manangement.#SAARCfightsCorona #IndiafightsCorona @aiims_rpr*, Twitter, 17 April 2020, https://twitter.com/ITECnetwork/status/1251116679788064769, accessed 25 May 2020.

Jaishankar, S. 2020. *Consignment (15 tonnes) of Indian medical relief for #COVID19 lands in Wuhan. Strong expression of our solidarity with the Chinese people at this difficult time. Thank you @IAF_MCC and @EOIBeijing for your efforts*, Twitter, 26 February 2020, https://twitter.com/drsjaishankar/status/1232662070837026817?lang=en, accessed 25 May 2020.

Jayakumar, P.B. 2020. 'ISA wants to solarise all un-electrified Primary Health Centres in member countries', *Business Today*, 12 June 2020, https://www.businesstoday.in/opinion/interviews/isa-wants-to-solarise-all-un-electrified-primary-health-centers-in-member-countries/story/406794.html, accessed 16 August 2020.

Katz, R., Kornblet, S., Arnold, G., Lief, E. and Fischer, J.E. 2011. 'Defining health diplomacy: Changing demands in the era of globalisation', *Milbank Quarterly*, 89/3, 503–23.

Kickbusch, I. 2013. 'Twenty-first century health diplomacy: A new relationship between foreign policy and health', in T. E. Novotny, I. Kickbusch and M. Told (eds.) *Twenty-first Century Global Health Diplomacy* (New Jersey: World Scientific), 1–40.

Kickbusch, I. and Behrendt, T. 2017. 'Global health diplomacy', *Oxford Bibliographies*, 27 March 2014, https://www.oxfordbibliographies.com/view/document/obo-9780199756797/obo-9780199756797-0101.xml, accessed 16 August 2020.

Kickbusch, I., Silberschmidt, G. and Buss, P. 2007. 'Global health diplomacy: The need for new perspectives, strategic approaches and skills in global health', *Bulletin of the World Health Organisation*, March 2007, 85/3, 230–32.

Krishnan, V. 2021. 'India's Covid-19 taskforce did not meet in February, March despite surge', *The Caravan*, 22 April 2021, https://caravanmagazine.in/health/india-covid-19-taskforce-did-not-meet-february-march-despite-surge-say-members, accessed 8 May 2021.

Lalwani, V. and Saikia A. 2021. 'India is running out of oxygen, Covid-19 patients are dying – because the government wasted time', *The Scroll*, 18 April 2021, https://scroll.in/article/992537/india-is-running-out-of-oxygen-covid-19-patients-are-dying-because-the-government-wasted-time, accessed 8 May 2021.

Laskar, R. 2020. 'As Trump threatens to cut WHO funding, India says Covid-19 should remain focus', *Hindustan Times*, 15 April 2020, https://www.hindustan-times.com/india-news/as-trump-threatens-to-cut-funding-for-who-india-says-focus-should-remain-on-covid-19-pandemic/story-xJXdfupz7I3TCN4tg8QtOL.html, accessed 24 July 2020.

MEA. 2005. 'India offers assistance for victims of hurricane Katrina', *GoI*, 3 September 2005, https://www.mea.gov.in/press-releases.htm?dtl/5387/In-, accessed 4 March 2020.

——. 2013. 'India-Haiti relations', *GoI*, February 2013, http://mea.gov.in/Portal/ForeignRelation/Haiti.pdf, accessed 7 March 2020.

——. 2015. 'Lok Sabha starred question No. 342. Answered on 12.08.2015', *GoI*, n.d., http://164.100.47.194/Loksabha/Questions/qsearch15.aspx?lsno=16, accessed 4 March 2020.

——. 2017. 'Lok Sabha starred question No. 342. Answered on 10.03.2017', *GoI*, n.d., http://164.100.47.194/Loksabha/Questions/qsearch15.aspx?lsno=16, accessed 4 March 2020.

——. 2020a. 'Video conference of leaders of SAARC countries', *GoI*, 16 March 2020, https://www.mea.gov.in/press-releases.htm?dtl/32540/Video_Conference_of_Leaders_of_SAARC_Countries, accessed 14 August 2020.

——. 2020b. 'Press release on the extraordinary Virtual G20 Leaders' Summit', *GoI*, 26 March 2020, https://www.mea.gov.in/press-releases.htm?dtl/32600/Press_Release_on_the_Extraordinary_Virtual_G20_Leaders_Summit, accessed 18 August 2020.

——. 2020c. 'Mission Sagar: India's helping hand across the Indian Ocean', *GoI*, n.d., 10 May 2020, https://mea.gov.in/press-releases.htm?dtl/32678/Mission_Sagar_Indias_helping_hand_across_the_Indian_Ocean, accessed 20 August 2020.

——. 2020d. 'Foreign Secretary's virtual address to MIT World Peace University, Pune on the importance of multilateralism in the time of a global pandemic – An Indian perspective' *GoI*, 11 May 2020, https://mea.gov.in/Speeches-Statements.htm?dtl/32683/Foreign_Secretarys_virtual_address_to_MIT_World_Peace_University_Pune_on_the_Importance_of_Multilateralism_in_the_Time_of_a_Global_Pandemic__an_Indian, accessed 17 August 2020.

——. 2020e. 'Foreign Secretary's virtual address to the National Defence College on "India's foreign policy options in the emerging world order"', *GoI*, 15 May 2020, https://www.mea.gov.in/Speeches-Statements.htm?dtl/32694/Foreign_Secretarys_virtual_address_to_the_National_Defence_College_on_Indias_Foreign_Policy_Options_in_the_Emerging_World_Order_May_15_2020, accessed 29 August 2020.

——. 2020f. 'Prime Minister addresses the virtual Global Vaccine Summit 2020', *GoI*, 4 June 2020, https://mea.gov.in/press-releases.htm?dtl/32733/Prime_Minister_Addresses_the_virtual_Global_Vaccine_Summit_2020, accessed 11 August 2020.

————. 2020g. 'eITEC programme on "COVID-19 – good governance practices in a pandemic" at National Centre for Good Governance (NCGG)', *GoI*, 7 August 2020, https://mea.gov.in/press-releases.htm?dtl/32879/eitec+programme+on+-covid19++good+governance+practices+in+a+pandemic+at+national+centre+for+-good+governance+ncgg, accessed 14 August 2020.

Modi, R. 2011. 'Offshore healthcare management: Medical tourism between Kenya, Tanzania and India', in E. Mawdsley and G. McCann (eds.) *India-Africa: Changing Geographies of Power* (Nairobi: Pambazuka Press),125–39.

Mohanty, S. 2020. 'India steps up health diplomacy to build new narratives in multilateralism', *South Asia Monitor*, 24 June 2020, https://southasiamonitor.org/spotlight/india-steps-health-diplomacy-build-new-narratives-multilateralism, accessed 25 July 2020.

NDB. 2020. 'New Development Bank Board of Governors statement on response to COVID-19 outbreak', 22 April 2020, https://www.ndb.int/new-development-bank-board-of-governors-statement-on-response-to-covid-19-outbreak/, accessed 13 June 2020.

Ngangom, T. and Aneja, U. 2016. 'Health is wealth: Indian private sector investments in African healthcare', *ORF Online*, 7 June 2016, https://www.orfonline.org/research/health-is-wealth-indian-private-sector-investments-in-african-health-care/#_edn8, accessed 1 June 2020.

Pandalai, S. 2020. 'Seizing the chance to chart "The India way"', *The Interpreter*, 12 June 2020, https://www.lowyinstitute.org/the-interpreter/seizing-chance-chart-india-way, accessed 16 August 2020.

Pant, H. and Mishra, A. 2020. 'India, China and fortifying the Africa outreach', *ORF Online*, 2 June 2020, https://www.orfonline.org/research/india-china-and-fortifying-the-africa-outreach-67203/, accessed 5 August 2020.

PIB. 2018. 'Foreign tourist arrivals in India for the medical purpose have shown a substantial increase from 2014 to 2016: Tourism Minister', *GoI*, 2 April 2018, https://pib.gov.in/Pressreleaseshare.aspx?PRID=1527299, accessed 17 August 2020.

PMINDIA, 2021. 'PM's address at the World Economic Forum's Davos Dialogue', 28 January 2021, https://www.pmindia.gov.in/en/news_updates/pms-address-at-the-world-economic-forums-davos-dialogue/, accessed 1 March 2021

Prabhu, S. 2021. 'Vaccine Maitri: Friendship gone wrong?', *ORF Online*, 4 May 2021, https://www.orfonline.org/expert-speak/vaccine-maitri-friendship-gone-wrong/, accessed 8 May 2021.

PTI. 2020a. 'Indo-US science and tech forum invites joint research proposals on COVID-19', *Indian Express*, 13 April 2020, https://www.newindianexpress.com/nation/2020/apr/13/indo-us-science-and-tech-forum-invites-joint-research-proposals-on-covid-19-2129481.html, accessed 4 July 2020.

————. 2020b. 'India co-sponsors resolution calling for equitable access to coronavirus vaccines', *Economic Times*, 24 April 2020, https://economictimes.indiatimes.com/industry/healthcare/biotech/healthcare/india-co-sponsors-resolution-calling-for-equitable-access-to-covid-19-vaccines/articleshow/75288563.cms?from=mdr, accessed 4 July 2020.

——. 2020c. 'First batch of eighty-eight nurses from India arrive in UAE', *Economic Times*, 10 May 2020, https://economictimes.indiatimes.com/news/politics-and-nation/first-batch-of-88-nurses-from-india-arrive-in-uae/articleshow/75655710.cms, accessed 4 July 2020.

——. 2020d. 'Ayurvedic practitioners in India, US planning joint COVID-19 trials: envoy', *NDTV*, 9 July 2020, https://www.ndtv.com/india-news/ayurvedic-practitioners-in-india-us-planning-joint-covid-19-trials-envoy-indian-ambassador-to-the-us-taranjit-singh-sandhu-2259598, accessed 7 August 2020.

——. 2020e. 'Over 6.87 lakh Indians have returned from abroad under Vande Bharat mission: MEA', *Economic Times*, 16 July 2020, https://economictimes.indiatimes.com/news/politics-and-nation/over-6-87-lakh-indians-have-returned-from-abroad-under-vande-bharat-mission-mea/articleshow/77002829.cms, accessed 13 August 2020.

Rajan, S.I. and Zachariah, K.C. 2019. *Emigration and Remittances: New evidence from the Kerala Migration Survey, 2018* (Kerala: Centre for Development Studies).

Reid, M., Goosby, E. and Kevany, S. 2019. 'Leveraging health diplomacy to end the tuberculosis epidemic', *Lancet*, 7/5, E561–E562.

RIS. 2017. 'Asia Africa Growth Corridor. Partnership for sustainable and innovative development: A vision document', n.d., http://ris.org.in/aagc/sites/default/files/Basic%20page%20files/1_Asia%20Africa%20Growth%20Coordior25052017.pdf, accessed 2 December 2019.

Sen, A. 2018. 'Health care: India resists pressure on forgoing "flexibilities" under TRIPS, *Hindu Business Line*, 11 January 2018, https://www.thehindubusinessline.com/economy/policy/health-care-india-resists-pressure-on-forgoing-flexibilities-under-trips/article9750696.ece, accessed 25 March 2020.

Serhan, Y. 2020. 'Indians aren't buying China's narrative', *The Atlantic*, 21 April 2020, https://www.theatlantic.com/international/archive/2020/04/india-china-pandemic-coronavirus-distrust/610273/, accessed 29 June 2020.

Trump, D. 2020. *The United States will be powerfully supporting those industries, like airlines and others, that are particularly affected by the Chinese Virus. We will be stronger than ever before!*, Twitter, 16 March 2020, https://twitter.com/realDonaldTrump/status/1239685852093169664, accessed 9 June 2020.

United Nations General Assembly. 2020a. 'Global solidarity to fight the coronavirus disease 2019 (COVID-19)', *UN*, 3 April 2020, https://undocs.org/en/A/RES/74/270, accessed 15 June 2020.

——. 2020b. 'International cooperation to ensure global access to medicines, vaccines and medical equipment to face COVID-19', *UN*, 21 April 2020, https://undocs.org/en/A/RES/74/274, accessed 15 June 2020.

Vijayan, P. 2020. *Wrote to Hon'ble @PMOIndia Shri. @narendramodi to bring his attention to the plight of Keralites in the Gulf region. We have assured that testing and quarantine needs of the Keralites who are returning will be undertaken by the State Government.*, Twitter, 13 April 2020, https://twitter.com/vijayanpinarayi/status/1249729223540924416?s=20, accessed 25 May 2020.

WHO. 2020. 'Seventy-third World Health Assembly, agenda item 3: COVID-19 response', 18 May 2020, https://apps.who.int/gb/ebwha/pdf_files/WHA73/A73_CONF1Rev1-en.pdf, accessed 15 June 2020.

——. 2021. 'Domestic general government health expenditure (GGHE-D) as a percentage of gross domestic product (GDP)', n.d., https://www.who.int/gho/health_financing/public_exp_health/en/, accessed 8 May 2021.

WTO. n.d. 'Compulsory licensing of pharmaceuticals and TRIPS', n.d., https://www.wto.org/english/tratop_e/trips_e/public_health_faq_e.htm, accessed 5 August 2020.

PART 4

Skilling, Knowledge Transfer and Indo-African Interactions

8

Precarious Partnerships: Tanzanian Entrepreneurs of Asian and African Descent

JACQUELINE HALIMA MGUMIA AND
CHAMBI CHACHAGE

Introduction

In his chairpersonship address to the then Dar es Salaam Merchant Chamber in 1964, M.M. Diwani, a Tanzanian businessman of Asian origin, presented radical proposals for redressing the historical imbalance between businesspeople of Asian and African descent. Among other things, he announced initiatives for imparting skills to, and partnering with, Africans. *Mwafrika* i.e. African, a Kiswahili newspaper, received this groundbreaking news with much excitement. '*Waasia wenye Maduka wataka Umoja na Waafrika*' ('Asian shop owners want Unity with Africans') it stressed in its headline (Ripota Wetu 1964: 1).

On the following day, its editorial, entitled '*Upatna wa Waasia na Waafrika*' (Partnership between Asians and Africans), also extolled such a long overdue need for the transfer of skills (Mwafrika 1964: 2). The editors saw it, albeit cautiously, as a new dawn for Tanzanians who considered themselves indigenous Africans and those who, through historic migration from South Asia to Tanzania, became citizens of the newly established African nation state. For them, it potentially ushered in a new era in which the two groups would identify with each other. Also known as the Indian subcontinent, this point of their origin marked the identity of the latter group to the extent that the Kiswahili terms *mhindi* for Indian came to be used interchangeably and even stereotypically with *muasia* for Asian (Delf 1963; Ghai and Ghai 1965; Mangat 1969; Tandon and Raphael 1984; Nagar 1995; Seidenberg 1996; Himbara 1997; Heilman 1998; Ranja 2003; Oonk 2013; Bishara 2017). This has been the case although some of them are not necessarily Indians in terms of originating from India.[1]

---

[1] Throughout this chapter the terms Asian and Indian are used interchangeably, especially when directly quoting Tanzania's entrepreneurs of both African and

More than half a century later, it appears that the transfer and partnership either did not occur or has not been sustainable over generations. 'I have written and spoken widely about this phenomenon,' a top African entrepreneur, Ali A. Mufuruki, stated, 'I don't know of any African Tanzanian who has grown as an entrepreneur from working closely with Indians'.[2] He was responding to our question on whether he was aware of knowledge, technology or skills transfer from Tanzanians of Asian origin to those of African origin that facilitated business start-ups.[3] 'The opposite', he concluded, 'seems to be true in the majority of cases.'

Similarly, a former chair of the parliamentary committee responsible for accounts of public companies, Zitto Kabwe, affirmed that there is no such thing. 'I have known some Indian businessmen for some years now; some of them are even my friends,' he elaborated, 'but I have not come across an African Tanzanian who has started businesses out of their business interactions.'[4] He then concluded: 'Personally, I can attest to introducing some African Tanzanians from my constituency to Indian Tanzanians to support their business ideas, but nothing materialised.' However, among contemporary business figures, some mutual interactions have been documented (Chachage 2018).

Therefore, our narrative is a fusion of historical and contemporary accounts on the relatively dominant role of Asians in business dealings in East Africa, which made it possible for them to be identified as a commercial class in Tanzania in the 1970s (Shivji 1975). The achievement of such

---

Asian/Indian origin who invoke them (cf. Mufuruki 2013: 1): 'You may wish to know if you do not know already that not many indigenous Tanzanians like myself can tell the difference between the numerous communities to which our fellow citizens of Asian origin belong. We see all Ismailis, Khoja Shia Ithnasheri, Hindus, Bohoras, Goans, Bangladeshis, Pakistanis, Baluchis, etc, as one community known as *Wahindi*'. Bryceson (1988: 75) also notes that in 1921, 'Indians in Tanganyika numbered 9,411' however she points out that this term and figure referred to 'people living in East Africa with Indian or Pakistani ancestry'.

[2] Ali A. Mufuruki to Jacqueline Mgumia, personal communication, 2 June 2019, Dar es Salaam.

[3] It is also important to note their religious diversity which, in some cases, coincides with their points of origins in India/Asia; for instance Brennan (2012: 46) notes: 'In 1931, the earliest comprehensive religious census of South Asians on the mainland (then Tanganyika), there were 14,390 Muslims (57.2 per cent); 7,762 Hindus (30.9 per cent); 1,722 Goans (6.8 per cent); 768 Sikhs (3.1 per cent); 215 Jains (0.9 per cent); 168 non-Goan Christians (0.7 per cent); 52 Parsi (0.2 per cent), and 6 Buddhists.'

[4] Zitto Kabwe to Jacqueline Mgumia, personal communication, 4 June 2019, Dar es Salaam.

an identity has partly been associated with historical exploitation through unequal trade relations and racial colonial structures. Conventional critiques posit that there is nothing mythical about Asian entrepreneurs; rather the reproduction of their business identity is through socialisation, apprenticeship and networking. Such processes have been criticised for being secretive and exclusive to the Asian community in Tanzania, leaving out the majority of Tanzanians who are of African origin. It is this narrative that we seek to unpack through Africans who have tapped Asians' knowledge directly and/or indirectly. Since it is a two-way process, we also look at some Asians who have also gained from African expertise. Since most of them are Tanzanian citizens, the African–Asian dichotomy is more of a racial than a national category even when both are conflated.

In this chapter we therefore provide an account of cases of knowledge transfer and partnership between entrepreneurs of Asian and African origins in Tanzania. In doing so, we unpack the conventional stereotype of entrepreneurs of Asian descent as sharing business knowledge and forging entrepreneurial partnership exclusively within their racial community at the expense of businesspeople of African origins. We contend that there have been working relationships between them that have led to the transfer of business knowledge, skills, capital, profit and labour, albeit developing around simmering and/or cyclic racial tensions in the Tanzanian business ecosystem

The chapter has two main sections. In the first, we revisit the historical legacy that led to the relative dominance of people of Asian descent in both wholesale and retail business in East Africa in general and Tanzania in particular. The second section focuses on Tanzania's large-scale entrepreneurs, such as Reginald Mengi and Christopher Gachuma, who, in one way or another, also benefited from business encounters with people of Asian descent and vice versa; it also focuses on Tanzania's intellectuals of capital, that is, advocates of promoting private capital and the private sector, such as Mufuruki and Juma V. Mwapachu, who have added value, in terms of knowledge and national capitalist network building, to businesspeople of Asian origin who make use of such networks.

Racial discourse in business

In October 2019, one of us witnessed a spontaneous conversation between a salesperson and a customer in a recently opened café at the state-of-the-art airport. The customer was unhappy with the service, given that the salesperson was serving sugar to customers on a saucer instead of in a packet. Defensively, the salesperson informed him that they did not normally do that; the situation was temporary as they had run out of sugar packets, but more were on their way. Unconvinced, he asked, rhetorically, in Kiswahili: '*Hii ni biashara ya mhindi au ya maskini?*' When translated directly, it reads: 'Is this a business of an Indian or of a poor person?' It is important to reiterate that in Tanzania the terms Asian (*Muasia*) and Indian (*Mhindi*) are generally used interchangeably to refer to people who originated – or look like those – from the South Asian countries of India and Pakistan (Anand and Kaul 2011; Brennan 2012). After reiterating his question, the customer said he knew what he was talking about as he also ran a business. Judging from his ensuing clarification, he meant an Indian businessperson would never allow their business to serve sugar in such an unprofessional manner. Both phenotypically and phonetically, the customer looked and sounded Indian. Stereotypically, he seemed authoritative in talking about Indians.

What is striking about this encounter is the historical legacy of the racial discourse it draws from when it invokes and contrasts *mhindi* and *maskini*. Although poverty cuts across racial lines, both the customer – a person of Asian descent – and the salesperson – a person of African origin – understood each other as far as what the term poor was in reference to: *Mwafrika* (African). To be politically correct in a country that has been legally averse to racialism and racism, the customer could not say, '*Hii ni biashara ya mhindi au ya mwafrika* (This is a business of an Indian or an African)?' However, and herein lies the irony, by using *maskini* to contrast *mwafrika* from *mhindi*, he was not only invoking an erstwhile racialist discourse in business, but also reaffirming its enduring stereotype (Kayamba 1932; Kayamba 1948; Mukajanga 1994).

The construction of this discourse of the Indian as the quintessential businessperson in contrast to the African in the case of East Africa dates back to precolonial times. However, as Chachage (2018) has noted, it was consolidated during colonial times through media such as *Mambo Leo*, whose name could literally mean 'Current Affairs', 'Today's Events', 'Contemporary Events' or 'Modern Things' (Sturmer 1998; Liebau et al. 2010; Suriano 2011; Ronnenberg 2012). In its second issue in 1923, for instance, the editor(s) of *Mambo Leo* devoted a cover story that chastised Africans for not being good in business in contrast to Asians, admonishing the former to learn from the latter. Our purpose in this section, however, is not to revisit the whole history of the racial engagement and disengagement between Asians and Africans during the colonial and precolonial times; rather, it is to draw attention to how current racial business discourses and practices reinvoke this genealogy, which is covered in the literature (Chittick 1980; Honey 1982; Middleton 2004; Chande 2005; Oonk 2013).

One of the earliest African entrepreneurs to experience this racial encounter during colonial times is Kleist Sykes (Said 1998). According to his granddaughter, he was convinced that 'the Asian way of doing' business 'was the best for improving himself, and if all other Africans could follow the same pattern, life would be better for them too' (Buruku 1973: 109). With the intent of learning from and cooperating with them, he even joined their retail trade association at a time when business associations and chambers of commerce were highly racialised. However, he found it difficult to accept their ways and opted to form a business association for Africans. Yet he continued to capitalise on the knowledge and practices, such as those pertaining to consolidating and diversifying business within the family, that he had observed from Asians' business dealings. It thus became sustained across generations.

As the Sykes's example underscores, business relations between Africans and Asians were difficult to establish in Dar es Salaam during colonial times. This was partly due to racial laws that demarcated the city into racialised zones. In line with the racial business discourse of the Asian man as the ideal businessman in contrast to the African man, the large part of Dar es Salaam's Central Business District (CBD) fell within the Asian zone. For Africans, this was mainly a no-go zone unless they were labourers and/or customers. As for Asians, they increasingly needed to rely on African labourers, who might be taken on as *vibarua* (casual labourers) or 'spanner boys', yet could end up being *fundi* (craftsmen). Competing with Asians in business, however, was thus a daunting task for Africans and it became even more so given that the colonial government also allowed Asian businesspersons to encroach upon the African zone. One other restriction that entrenched the racial business discourse was a law – The Credit to Natives (Restriction) Ordinance of 1923 – that prohibited Asians from extending credit to Africans. Hence, business cooperation was racially circumscribed.

It is this background that continued to shape business relations in the early postcolonial period. Although decolonisation seemed to promise a reversal of fortunes for aspiring African entrepreneurs, the racial legacy favoured Asian entrepreneurs. Diwani's clarion call in 1964 was thus an attempt to mobilise the Asian business community to assist in rectifying this situation for mutual benefit and in response to the demands from Africans. Even though his radical proposals hardly materialised, there were some relative successes in terms of intent. For instance, as Chachage (2021) observes, their chamber managed to sponsor the establishment of a joint Asian and African business enterprise mainly to train and initiate willing Africans in trade and commerce. Ten experienced Asian firms committed themselves as shareholders to this joint venture known as Amalgamated Commercial Enterprise of Tanzania

(ACOTA) and sought African shareholders. Its head was Philbert Mutabuzi, an African who also led the then-national chamber of commerce that was mostly African.

Thirty years later, when a maverick opposition politician, Reverend Christopher Mtikila, incited an African mob to attack Asian businesses in Dar es Salaam, they were also drawing from this racial business discourse coupled with other stereotypes of Asian businesspeople. Due to the continued dominance of Tanzanians of Asian origin in business during the Liberalisation, Marketisation and Privatisation (LIMP) period in the 1990s, debate on the indigenisation of business resurfaced leading to these 'racial tensions' that Mtikila capitalised on through his hate speeches in public rallies about how Indian businesspeople allegedly stole from Africans (Mukajanga 1994: 1). In a way it was a testament to a failure to rectify the historical legacy of invoking race in business. However, it is important to note that throughout the postcolonial era there have been some Africans with relatively fruitful business exchanges with Asians. As we shall notice in the next section, such relations started in the early postcolonial period.

Racial partnership in business

In a touching tribute to Mufuruki on 10 December 2019 at the Julius Nyerere International Conference Centre, Sanjay Rughani, a Tanzanian entrepreneur of Asian origin, recalled how the departed 'champion and the voice of private sector' had impacted on both his personal and professional life as an entrepreneur.[5] Rughani had taken over from Mufuruki as the chair of the CEO Roundtable of Tanzania (CEOrt) and was thus using this solemn occasion to celebrate the deceased's impact, not only on the wider business community, but also on individuals from diverse backgrounds (Zacharia 2018). CEOrt is an organisation that was started in 2000 by a small group of Chief Executive Officers (CEOs) with the main objective of creating 'a forum through which industry leaders within the Tanzanian private sector could constructively engage with government, its development partners and other stakeholders with a view to creating a more conducive environment for business to prosper and for the country to develop' (CEOrt 2014; CEOrt 2020). Reminiscing on institutional transition, Rughani had this to say on Mufuruki's influence:

---

[5]   This and subsequent quotes from Rughani are based on our transcription of the tribute that he presented live during the funeral (see Azam TV 2019).

As a Tanzanian myself, I have known of Ali for many, many years. However, in the last three and a half years, he moved from being a man I looked upon, I admired and really felt from a distance to him becoming a friend, a mentor, and a coach who inspired me. And maybe I feel Ali actually conned me to take off from him as a chairman of CEO Roundtable. I remember one day, Ali giving me a call and telling me that we have talked as a board, and I was not there in that board meeting, and I think that it is the right time for you to take a much bigger leadership role beside what you are doing for Standard Chartered Bank. And, I actually asked him, Ali, what is happening to you? Why don't we talk about this? So, a couple of weeks later I went to Ali's office and I asked him, Ali, how will this work? And how am I expected to fill up your shoes? To that Ali said, the association requires change, I have been hanging on for a bit too long and, Sanjay, who says you need to fill my shoes? You need to make your shoes (Zacharia 2018).

What is particularly striking in this tribute is that it corroborates what Mufuruki told us two months before his demise that counters the conventional narrative about the relationship between businesspeople of African and Asian origin in Tanzania as far as business knowledge transfer and partnership are concerned.[6] For Mufuruki, in most cases it is the latter that benefitted from the former. And here was one, Rughani, a successful corporate leader, affirming this a few months later. 'In every interaction I had with him,' Rughani recalled in reference to Mufuruki, 'I always took away some learning' (Azam TV 2019). As the founding chair of CEOrt, Mufuruki managed to assemble leading business minds of African, Asian and European origin in an elite entrepreneurship network that fostered circulation of business and management knowledge while opening space for partnership across race.

Mufuruki's success in forming such a multiracial association of captains of commerce and industry partly stems from his reading of the racialised business history that pitted Asians against Africans. 'If you ask me,' he remarked in a keynote address at the launch of the Ismaili Professionals Network in 2013, 'a community, like the Ismaili, has continued to thrive but their embrace of change and social integration in Tanzania remains tenuous at

---

[6] Ali A. Mufuruki to Jacqueline Mgumia, personal communication, 2 June 2019, Dar es Salaam.

best if not absent altogether' (Mufuruki 2013: 1).[7] He then reiterated that deeper 'social integration into Tanzanian society must be a priority for the network' (Mufuruki 2013: 1). Acutely aware of such disjuncture, he admonished their network:

> You must look at the endless stream of opportunities that come with opening up your community to other Tanzanians, beyond welcoming them to your mosques. Think about having them in your homes, in your businesses and other social engagements. Think about being involved in local politics and being representatives not only of your community's interest, but of the interests of all of us. Let your economic power serve the interest of the wider community of Tanzanians (Mufuruki 2013: 1).

Mufuruki practised what he preached in regard to transcending the historical racial divide in business and related personal interactions. For instance, his successor recalls how his dealings with him reached beyond the confines of CEOrt. 'On his last visit to Canada', Rughani recalls, 'he really touched me and my wife, Melly, because he actually took time to invite my son to have lunch with him and his family' (Azam TV 2019). A young entrepreneur of Asian origin, Rahim Mawji, also recalls how Mufuruki was inspirational in enabling him to start an entrepreneurship business – Samora Ventures – in Dar es Salaam in collaboration with Samuel Killewo, a Tanzanian of African descent.[8] Their encounter, however, was two-way as Mufuruki also credited Mawji as the one who inspired the kickstarting of a mutual collaboration that led to the publication of their book on *Tanzania's Industrial Journey*:

> During the month of October 2014, I received an email from a Tanzanian student at Harvard University who wanted to interview me as part of his research on leadership development in Africa. He had read my lecture, at Strathmore Business School, titled 'What Africa needs is transformational leadership' and thought that it resonated with the objectives of his research … In the end, we managed to meet in person for the first time on 24 December 2014 at a food joint outside Bukoba Airport. Throughout our conversation that lasted just under one hour, I was struck by the intensity and intelligence of my young visitor. He asked very tough questions … We agreed to continue our conversation online and that is how my friendship

[7] It is instructive to note that, in regard to nationalisation, the socialist regime was harsh towards, but also lenient on some Ismaili business activities (see Kaiser 1996; Heilman 1998 and Kassum 2007).

[8] Rahim Mawji to Chambi Chachage, personal communication, 15 January 2020, Dar es Salaam

with Rahim Mawji began ... Towards the end of 2015, two good friends of mine joined our conversation. Gilman Kasiga, an engineer turned business executive, and Moremi Marwa, the youngest Tanzanian to be appointed CEO of the Dar es Salaam Stock Exchange, added a more practical dimension to the theoretical debate that Rahim and I had engaged in for a year. Before long, we knew we needed to move from asking questions to providing answers and that is how the idea of this book was born (Mufuruki et al. 2017: x–xi).

However, Mufuruki was as cognisant as he was critical of the racial business legacy. In a retreat with leaders of the leading opposition party in 2014, he recalled how Tanzanians of African descent who aspired to do business were discouraged while Tanzanians of Asian origin continued with business that the government did not regulate during the socialist period. By this, he meant some of the Asian businesses that were neither fully nationalised nor strictly controlled during the *Ujamaa* period following the Arusha Declaration on Socialism and Self Reliance in 1967.[9] As a result, he contended, once again, as in the case of the postsocialist period, that the Asians became 'very influential in the running of the economy of our country' (Mufuruki et al. 2017: x–xi). It is this imbalance that CEOrt have been attempting to redress as a forum for their exchange of entrepreneurial expertise beyond racial lines.

The late Mengi (2018), arguably the leading African entrepreneur in Tanzania prior to his death in 2019, also had to associate his journey to success with Asians. When he started his first business of ballpoint pens, he flew to Mombasa in Kenya to meet with a manufacturer of Asian descent to ask him if he could buy pen components on credit and repay after he assembled and sold them. However, the manufacturer declined. Mengi travelled back to Dar es Salaam and met a friend of Asian descent who knew the manufacturer in Mombasa. He told him that Mengi was a reliable person, a man of his word who would honour his promise. 'After a while,' he recalls, 'the supplier agreed to sell the components to me' (Mengi 2018: 170). It is also a businessperson of Asian descent who provided him with a premise in the industrial area. He recalls:

---

[9] The Asian commercial class suffered some setbacks but did not disappear during the socialist period (1967–91) and, in some cases, even thrived through capitalising on the economic crises of the 'lost decades' of the 1970s and 1980s. For an extensive discussion on this contentious topic and period (see Ghai and Ghai 1965; Mamdani 1975; Shivji 1975; Honey 1982; Tandon and Raphael 1984).

The business became bigger and the bedroom became too small. I moved to the living room and then to the garden. I needed an industrial building when the garden also became too small, but I could not afford the rent for this. I asked the owner of an industrial building to rent me part of the outer wall of his building, which he did, although he thought I was crazy. I bought iron sheets, built a sizeable shack against the wall and started from there. I diversified into importation of marker pen components. In the first year I made my first million dollars (Mengi 2018: 163).

Mwapachu, on his part, spent some time in India where, according to his curriculum vitae, he was a Minister Counsellor, Deputy Head of Mission and Head of Chancery at the Tanzania High Commission in New Delhi in the late 1970s. He also obtained his Post-Graduate Diploma in International Law, International Institutions and Diplomacy at the Indian Academy of International Law and Diplomacy there. A few years after his return to Tanzania, he became Managing Director of Tanzania's JV Group of Companies, considered to be the largest private sector group in the 1980s and 1990s owned by businesspeople of Asian origin (Chachage 2018). As the co-founder of the Confederation of Tanzania Industries (CTI) in the early 1990s, he was instrumental in creating a space that brought together businesspeople of African and Asian descent (Lofchie and Callaghy 1995; Mwapachu 2005; Mwapachu 2018).

This was a time when the racial discourse of indigenisation was hotly debated in relation to the dominance of captains of commerce and industries of Asian origin in Tanzania. As Chachage (2018) has noted, Mwapachu founded a magazine known as *Change* around the same time and devoted nine pages of its inaugural issue to interview two prominent businesspeople of Asian and African origin, respectively, on the sensitive topic. The overall aim in interviewing both of them was to enable the country to achieve what he envisioned as 'some racial balance in the wealth creation process' (Mwapachu 1993: 5).

Tanzania has thus come a long way since the colonial times when Sykes could hardly partner with businesspeople of Asian descent on an equal footing. In the postcolonial dispensation, especially the postsocialist one, someone like Gachuma with his CMG Group is able to forge a business partnership with Jayesh Shah of Sumeria Group. In 1986 they 'founded, built and developed Nyanza Bottling Company Limited (NBCL)' (Business Excellence n.d.). He is said to be an 'equal shareholder' since 'its inception' (Business Excellence n.d.). This partnership and his other position, as chair of Tanzania Cotton Association (TCA), have opened doors for more interactions with India and partnership with its business community in both countries (High Commission of the United Republic of Tanzania – New Delhi 2019). Through its initiative known as Indian Business Forum (IBF), the High Commission of India in Tanzania has been instrumental in (re)connecting business communities of both descents – African and Indian – as well as both nationalities and citizenships – Tanzanian and Indian (IBF 2020). This is the case given that not every Person of Indian Origin (PIO) in Tanzania is a Tanzanian citizen as some are also foreign investors from countries other than India.[10]

Conclusion

This chapter has traced the relationship between businesspeople of African and Asian descent in the context of business cooperation and knowledge sharing from the precolonial and postcolonial era. Such relationships have continued to be predicated on racial discourse. For some businesspeople of African descent who are already established, the need has been to forge business networks and interactions with businesspeople of Asian descent. In such cases, however, the needs have been mutual.

What sustains such business relationships in the context of continued racial discourses and stereotypes perpetuated by both groups, then, is the mutual dependence. Such relationships are more balanced as both parties are relatively at par and thus mainly operate on the basis of mutual business interests. However, those of Asian descent continue to dominate big business; hence mutual trust remains a challenge. Nevertheless, business knowledge transfer and/or partnership continue across the racial line.

Bibliography

Anand, D. and Kaul, N. 2011. 'A disruptive ethnography of Tanzanian-Indians', *South Asian Diaspora*, 3, 183–95.

Azam TV. 2019. *Live | Shughuli Ya Kuaga Mwili Wa Marehemu Ali Mufuruki Ukumbi Wa Jnicc*, YouTube, 9 December 2019, https://www.youtube.com/watch?v=Vy900-UUAtno&ab_channel=AzamTV, accessed 20 May 2020.

Bishara, F.A. 2017. 'Making Africa Indian', in F.A. Bishara (ed)., *A Sea of Debt: Law and Economic Life in the Western Indian Ocean, 1780–1950*, Asian Connections (Cambridge: Cambridge University Press), 150–68.

Brennan, J.R. 2012. *Taifa: Making Nation and Race in Urban Tanzania* (Athens: Ohio University Press).

[10]   For an extensive analysis of PIOs in Africa, see a chapter entitled 'Hands across the Water: Indian Engagement in Africa' by Taylor (2010).

Bryceson, D.F. 1988. 'Food insecurity and the social division of labour in Tanzania, 1919–1985' (Unpublished Ph.D. dissertation, University of Oxford).

Buruku, D.S. 1973. 'The townsman: Kleist Sykes', in J. Iliffe (ed.), *Modern Tanzanians: A Volume of Biographies* (Dar es Salaam: East African Publishing House), 95–114.

Business Excellence. n.d. 'Nyanza Bottling Company Limited', n.d., https://www.bus-ex.com/article/nyanza-bottling-company-limited, accessed 7 June 2020.

CEOrt (CEO Roundtable of Tanzania). 2014. 'CEOrt Annual Report 2014', *CEOrt*, 24 November 2015, https://fliphtml5.com/qoly/trnw/basic, accessed 17 May 2020.

——. 2020. 'About us', *CEOrt*, n.d., https://ceo-roundtable.co.tz/about-us/, accessed 17 May 2020.

Chachage, C. 2018. 'A capitalising city: Dar es Salaam and the emergence of an African entrepreneurial elite (*c.* 1862–2015)' (Ph.D. dissertation, Harvard University).

——. Forthcoming. *Africanising Capital: Emergence of Black Entrepreneurs in Eastern Africa*.

Chande, J.K. 2005. *A Knight in Africa: Journey from Bukene* (Newcastle: Penumbra Press).

Chittick, N. 1980. 'Indian relations with East Africa before the arrival of the Portuguese', *The Journal of the Royal Asiatic Society of Great Britain and Ireland*, 112, 117–27.

Delf, G. 1963. *Asians in East Africa* (London: Oxford University Press).

Ghai, D.P. and Ghai, Y.P. 1965. 'Asians in East Africa: Problems and prospects', *Journal of Modern African Studies*, 3, 35–51.

Heilman, B. 1998. 'Who are the indigenous Tanzanians? Competing conceptions of Tanzanian citizenship in the business community', *Africa Today*, 45, 369–87.

High Commission of the United Republic of Tanzania – New Delhi. 2019. 'Remarks by Ambassador Baraka H. Luvanda at the Occasion of the Tanzania Cotton Trade Mission to India, Tanzania High Commission, New Delhi, 18 Dec 2019', *Government of Tanzania*, 18 December 2019, https://www.in.tzembassy.go.tz/resources/view/remarks-by-ambassador-baraka-h-luvanda-at-the-occasion-of-the-tanzania-cotton-trade-mission-to-india-tanzania-high-commission-new-delhi-18-dec-2019, accessed 7 May 2020.

Himbara, D. 1997. 'The "Asian question" in East Africa', *African Studies*, 56, 1–18.

Honey, M. 1982. 'A history of Indian merchant capital and class formation in Tanganyika: c. 1840–1940' (Unpublished Ph.D. dissertation, University of Dar es Salaam).

IBF. 2020. 'Information', n.d., http://ibf.co.tz/information/, accessed 29 May 2020.

Kaiser, P. 1996. *Culture and Civil Society in an International Context: The Case of Aga Khan Health Care and Education Initiatives in Tanzania* (London: Praeger).

Kassum, A.N. 2007. *Africa's Winds of Change: Memoirs of an International Tanzanian* (London: IB Tauris).

Kayamba, H.M.T. 1932. 'The modern life of the East African native', *Africa Journal of International African Institute*, 5, 50–60.

——. 1948. *African Problems* (London: Lutterworth Press).

Liebau, H., Bromber, K., Lange, K., Hamzah, D., and Ahuja, R. 2010 (eds). *The world in World Wars: Experiences, perceptions and perspectives from Africa and Asia* [Studies in Global Social History, 5] (Leiden and Boston: Brill).

Lofchie, M.F. and Callaghy, T. 1995. 'Diversity in the Tanzanian Business Community: Its Implications for Economic Growth', *UCLA College of Social Sciences*, December 1995, http://www.sscnet.ucla.edu/polisci/faculty/lofchie/tanzaniabusinessstudy.pdf, accessed 29 May 2020.

Mamdani, M. 1975. 'Class struggles in Uganda', *Review of African Political Economy*, 2, 26–61.

Mangat, J.S. 1969. *A History of the Asians in East Africa, c. 1886 to 1945* (Oxford: Clarendon Press).

Mengi, R.A. 2018. *I Can, I Must, I Will: The Spirit of Success* (Dar es Salaam: IPP Limited).

Middleton, J. 2004. *African Merchants of the Indian Ocean: Swahili of the East African Coast* (Long Grove: Waveland Press).

Mufuruki, A.A. 2013. 'Embracing change is key to success in today's multi-cultural world', *Keynote address at the launch of Ismaili Professionals Network*, June 2019, Dar es Salaam.

Mufuruki, A.A., Mawji, R., Kasiga, G. and Marwa, M. 2017. *Tanzania's Industrialisation Journey, 2016 – 2056: From an Agrarian to a Modern Industrialised State in Forty Years* (Nairobi: Moran Publisher).

Mukajanga, K.D. 1994. 'The resurgence of racial tensions in Tanganyika 1991–1994: The Gabacholi phenomenon' (Unpublished BA dissertation, University of Dar es Salaam).

Mwafrika. 1964. 'Upatna wa Waasia na Waafrika', 18 August 1964, 2.

Mwapachu, J.V. 1993 'Indigenisation: Jump start or racist ploy,' *Change* 1, January 1993, 5.

——. 2005. *Confronting New Realities: Reflections on Tanzania's Radical Transformation* (Dar es Salaam: E & D Limited).

——. 2018. *Tanzania in the Age of Change and Transformation* (Dar es Salaam: E & D Vision Publishing).

Nagar, R. 1995. 'Making and breaking boundaries: Identity politics among South Asians in post-colonial Dar es Salaam' (Ph.D. dissertation, University of Minnesota).

Oonk, G. 2013. *Settled Strangers: Asian Business Elites in East Africa (1800–2000)* (New Delhi: Sage Publications).

Ranja, T. 2003. 'Success under duress: A comparison of the indigenous African and East African Asian entrepreneurs', September 2003, *SSRN*, ESRF Globalisation Project Paper Series, https://ssrn.com/abstract=904388, accessed 1 June 2020.

Ripota Wetu. 1964. 'Waasia Wenye Maduka Wataka Umoja na Waafrika', *Mwafrika*, 17 August 1964, 1.

Ronnenberg, R. 2012. '"House of believers": Irony and commensurability in Tanganyikan colonial discourse', *African Identities*, 10, 33–54.

Said, M. 1998. *The Life and Times of Abdulwahid Sykes (1924–1968): The Untold Story of the Muslim Struggle against British Colonialism in Tanganyika* (London: Minerva Press).

Seidenberg, D.A. 1996. *Mercantile Adventurers: The World of East African Asians, 1750–1985* (New Delhi: New Age International).

Shivji, I.G. 1975. *Class Struggles in Tanzania* (Dar es Salaam: Tanzania Publishing House).

Sturmer, M. 1998. 'The media history of Tanzania', *Ndanda Mission Press*, n.d., https://tanzania.mom-rsf.org/uploads/tx_lfrogmom/documents/12-1508_import.pdf, accessed 1 June 2020.

Suriano, M. 2011. 'Letters to the editor and poems: *Mambo Leo* and readers' debates on Dansi, Ustaarabu, respectability, and modernity in Tanganyika, 1940s–1950s', *Africa Today*, 57, 39–55.

Tandon, Y. and Raphael, A. 1984. *The New Position of East Africa's Asians: Problems of a Displaced Minority* (London: Minority Rights Group).

Taylor, I. 2010. *The International Relations of Sub-Saharan Africa* (New York: Bloomsbury Publishing).

Zacharia, A. 2018. 'New CEOrt outlines his priorities', *The Citizen*, 13 June 2018, https://www.thecitizen.co.tz/news/New-CEOrt-outlines-his-priorities/1840340-4610556-1307binz/index.html, accessed 3 May 2020.

9

The Trumpets and Travails of 'South–South Cooperation': African Students in India since the 1940s

GERARD MCCANN

In his 1966 memoir, the Kenyan writer R. Mugo Gatheru recalled his time as a student in newly independent India. His stay at the University of Allahabad in 1949 on a recently created Indian Council for Cultural Relations (ICCR) scholarship was 'a tremendous experience to me emotionally and psychologically. There, for the first time in my life, I felt a free man – free from passes or being pushed here and there as if I was an undesirable animal' (Gatheru 1966: 130). Gatheru was in the first cohort of tens of thousands of Africans who would study in India over the next seventy years. Such opportunities signalled, framed and were the anti-colonial solidarities that characterised Indo-African relations under India's first Prime Minister, Jawaharlal Nehru, in the 1950s. This historical conviviality became repurposed under the rejuvenated 'South–South cooperation' of the India-Africa Forum Summits (IAFS) from 2008 onwards as India–Africa economic cooperation grew apace in the twenty-first century.

The presence of African students in India anchored the continuities – rhetorical and very real – of the united Indo-African community over the postcolonial period. It was also an era in which New Delhi argued for the consistency of its human resource-centred outreach to Africa. These were policies formed in deliberate contrast to former colonial and neo-colonial Western powers, who dealt in coercive 'tied' economic aid, and other emerging Asian donors, notably China, rolling out large infrastructure projects from the 1960s and with notable speed in the 2000s as competition for African exports, commercial opportunities and political alliances intensified. The assertion of moral exceptionalism in India's Africanist foreign policy became encapsulated in the frequently cited words of Mahatma Gandhi, who himself developed as a political thinker on African soil at the turn of the twentieth century. In 1946, he predicted that 'the commerce between India and Africa will be of ideas and services, not of manufactured goods against raw materials after the fashion of the Western exploiters' (Gandhi 1946: 282). Educational cooperation – the commerce of ideas – was a cornerstone of India's significant ideological and material commitment to African partners in the era of decolonisation. At the same time, this work buttressed India's self-proclaimed leadership within the 'Third World' and successor 'Global South'.

There was much to Gandhi's foresight. Through official schemes under ICCR at India's historic seats of learning from the late 1940s, Indian Technical and Economic Cooperation (ITEC) from 1964 and specialist sectoral institutes across Africa in the new millennium, India boasts an unbroken record of supplying substantial educational opportunities for African citizens in the cause of solidarity. India's Africa-facing development programmes of the late colonial and early postcolonial periods endure to this day. From their outset, a targeted attention to vocational training for Africans at Indian institutions aimed, in the words of the strategic framework of the third IAFS in 2015, 'to boost Africa's capacity in areas such as engineering, medical, technology, agriculture as well as emerging areas' (MEA 2015: 8). At IAFS 2015, Nkosazana Dlamini Zuma, Chairperson of the African Union Commission, stressed the educational 'investments in people, our most precious resource' were central to the visions of Gandhi, Jomo Kenyatta and Nelson Mandela. 'An emphasis on greater access to science, engineering, mathematics and technology' through enhanced India–Africa collaboration today would unleash an 'African skills revolution' built on the dreams of those founding fathers (Zuma 2015: 4).

The shared histories of colonial oppression and colonial underdevelopment – and India's success in creating solutions to postcolonial developmental challenges through its 'Green Revolution' over the 1960s and information technology achievements in the 2000s – underpinned such cooperation as India–Africa economic ties thickened from the late 1990s. In 2010, India's 'year of Africa', Malawi's President Bingu wa Mutharika declared that 'I consider myself a Delhiwala, I am a product of India' on the occasion of Indian Vice President Hamid Ansari's tour of Malawi, Zambia and Botswana (Deccan Herald 2010). Mutharika had studied for five years at Shri Ram College, University of Delhi, earning BA and MA degrees in commerce and economics in 1961 and 1963. His achievements have been commemorated since 2014 at the annual graduation ceremonies of the Association of African Students in India (AASI).

History mattered. The recitations of personal, human-focused Indo-African cooperation that propelled the career of Mutharika – partnerships grounded in emotive and powerful anti-colonial histories – served to present and anchor the diplomacy of rejuvenated India–Africa relations in the twenty-first century. India sought markets, resources and geopolitical friends in Africa. African leaders searched for economic opportunities from a new range of suitors unavailable through empire, within Cold War environments and under oppressive structural adjustment programmes over the 1980s. A rhetoric of 'win–win' partnership, rooted in those durable anti-imperialist solidarities, pervaded Indo-African diplomatic meetings under the banner of New Delhi's new 'Focus Africa' programme from 2002 and, more fully, under the grander IAFS from 2008.

However, as Emma Mawdsley suggests of India's contemporary aid diplomacy in Africa, this 'symbolic regime' also served to 'euphemise or obscure the realpolitik of South–South relations' as New Delhi confronted the uneasy realities of new commercial ambitions set against the ideals of the past. By necessity, India's strategies to secure African resource and market access replicated those of Western and Asian competitors in this 'new scramble for Africa' (Mawdsley 2012a). Such transitions augured a departure from the putative morally exceptional foreign policy of the Gandhi–Nehru era, despite the persistent language of continuity in historical 'Third Worldist' partnership and mutual gain within the new 'Global South'. Rhetoric and practice appeared to diverge in India's Africanist designs for some commentators (Malghan and Swaminathan 2008).

Such tensions were not, however, entirely the product of the neoliberal world. Alongside his sense of existential freedom in the late-1940s, R. Mugo Gatheru lamented the racialised tutelary condescension of some tutors and fellow students in Allahabad. The lived experiences of Africans in India seemed, in some measure, to call into question the received high-political narratives of Afro-Indian solidarity. Numerous reports of anti-African prejudice in Indian cities emerged in the global press from 2015. The Bengaluru photographer Mahesh Shantaram's evocative portraits of African students in contemporary India shed light on the 'everyday phenomenon' of racism in India. For Shantaram, 'Africans are seen as not having agency, the *auqaat*, to act in public environments or even speak against Indians when they feel wronged by them. Their problems are not theirs – these problems are a problem of Indianness and the Africans are just caught up in this shit. Africans just hold up a mirror to Indians who act in these petty and evil ways and show us who we really are' (Guha 2017). Shantaram's work exposed something more visceral and hierarchical in the guts of relationships between Africans and Indians.

The social histories of African students in India provide one means to reflect upon the complex, textured nature of Indo-African connections, and from vantage points beyond diplomatic podiums or canonical nationalist historiographies. Through a very brief historical account of African student presence in India, this chapter surveys both the harmonies and fault lines of Indo-African relations since the late 1940s. It underlines the crucial importance of how educational cooperation shaped mutual anti-colonial visions for African and Indian nationalists in the first decades of independence and thereafter. But such political and technocratic proximity was not as consistently undergirded by intimacy between African and Indian citizens as these relationships unfolded amidst complicated Afro-Asian histories under empire and into the postcolonial world. The Indian state lauds its long, durable and people-centred development assistance to African states for good reason. In profoundly human ways, more divisive interpersonal tensions between African and Indian citizens interrogate more comfortable accounts of that Indo-African fraternity over the last half century.

Technocracy and anti-colonialism in India's early African studentships

In 1948, Nehru dispatched Apa Pant as India's first High Commissioner to East Africa with twin missions to solder India's estranged East African diaspora to the new Indian nation state and to assist African politicians in support of their own struggles for liberation (Sutton 2007). Over his six-year term, Pant tirelessly promoted new ICCR scholarships, a key pillar of India's engagement with Africa and a talismanic marker, in New Delhi at least, of Indian-led anti-colonial solidarity. The charismatic Pant befriended Kenya's nationalist elite, for example sponsoring Mbiyu Koinange's tour of India in 1949. The founder of the landmark Independent African Schools Movement, son of a prominent Kikuyu chief and close ally of Jomo Kenyatta, Koinange spent a month observing India's progress in educational advancement for application at home in central Kenya (Pant 1987).

East African leaders enthusiastically seized these opportunities to scramble technocratic education as a form of local anti-colonialism in the context of colonial underdevelopment. In September 1946, Kenyan activists from the Kenya African Union, Kikuyu Central Association and newspaper *Ramogi Luo* wrote to Nehru to congratulate him on the establishment of his interim government in advance of Indian independence. They praised Gandhian non-violence and India's achievement of freedom as a wider 'historic moment for the emancipation of the oppressed and downtrodden coloured people of the whole world'. They soon cut to the chase to demand Indian commercial, agricultural and technical instruction because 'we have been kept pitifully backward educationally'.[1] In 1948, Chief Petro of the Wachagga ethnic group in Kilimanjaro similarly called for Indian scholarships for his subjects to address the paucity of non-missionary, skilled education in northern Tanganyika.[2]

East African institutions and individuals inundated Pant with applications – some three hundred in the first year of the scheme alone – competition that troubled an anxious British colonial state looking on with their own nascent post-war developmental agendas.[3] In December 1953, over a hundred African scholars attended a student conference in New Delhi, while four ICCR zonal offices in Aligarh, Benares, Bombay and Madras administered student welfare and annual holiday camps in Mahabaleshwar, Kodaikanal, Simla and Darjeeling hill-stations. Student numbers grew. By 1965, half of the 5,000 overseas students in India hailed from Africa, and with specific opportunities for women, through old ICCR scholarships and the new ITEC programme (Indian Council for Africa 1967: 36–43).

Several of the recipients would combine their studies in independent India with overt political activism in locations away from the direct control and deep surveillance of the British colonial state. Jean-Marie Seroney, a prominent Kenyan MP in the 1970s and the first Kenyan to graduate in law, studied at the University of Allahabad in the early 1950s during which time he contributed to the *Indian Review* equating the evils of apartheid with settler colonialism in Kenya (Seroney 1950; Sang 2015). In 1953, Munukayumbwa Sipalo, a Northern Rhodesian law student and leader of the All-India African Students Federation, established a new 'Africa Bureau' in Delhi, which aligned to the internationalist Asian Socialist Conference in Burma. In 1956, he opened an 'African Liberation Committee' in Cairo in collaboration with the fledgling Afro-Asian Peoples' Solidarity Organisation under Gamal Abdel Nasser. Sipalo's mobility and ability to plug African and South Asian contacts into broader networks of decolonisation – as his comrades at home continued to suffer the brutalities of settler colonialism – occurred in part because of his studies in India and the networking possibilities this afforded (Milford 2019: 77–85).

Alongside such formal political organisation, the pedagogy of India's African studentships provided an equally important mode of activism: the

1   National Archives of India (NAI), New Delhi: 25–25/46–O.S.I: Henry Muoria, George Ndegwa, George Karioki, Zabula, and Mbiyu Koinange to Jawaharlal Nehru, 16 September, 1946.
2   NAI: 18–68/49–AFRII: Apa Pant to Subimal Dutt, 18 October, 1949.
3   NAI: 20–24/48–O.S.I: Pant to Dutt, 28 August, 1948.

improvement of technocratic skills as applied forms of anti-imperialism. Mutharika read economic theory at the Delhi School of Economics in the early 1960s. Somali novelist Nuruddin Farah graduated in philosophy and literature from Panjab University, Chandigarh, in 1970. They became famous men after stellar achievement in traditional academic disciplines. A large number of African students in India undertook specialised vocational courses in a catholic range of Indian institutions such as the Wardha Cottage Industry School; the Jadavpur Soap Works, Calcutta; the Leather Technical Institute, Madras; and Bengal Tanning Institute. Such apprenticeships informed the planning of African postcolonial economies as the momentum of independence quickened over the 1950s.

In 1953, future Kenyan Vice President, Jaramogi Oginga Odinga, toured India sponsored by ICCR. His report (first published in Dholuo as *Dweche Ariyo e India*) showed as much veneration for Indian railways, urban planning and universities as for Gandhi's life and works (Oginga Odinga 1966). On his 1958 state visit to India, Prime Minister Kwame Nkrumah extolled Indian achievements in civil engineering as his own plans for the Volta Dam took shape following Ghanaian liberation in 1957 (India News 1959). Diverse Afro-Asian educational cooperation was not just a tool to attain African independence but also to construct its content.

'Anti-colonial politics was development and vice versa', and African students in India were central – rhetorically and materially – to that dyad (McCann 2019). Crucially, this was driven by African demand, as well as Indian soft power supply. In the late 1950s, Oginga Odinga and Tom Mboya, among the first African elected members of the Kenyan Legislative Council, held reserved places on the selection committee for Indian government scholarships, alongside Julius Kiano, the first Kenyan to gain a PhD (in California) and first African lecturer at the Royal Technical College in Nairobi. Kiano insisted medicine, agriculture and civil engineering must be the priority degrees in India.[4] This dovetailed with other global educational opportunities in technical training grasped by African leaders. Over the 1960s, thousands of Africans would study industry, trade unionism and *kibbutz* agriculture at Israel's Afro-Asian Institute for Labour Studies and Cooperation in Tel Aviv. In 1964, E.J. Mangame, president of the African Students' Association of Israel, lamented that 'when a country gets independence it is a sad thing to see a large number of graduate administrators and lawyers, a handful of

---

[4]   Kenyan National Archives: OP/EST/1/697: Minutes of meeting of the Indian Scholarships Local Selection Committee, India House, Nairobi, 23 September 1958.

doctors and a few or no engineers at all' (Mangame 1964: 24–5). India's scholarships, most commonly folded into generalist Nehruvian narratives of 'non-aligned' solidarity, held more pragmatic and local anti-colonial utility for African nationalists.

This success led to a proliferation of official schemes for African students in India under ICCR, the Special Commonwealth African Assistance Programme (SCAAP) from 1960 and ITEC after 1964. In 2019, around half of the nine hundred annual ICCR scholarship slots went to Commonwealth African nations to fund longer-term courses and degrees (King and King 2019: 401). The short-term, vocational training courses under ITEC – with some 13,000 places annually by 2019, around 40 per cent of which go to African trainees – fulfilled many of the technocratic aspirations described by Mangame in the 1960s (King and King 2019: 403; King 2019: 11; Chaturvedi 2016). The diversification of the African student body away from African nations with historical Indian Ocean links to India – such as Kenya, Tanzania and Uganda – to include West African and Central African scholars was notable, even if the bulk of scholarship recipients continued to hail from Anglophone Africa (Dubey 1990). The claims that New Delhi's human resource approach acted to tangibly help Africans realise the promises of nation-building could not be denied. The tenacity of these schemes over the decades underlined India's sustained material commitment to Afro-Asian cooperation.

The quotidian travails of India's African students

The celebratory tales of anti-colonial comradeship, revealed in abundance in state archives, did not always resemble the experiences of those African students living in India. These more tense and intimate dynamics are more difficult to capture. In 1956, the British Council representative in Bombay (now Mumbai) reported unhappiness in the city's African student population given their negative assessments of the quality of education received, poor state of infrastructure, aloofness of (often much younger) Indian peers and what they considered to be paltry stipends.[5] Some East Africans in the 1950s and 1960s concurred with such observations, complaining that India's laudable anti-colonial credentials were not matched by the academic content of its curricula. Some came to reflect on the superiority of higher educational

---

5   The UK National Archives: DO/35/5347: J.R. Williams, Office for British High Commissioner to India, New Delhi, to R.C. Ormerod, Commonwealth Relations Office.

institutions at home, such as Uganda's Makerere College/University which several East African students attended before postgraduate work overseas, relative to Indian institutions. Many young Africans indeed turned down Indian university places if opportunities in Europe or the US could be secured (Milford 2019: 77). Gatheru's time as a student in independent India was, in part, imaginative liberation from the 'raw' colonialism of settler Kenya. He also confessed ulterior motives for selecting to study in South Asia: 'my mind was not really on India. India was a means to an end. My sights were set upon America' (Gatheru 1966: 127).

Gatheru did enjoy his time in India and recalled the kindness of many he met. But he also commented on the condescension of some hosts who were not easily receptive to criticisms, noting that 'they were very sensitive and always wanted to dominate whenever we had a discussion'. Unwanted attention, even abuse, from members of the Indian public led him and fellow Kenyan students to 'almost suspect them of being a pathologically colour-conscious people'. The Kenyans raised the issue with the local editor of the *Amrita Bazaar Patrika* newspaper to publish a complaint about the quotidian behaviour of Indian citizens towards African students in Allahabad (Gatheru 1966: 127).

At a grander geopolitical stratum, scholars such as Antoinette Burton highlight hierarchicalisation in India's relations with Africa in the mid-twentieth century. Nehru:

> believed it [India] was *prima inter pares* in civilisational terms, and he arguably viewed a decolonizing Africa as a set of successor states to the Raj over which independent India would seek market advantage and to which it would offer geopolitical tutelage … Nehruvian postcolonial imaginary carried racial hierarchies of brown over black into diplomacy and global strategy in the first quarter of the cold war (Burton 2010: 354).

Such controversial assessments build on a diverse corpus of scholarship that probes notions of a 'Greater India' in Africa; networks forged by diaspora and transnational Indian nationalism within the British imperial Indian Ocean (see Metcalf 2007; Brennan 2012; Aiyar 2015). The complexities of Indo-African communion begin to surface for the postcolonial aftermath and in spaces beyond the high-diplomatic settings of the 1955 Bandung conference and Non-Aligned Movement.

The singular ideological position of education within orthodox narratives of India–Africa affinity shifts as the lives and reminiscences of African students in India start to emerge. Timothy Nicholson's work on the testimonies of East Africans in India during the 1950s and 1960s foregrounds the emotive disconnect between lofty Nehruvian dreams of Afro-Asian friendship and the real-world experiences of Africans in urban India. Nicholson concludes that for many young African men the defining experience of their sojourn became bitterness towards India and disappointment in transnational anti-colonialism, given that they were:

> met with alienation by the Indian public who, in the new zones of contact, reproduced colonial anxieties and fears of African intimacy … the fears of miscegenation within much of the Indian population, with the surveillance, policing and monitoring of Indian women enacted to prevent such intimate contact failing to control the perceived threats represented by African male students … the wider community felt themselves to be under threat by African students, reflecting the colonial stereotypes that portrayed Africans as sexual predators and savages (Nicholson 2017: 616).

Numerous press reports attested to these tensions of intimacy. In February 1955, five students from East and Central Africa petitioned the Delhi Rotary Club on 'the immense psychological torture' of the daily discrimination they faced in the classroom and on the street. They bemoaned that 'if India is against colonialism, it should not discriminate against colonials of darker hue'. They argued that this prejudice bordered on the suffering endured by South African Indians under apartheid about which black Africans had been outraged, inspired by Gandhi's legacy and Nehru's anti-racist speeches at the United Nations (Times of India 1955: 5).

In May 1967, several Ugandan students were assaulted at a cinema in Poona after their protests at the screening of a film, *Naked Flesh,* that lasciviously portrayed African 'barbarism'. G.W. Limbanga, president of the African Students' Association of Bangalore, raged at the decision to publicly show this 'cheap entertainment at the expense of African personality. We will not sit back and see Mother Africa insulted'. He wrote to the editor of the *Times of India* urging the paper to denounce letters it had published from Indian citizens that condescended the African protesters as 'immature' and 'ungrateful' to their Indian sponsors (Times of India 1967: 3). In February 1968, one African student succinctly pointed out to ICCR 'that Indian homes are too orthodox to admit Africans but not too orthodox to welcome white-skinned students' (Times of India 1968). He received a lukewarm response. The strapline Nehruvian evocation of Africa's special place in a harmonious decolonising world did not match the realities of being an African in India in the eyes of those students.

The mixed intimacies of India–Africa partnership in the twenty-first century

The successes and travails of African students in India remain distinct strands in assessments of rejuvenated India–African partnerships of the twenty-first century. Contemporary avatars of the academic and vocational schemes provided by India since the 1940s are key tenets of the IAFS process. India's arguments that its approaches are especially appropriate to African challenges – because of shared histories of colonialism and postcolonial development – are grounded in mutual and meaningful appreciation of the sustained and fruitful Indo-African educational relationships described above (Mawdsley 2012b). On the other hand, critics note the reductive nature of India's engagements with 'Africa' under Prime Minister Narendra Modi (and indeed his Congress opponents before him), which relies on an instrumental and ambivalent use of anti-colonial history and the reification of neoliberal hierarchies to privilege Indian agency over African voices (Davis 2018).

The African student criticisms of the 1950s and 1960s about racist prejudice, the quality of Indian education and questionable global comparative advantage of Indian degrees dictated a contraction of African interest in Indian studentships into the 1970s. The economic crises that confronted numerous African states in the 1970s and 1980s, as well as India's own autarkic turn in that period, compounded the retrenchment of Indo-African connection. The relative reduction in African student numbers in India continued into the age of liberalisation in the 1990s and 2000s, realities rubbing up against celebrations of rapidly expanding Indo-African economic partnership under 'Focus Africa' and IAFS. P.J. Lavakare and K.B. Powar estimated that in 1991, 6,222 Africans studied in India, some 48 per cent of the total number of international students. By 2009, 3,128 Africans attended Indian colleges, 20 per cent of the total international student body (Lavakare and Powar 2013: 22). By 2017, estimates of African student numbers in India varied from around five thousand to ten thousand in the absence of authoritative statistics, an international student body dwarfed in size by attendees from neighbouring Afghanistan, Bangladesh, Bhutan, Nepal and Sri Lanka. These numbers excluded those on short-term (one to three month) training courses under ITEC (King 2019: 10–12).

These trajectories suggested a more complicated picture of the relationship between historical conviviality and future growth applauded in India's flagship developmental activities in Africa such as the 'Pan-African e-Network' established in 2004. Lavakare and Powar attributed the decline of the African student population to cumbersome Indian bureaucracy, continued negative

African perceptions of Indian educational institutions in the global market-place, aggressive marketing by universities in the Global North and marked improvements in African higher education, notably in South Africa. They called for more muscular joint-ventures between Indian and African universities within governmental frameworks, especially through the African Union, and via burgeoning non-governmental channels (Lavakare and Powar 2013: 24–33).

Such initiatives multiplied as the Government of India committed more resources to India–Africa policy in the mid-2000s. In 2008, New Delhi vowed to establish nineteen (and one hundred in 2015) more African training institutes drawing on India's technical prowess, although the scale of implementation did not match these promises (King 2019: 23–24). But, those that were built – such as the Ghana-India Kofi Annan Centre of Excellence in ICT founded in 2003 – did translate the technical partnerships of the 1960s into twenty-first century form. Within higher education, the Indian Consul-General in Johannesburg became an ex-officio member of the Advisory Board of the Centre for Indian Studies in Africa (CISA) at the University of the Witwatersrand, South Africa, founded in 2007.

The Indian Confederation of Indian Industry (CII), tellingly a key driver of India's Africa policy over the last two decades, keeps up this momentum. In August 2019, CII hosted an India-Africa Higher Education and Skill Development Summit to encourage Indian education providers with access to African officials, businesspersons and civil society leaders to establish 'quality, publicly-funded colleges and universities of higher and technical education, modelled on the Indian institutes of technology and of science' towards African skill development. The CII stated that:

> in many ways the problems in Africa, as far as education is concerned, are similar to those in India though there is a difference in scale and magnitude … Africa could also draw lessons from India's massive expansion of tertiary education, which generated a human capital base with highly developed science, technology, engineering and mathematics (STEM) expertise that allows export of scientists and technologists (Kokutse 2019).

African leaders appeared to be on the same page. In March 2019, at the fourteenth CII-EXIM Bank India-Africa Project Partnership Conclave, Ghana's Vice President Mahamudu Bawumia stressed his ambitions to transform Ghana into West Africa's pharmaceutical hub and grow ICT capacity in concert with India's world-leading universities and companies. 'We have an ambitious agenda to industrialise and add value to every resource and since India has a lot of experience in industrialisation, we believe that the nation can help us fulfil our dream of industrializing Ghana... We would like to set up similar kinds of medical institutions that are present in India' (Ansah 2019). The virtues of applied technical alliances – and accompanying tutelary language of Indo-African connection redolent of the mid-twentieth century – seem alive and kicking, repurposed for the digital age.

However, as in the 1950s and 1960s, and beyond the boardroom, the spectre of discrimination against members of the African student body in India called into question the convivial nature of Indo-African community. From 2015 to 2017, media outlets across the world published repeated reports of violence against African students in cities across India (Anand and Raj 2017). In February 2016, global news agencies syndicated the story of a 21-year-old female Tanzanian student attacked in Bengaluru. After a Sudanese student ran over an Indian pedestrian, a group assaulted a passing car of Tanzanian students, setting the vehicle alight before beating and stripping the woman (Al Jazeera 2016).

The murder of Congolese student Masonda Ketada Olivier in Delhi in May 2016 propelled the issue into the diplomatic sphere. The Eritrean Ambassador to India, Alem Tsehaye Woldemariam, announced that the envoys of forty-two African countries would boycott India's 'Africa Day' celebrations in protest at the abuse facing their citizens. He stated that 'the Indian government is strongly enjoined to take urgent steps to guarantee the safety of Africans in India including appropriate programmes of public awareness that will address the problem of racism and Afrophobia in India' (PTI 2016). The mollifying words of the Indian Minister of External Affairs about the 'historically close relationship' between India and Africa only served to intensify African remonstration. In the face of continued attacks and a lack of official redress, in March 2017 AASI declared that given 'the failure to secure the lives of African students and to ensure maximum security in areas where African students live, we will write to the African Union to cut all bilateral ties with India' (Roy 2017). Such episodes publicly debunked unproblematic narratives of Indo-African harmony as the voices of African citizens, rather than Indian leaders, became heard.

Conclusion

In the 1950s and 1960s, the experiences of Africans studying in locations beyond European empire – in Asia, the Americas or eastern Europe – 'empowered them' and showed imperial power 'to be anachronistic' (Branch 2018: 830). India's specific and sustained commitment to African educational partnership during the maelstroms of decolonisation and through revitalised

India–Africa engagements today have proved transformative. In soldering anti-colonial activism to technocratic progress these relationships have been profoundly meaningful for African and Indian participants for well over half a century. The continuities of these connections are real. They matter. It is, however, also clear that the legacies of complex racial histories between Indians and Africans, forged especially by colonial rule but also beyond, have not been well illuminated thus far. Fractious histories of South Asian diaspora in East Africa over the twentieth century condition contemporary India–Africa association in ways that reveal contestation as well as collaboration (McCann 2010). So too have the negative experiences of African students in India and the tutelary dynamics of Indo-African connection at large tarnished more comfortable assessments of 'South–South' fraternity from the 1950s to the present day. The Indian government's refurbishment of the historic Gandhi Memorial Library at the University of Nairobi from 2016 to 2019 occurred alongside the 'Gandhi Must Fall' movement at the University of Ghana from 2016 to 2018 (Vittorini, this volume). Incorporating the historical experiences of African students in India into the imagination of India–Africa relations frames the tensions, as well as Afro-Asian bonds, of the postcolonial era. Such social histories serve to complicate high-political narratives of Indo-African geopolitical solidarity. They might also become means to debate and clarify the promise of these relationships that have enriched the lives of many young citizens, such as R. Mugo Gatheru breathing in that air of freedom and possibility in Allahabad in 1949.

Bibliography

Aiyar, S. 2015. *Indians in Kenya: The Politics of Diaspora* (Cambridge: Harvard University Press).

Al Jazeera. 2016. 'Shock in India over mob attack on Tanzanian student', 5 February 2016, https://www.aljazeera.com/news/2016/02/anger-india-mob-attack-tanzanian-student-160205141006483.html, accessed 25 August 2019.

Anand, G. and Raj, S. 2017. 'Attacks against African students rise in India, rights advocates say', *The New York Times*, 29 March 2017, https://www.nytimes.com/2017/03/29/world/asia/african-students-india-mob-attacks.html, accessed 15 October 2019.

Ansah, M. 2019. 'We'll partner with India to make Ghana pharmaceutical hub – Bawumia', *CNR Citi Newsroom*, 17 March 2019, https://citinewsroom.com/2019/03/well-partner-with-india-to-make-ghana-pharmaceutical-hub-bawumia/, accessed 29 October 2019.

Branch, D. 2018. 'Political traffic: Kenyan students in eastern and central Europe, 1958–1969', *Journal of Contemporary History*, 53/4, 811–31.

Brennan, J. R. 2012. *Taifa: Making Nation and Race in Urban Tanzania* (Athens: Ohio University Press).

Burton, A. 2010. 'Epilogue. The sodalities of Bandung: Towards a critical twenty-first century history', in C. J. Lee (ed.), *Making a World After Empire: The Bandung Moment and its Political Afterlives* (Athens: Ohio University Press), 351–61.

Chaturvedi, S. 2016. *The Logic of Sharing: Indian Approach to South-South Cooperation* (New Delhi: Cambridge University Press).

Davis, A. E. 2018. 'Solidarity or hierarchy? India's identification with Africa and the postcolonial politics of race', *India Review*, 17/2, 242–62.

Deccan Herald. 2010. 'I am Deliwala, a product of India: Malawi president', 8 January 2010, https://www.deccanherald.com/content/45683/i-am-delhiwala-product-india.html, accessed 17 October 2019.

Dubey, A. 1990. *Indo-African Relations in the Post-Nehru Era* (New Delhi: Kalinga Publications).

Gandhi, M. K. 1946. 'Discussion with negro soldiers', *The Harijan*, cited in *Collected Works of Mahatma Gandhi LXXXIX* (New Delhi: Ministry of Information and Broadcasting, Government of India), 282.

Gatheru, R. M. 1966. *Child of Two Worlds: A Kikuyu's Story* (London: Heinemann).

Guha, D. 2017. 'In these portraits of Africans, an unflattering picture of India', *The Wire*, 5 June 2017, https://thewire.in/culture/portraits-africans-unflattering-picture-india-mahesh-shantaram, accessed 22 December 2019.

Indian Council for Africa. 1967. *India and Africa: Perspectives of Cooperation* (New Delhi: Haya Hindustan Press).

India News (Accra). 1959. 'Bhakra dam fascinates Prime Minister Nkrumah', 15 January 1959.

King, K. 2019. 'India-Africa cooperation in human resource development: Education, training and skills, *MP-IDSA*, Occasional paper no. 51, April 2019, https://idsa.in/system/files/opaper/ind-africa-cooperation-op-51.pdf, accessed 8 October 2019.

King, K. and King, P. 2019. 'India's south-south cooperation in human resource development', *The Roundtable: The Commonwealth Journal of International Affairs*, 108/4, 399–409.

Kokutse, F. 2019. 'HE summit hopes to lure more African students to India', *University World News*, 20 July 2019, https://www.universityworldnews.com/post.php?story=20190717134920281, accessed 17 September 2019.

Lavakare, P.J. and Powar, K.B. 2013. 'African students in India: Why is their interest declining?', *Insight on Africa*, 5/1, 19–33.

McCann, G. 2010. 'Ties that bind or binds that tie? India's African engagements and the political economy of Kenya', *Review of African Political Economy*, 27/126, 465–82.

——. 2019. 'Where was the *Afro* in Afro-Asian solidarity? Africa's "Bandung Moment" in 1950s Asia', *Journal of World History*, 30/1–2, 89–123.

Malghan, D. and Swaminathan, H. 2008. 'Material and moral foundations of India's Africa policy', *Economic and Political Weekly*, 43/19, 21–24.

Mangame, E.J. 1964. 'The African youth', *The African Student: Magazine of the African Students Association of Israel*, 6, 23–25.

Mawdsley, E. 2012a. 'The changing geographies of foreign aid and development cooperation: Contributions from gift theory', *Transactions of the Institute of British Geographers*, 37/2, 256–72.

———. 2012b. *From Recipients to Donors: Emerging Powers and the Changing Development Landscape* (London: Zed Books).

MEA. 2015. 'Third India-Africa Forum Summit: Partners in Progress: Towards a Dynamic and Transformative Development Agenda', *GoI*, 29 October 2015, http://mea.gov.in/Uploads/PublicationDocs/25981_framework.pdf, accessed 22 December 2019.

Metcalf, T.R. 2007. *Imperial Connections: India in the Indian Ocean Arena, 1860–1920*, (Berkeley: University of California Press).

Milford, I. 2019. 'Harnessing the wind: East and Central African activists and anti-colonial cultures in a decolonising world, 1952–64' (Unpublished Ph.D. dissertation, European University Institute).

Nicholson, T. 2017. 'Students, sex, and threatened solidarity: East African bodies and Indian angst, 1955–1970', *Journal of World History*, 28/3–4, 615–74.

Oginga Odinga, A. 1966. *Two Months in India* (Nairobi: New Kenya Publishers).

Pant, A. 1987. *Undiplomatic Incidents* (Hyderabad: Sangam Books).

PTI. 2016. 'Murder of Congolese national: African countries want "Africa Day" put off', 26 May 2016, *Indian Express*, https://indianexpress.com/article/india/india-news-india/congolese-nationals-killing-african-countries-seek-deferment-of-africa-day-celebrations-by-india-2818384/, accessed 8 October 2019.

Roy, S. 2017. 'The ugly side of being an African student in India', *NPR*, 4 April 2017, https://www.npr.org/sections/goatsandsoda/2017/04/04/522453520/the-ugly-side-of-being-an-african-student-in-india?t=1591780095166, accessed 5 October 2019.

Sang, G. 2015. *Just for Today: The Life and Times of Jean-Marie Seroney* (Coventry: Dolman Scott).

Seroney, J-M. 1950. 'Threat of South African fascism to East Africa', *Indian Review*, 51.

Sutton, D. 2007. '"Divided and uncertain loyalties": Partition, Indian sovereignty and contested citizenship in East Africa, 1948–55', *Interventions*, 9/2, 276–88.

Times of India. 1955. 'Colour prejudice prevails in India', 7 February 1955.

———. 1967. 'African students', 22 May 1967.

———. 1968. 'Foreign students', 11 February 1968.

Zuma, N. D. 2015. 'Statement of Dr. Nkosazana Dlamini Zuma, Chairperson of the African Union Commission at Third India-Africa Forum Summit, New Delhi', *GoI*, 29 October 2015, http://iafs.gov.in/downloads/speeches/african-union-29th.pdf, accessed 7 October 2019.

Archival Sources

Kenyan National Archives. OP/EST/1/697: Minutes of meeting of the Indian Scholarships Local Selection Committee, India House, Nairobi, 23 September 1958.

National Archives of India (NAI), New Delhi. 25–25/46–O.S.I: Henry Muoria, George Ndegwa, George Karioki, Zabula, and Mbiyu Koinange to Jawaharlal Nehru, 16 September, 1946.

——.20–24/48–O.S.I: Pant to Dutt, 28 August, 1948.

——.18–68/49–AFRII: Apa Pant to Subimal Dutt, 18 October, 1949.

The UK National Archives: DO/35/5347: J.R. Williams, Office for British High Commissioner to India, New Delhi, to R.C. Ormerod, Commonwealth Relations Office.

Conclusion

Reflections on India–Africa Studies, Development Cooperation and Soft Power

KENNETH KING AND MEERA VENKATACHALAM

On 10–12 February 2020, the India International Centre (IIC) ran a conference in Delhi on 'Understanding Africa: Continuity and change'. Within a month, there was certainly change in both India and Africa as the Coronavirus (Covid-19) pandemic struck. Several key Indian institutions concerned with South–South knowledge transfer, such as Indian Technical and Economic Cooperation (ITEC) and the Indian Council for Cultural Relations (ICCR), found their scholarship and training programmes frozen. Suddenly, the 14,000 short-term training slots of ITEC and the 3,000 scholarship places of the ICCR were on hold. The ITEC website had a single message running continuously: 'Currently only e-ITEC courses are being offered' (ITEC, 2020). It would appear that the only upcoming courses were focused on 'Good governance practices in a pandemic' (ITEC 2020). By contrast, the ICCR saw in the pandemic the relevance of Indian philosophy: 'Let's therefore rededicate ourselves to the task of evolving an enlightened understanding of the idea of India, and thereby make a significant contribution to India's soft power' (ICCR 2020).

Capacity building, which is such a critical aspect of India's development cooperation, looks set to be very directly affected. Not only are its 'flagship' ITEC and ICCR offerings almost completely closed for the moment by travel and lockdown decisions, or have gone online, but also a majority of the other people-to-people exchanges have been stopped or have gone virtual. In the short term, the sudden absence of international students and their foreign student fees will make a massive difference to institutional sustainability in some countries. However, Indian higher education which only attracts 0.7 per cent of the global international student body may not be very severely affected by this particular dimension of student mobility. The other most conspicuous casualty of the pandemic has been the postponement of the fourth India-Africa Forum Summit (IAFS IV) which was to have taken place during 2020. Equally, the ambitious programme to 'Study in India' might expect to be paused or drastically altered just two years after it started in 2018, though currently the website has not announced this (MOE 2020a).

More generally with the extent of expected damage to economic activity within India, it may well be that the activities of the Ministry of External Affairs (MEA) will be directly affected, in line with what is anticipated by other aid donors. However, on the more positive side, the Covid-19 crisis has arguably pushed forward some of the Government of India's cooperation policies in human resource development (HRD). The online offerings of the Ministry of Education (MOE) such as SWAYAM and of the MEA such as e-VidyaBharati and e-ArogyaBharati (e-VBAB) will have become more attractive (King, this volume; Duclos, this volume). For instance, the SWAYAM website carries the current Covid-19 alert: 'Let Covid-19 not stop your learning. Continue with SWAYAM' (MOE 2020b). The e-VBAB global projects could be rapidly expanded beyond the present number of eighteen partner African countries to cover the whole of Africa and the present number of scholarships to include the whole of the continent (MEA 2020).

The focus on capacity building, knowledge transfer and cultural diplomacy

In this volume's focus on the human resource lens in India–Africa relations, it has been noted that policymakers today frequently link Indian capacity building and 'development diplomacy' to a long-standing and 'strong civilisational underpinning'. Such diplomacy is traced back to Vivekananda in the nineteenth century, who is said to have captured the essence of development diplomacy – 'Each nation must give in order to live' (quoted in Tirumurti 2020: 4). This 'national habit and civilisational identity' are then illustrated in a long Indian history of knowledge sharing:

> Throughout history, India has always partaken with others our knowledge, science, mathematics, astronomy, philosophy, music, the arts – indeed every aspect of human activity.
>
> But given how…countries used to flock to India to trade, and more importantly, to learn from us, we should probably have coined the phrase 'South-North cooperation' as opposed to North-South Cooperation (Tirumurti 2020: 4).

This historical claim to India's knowledge sharing priority through the ages, in its ancient universities such as Nalanda, translates into the desire to present India as a 'teacher of the world' (*vishva guru*):

Indian leaders would like India to play the role of 'vishva guru', as they feel that it is endowed with spiritual and other values that could help in promoting civilisational dialogue among peoples and nations (Sahai 2019: 508).

Since Modi's premiership in 2014, this notion that 'India is not just a country but a civilisation' (Tirumurti 2020: 5) has translated into a new emphasis on the marketing of older, indigenous knowledge systems. For example, the new Ministry of AYUSH promoted Ayurveda, Yoga, Unani, Siddha and Homoeopathy, and several of these systems duly appear as 'niche courses' on the 'Study in India' website (MOE 2020b).

The *vishva guru* notion powerfully supports the view that the provision of knowledge is central to 'the idea of India'. Knowledge sharing thus becomes an activity in which India should expect to become world class: 'Even more importantly, the depth and resilience of our people-to-people links are continuously reinforced through some of the largest capacity building programmes anywhere in the world' (Tirumurti 2020: 5). This is felt to be particularly the case of India's educational aid to Africa, according to the Ministry of External Affairs in launching e-VidyaBharati (e-Knowledge India).

The aspect of development diplomacy, therefore, which has been given a central place in many chapters in this volume could be described as 'cultural diplomacy'. Older accounts of the India–Africa focus such as *India in Africa* (Mawdsley and McCann 2011) do not have the terms 'education' or 'human resource development' in their index. Another account, in the case of *India and Africa's Partnership*, contains a whole chapter on economic diplomacy but has no parallel analysis of the discourse on cultural diplomacy (Taylor 2016).

The topic has, however, begun to gain traction with the publication of Paramjit Sahai's book on *Indian Cultural Diplomacy: Celebrating Pluralism in a Globalised World* (Sahai 2019). This directly deals with the current status and greater potential of several of the institutions or 'key cultural diplomacy vehicles' that have been discussed in our chapters (Sahai 2019: 501). None of these is more salient than international student mobility, and within that the claim of attractiveness to African students of the opportunities associated with iLearn, the successor to the Pan-African e-Network (MEA 2020).

Here it must be recalled that despite the claimed ambitions to be the 'teacher of the world', only some forty thousand international students come to India, and, of these, only some ten thousand come from Africa. E-Knowledge India and e-Health India reach out to the whole of Africa, but, as has been mentioned earlier, on the website the invitation to the whole of Africa can be contrasted with the evidence that only eighteen out of fifty-four African countries are currently named as partners (MEA 2020). The current number of African students in India, both public and private, are less than the number of students from Sub-Saharan Africa going to South Africa. Thus, there has to be a sea-change as Sahai acknowledges:

> India has to emerge as a destination country for foreign students; its present share is only 0.7 per cent, while Indian students abroad comprise 4 per cent of foreign students' population. Our education institutes have to become not only competitive, but also provide open, friendly and conducive environments. Hopefully, the new Education Policy would also focus on Education Diplomacy. We need to make a concerted drive to achieve the target of 200,000 students by 2023, under the 'Study in India Programme' (Sahai 2019: 501–02).

Imagining and researching the realities of India–Africa relations

Too much of the India–Africa discourse remains at the rhetorical level. There are pages of claims about solidarity, people-to-people links, and South–South cooperation, including coffee table books produced by the MEA on India–Africa (King 2019: 33–34). But too little of the modalities of human resource development is illustrated in detailed practice. Arguably, there are the beginnings of this in the chapters in this volume, but much remains to be researched.

One example would be the absence of any detail on the India–Africa institutes provided to Africa over the last two decades and more. Several of these, such as Ghana's Kofi Annan Centre of Excellence in ICT have been in place for years, and the same is true of the Rajiv Gandhi Science Centre in Mauritius from 2004, and also its Mahatma Gandhi Institute from 1976. But very little is known about how they are perceived locally, and how they are utilised by surrounding communities. The same would be true of the many India–Africa institutes offered to Africa at the first India-Africa Forum Summit in 2008. No analysis exists, for example, of the India-Africa Institute of Educational Planning and Administration in Burundi, nor of the India-Africa Institute of Foreign Trade in Uganda, or indeed of any of the nineteen institutes offered to Africa at the first summit (King 2019: 23).

Another area of potentially crucial significance in India–Africa understandings is the growth of Indian trade and commerce in Africa. Very little is known about how Nairobi's industrial area came to be dominated by Indian businesses. What, if any, are the connections with the itinerant entrepreneurs from India who opened stores across Kenya, Tanzania and Uganda during the colonial period? What are the links between the early Indian informal sector in Eastern Africa and the rise of local African entrepreneurs? To what extent is Indian industry today in Kenya, and in other countries such as Tanzania, connected to these early settlers, many of whom became citizens of their host countries at independence, or to expatriate Indians who arrived many years after independence? Beyond the histories of early Indian entrepreneurs, there is also a lack of detail on major Indian enterprises and Indian entrepreneurs. Some of the history of early enterprise is available in accounts such as Mangat's *A History of the Asians in East Africa* (1970). In addition, there is reportedly a significant presence of Indian itinerant traders in West Africa, and African traders in India, engaged in trading textiles, accessories, electrical goods and consumer goods (Venkatachalam et al. 2020). Significant Nigerian communities have sprung up in Indian metropolises over the last two decades (Gill 2019). Nigerians have brought with them food, music, Nollywood (Nigerian films) and their very own brand of Pentecostal Christianity, and are engaged in a lively process of interaction with, and assimilation into their host communities in India. All of these are vastly under-reported.

The current role of Indian multinationals such as Tata and Airtel across Africa also remains unresearched. Some of the developments in agriculture – by a range of players from the private sector to NGOs and government – have recently become available (Modi and Venkatachalam 2021). There is also some detail on the impact on clothing of Indian enterprises (McCormick 2008; Venkatachalam et al. 2020). But for much of Indian investment in Africa there is still a substantial gap compared to what is known about Chinese investment in the continent.

Another unresearched area of Indian engagement with Africa was the very large number of Indian secondary school and university teachers present in many African countries from the time of their independence. These came largely from different communities in India than those who travelled to Africa as traders. The great majority of these cannot be considered as part of an Indian aid or charity project; they were mainly individual responses for self- and family improvement. But the sheer scale of their presence for six decades is worthy of research attention.

Not unconnected with the thousands of Indian teachers working in Africa is the need for a critical analysis of African students and travellers in India. Currently, there is no easily accessible equivalent for India of the Ghanaian Hevi's account of *An African Student in China* (Hevi 1963; King 2013). A good deal of the little that is currently available consists of accounts of prejudice encountered in India. By contrast there is too little detail on the experience of actually studying and living in India, as captured by Gatheru in his chapter

'Brown man's world' (Gatheru 1966; McCann, this volume). Equally, there is very little insight into African student perceptions of the Indian diasporas in Africa, or of the experiences of individuals invited officially to India through ITEC or ICCR (Oginga Odinga 1966). Nor are there more than a handful of accounts of the African communities in India which are to be found in Mumbai, Delhi, Chennai, Bengaluru and Hyderabad (e.g. Gill 2019).

Differentiating 'Asians' in Africa

Confusingly, African perspectives about Indians are often subsumed by the term 'Asians'. This usage goes back a long way, as for example with Delf's book for the Institute of Race Relations called *Asians in East Africa* (1963). Usage differs across the Francophone and Lusophone regions and also from Western to Eastern Africa. This generalising tendency does, however, mean that there are many challenges for Africa in differentiating the local, long-term resident Indian populations, many of whom are citizens of African nation-states, and the body of expatriate Indians, most of whom have come since the 1990s.

It is of course equally the case that in India many Africans are not identi-fied as being from a particular country. The commonly used generic term for Africans in India is Hapshi, a corruption of Habesha, or Ethiopia – the result of the historical memory of the large-scale presence of Ethiopians in India on account of thriving trade, commerce and the institution of elite slavery, which enabled many Ethiopians to establish themselves among Indian courtly elites (Bhatt 2018). The presence of the Siddis, a visibly African community, descendants of African slaves who were brought to Gujarat and the Deccan until the early twentieth century, has further informed the popular Indian imagination about Africa (Bhatt 2018). In contemporary India, African sojourners are often all referred to as 'Nigerians', as the latter account for the largest settled African community in India.

Leaving aside the presence of Bangladeshis and Pakistanis in Africa, there is a huge range of different Indian communities within those countries of Africa with significant diasporas. They have their temples, mosques, gurdwaras and churches, and a complex array of different community associations. These diasporas are layered, ranging from fourth and fifth generation Africa-born Africans of Indian origin to contemporary first-generation immigrants. The sheer complexity of the diasporic Indian communities along with their more recent expatriates is such that it would be invaluable to have ethnographies of India's early trading communities in Ethiopia, the composition of Indians in Nairobi's industrial area, or the extent of Indo-African skill transfer in the informal sectors of Dar es Salaam or Kampala.

Unpacking the instruments of India's collaboration with Africa

There would be plenty of scope also to analyse in much more detail the Indian and African sides of the main instruments of India's cooperation with Africa. For example, Lines of Credit (LoCs) are a critical feature of India's aid system, and these LoCs usually require that 75 per cent of the credit be tied to the use of Indian companies. All too often the total amount of the LoCs provided to individual countries in Africa is given, e.g. USD 10 billion over five years promised at the IAFS III in 2015, but there is no indication of which Indian companies or parastatal Indian firms have got the contracts to deliver the LoCs, or with which local company or parastatal firm they are collaborating in Africa. A telling example may be seen in the listing of no less than fifteen pages of LoCs given to different African countries, with the total sums involved, and their sectoral purpose, but no information on the firms involved either in India or in Africa (Dubey and Biswas 2016: 183–97).

Similarly, with the Indian 'commitment to provide 50,000 slots for capacity building over five years' for Africa from 2015, there is no breakdown of this total into short-term training and long-term scholarships (Tirumurti 2020: 6). In fact, the great majority of slots promised were only for short-term ITEC awards, and not for undergraduate or postgraduate training.

Although Prime Minister Modi did outline the beginnings of an African policy in the 'Ten guiding principles for India-Africa engagement' in Uganda in July 2018 (MEA 2018), it should always be recalled that the countries immediately surrounding India, with the exception of Pakistan, remain central to India's aid priorities: 'Our neighbours naturally remain our closest development partners. Ours are ties of blood, history, geography, resources, language, and culture ... "Neighbourhood first" is put into visible action by India' (Tirumurti 2020: 7). Compared with this visible action in the neighbourhood, it is argued that publicising these ten elements is just a first stage: 'The work, however, should not stop in merely articulating the principles. India should set out to develop an Action Plan for each of the principles' (Viswanathan and Mishra 2019).

In April 2021, at the Raisina Dialogue, India's most influential conference on geopolitics and geo-economics, External Affairs Minister S. Jaishankar declared that 'India must rise as an Enlightened Power, which not only organises its own rise, but facilitates the rise of others' (Bagchi 2021). In recent years, Indian think tanks and policymakers have begun advocating for the use of 'smart power', which integrates the discretionary use of both soft power and hard power (Mathoo 2014). As economic diplomacy and regional security assume centre stage in foreign policy, some Indian stakeholders have begun to argue for a rethinking of the modalities and *modus operandi* of soft power, to effectively build multilateral coalitions and partnerships in the neighbourhood and beyond. How this will affect India's multilayered engagement with Africa, remains to be seen.

Covid-19 and India's soft power

In May 2021, India began to report above 400,000 cases of Covid-19 daily in a deadly second wave of the pandemic (Worldometers 2021), just as this volume was being finalised. The ongoing events in India have dealt a serious blow to India's reputation as an emerging powerhouse of medical innovation, a *vishva guru* and the 'pharmacy of the developing world'.

The lethal second wave of the Covid-19 pandemic was caused in part by the government's triumphalism and miscalculations. In March 2021, Health Minister Harsh Vardhan prematurely (and erroneously) declared that India was in the 'endgame' of the pandemic (PTI 2021). Mass election rallies were then held in a number of states – in Assam, West Bengal, Kerala and Tamil Nadu in March and April 2021. The government allowed millions of devotees to congregate for the holy Kumbh Mela festival on the banks of the Ganges in mid-April.

The impoverishment of the country's health infrastructure became apparent, as did disparities between India's states, between the rich and poor, and between urban and rural populations. The escalation in Covid-19 infections resulted in an acute shortage of hospital beds, medical equipment, drugs, blood and oxygen. Medical personnel were unable to handle the enormity of the crisis. Indians took to social media platforms – Facebook, WhatsApp and Twitter – to network with each other and secure information about the availability of these life-saving resources. In early May, India began reporting a daily death toll of about four thousand (Worldometers 2021), though experts warned that the figure was actually much higher. Crematoriums in New Delhi had run out of wood, while burial grounds began turning away the families of the deceased (Lalwani and Johari 2021). The author-activist Arundhati Roy (2021) described the situation as a 'crime against humanity'.

Petitions demanding the resignation of Prime Minister Modi circulated on social media, with criticism emerging even from his staunchest supporters in his constituency in Varanasi (Pandey 2021). Some Indian analysts argued that Modi was not solely to blame for this tragedy; rather it was serial under-investment in the public infrastructure accompanied by privatisation of key sectors, which had been in motion since India embarked on its journey of neoliberal reforms in the 1990s (Krishnan 2021). India's vaccination drive, which had begun triumphantly in March 2021, came to a standstill, as the two vaccine producing companies in India – the Serum Institute of India (SII) and Bharat Biotech (BB) – blamed the internal vaccine shortages on soaring domestic demand, inability to source some raw materials from over-seas and disagreement with the government pricing regimes. The dramatic increase in domestic demand was unanticipated by the Indian government; they then proceeded to halt large exports of the AstraZeneca vaccine of the SII, including vaccines for the UN-backed Covax scheme which provides doses to low- and middle-income countries (Thakur 2021).

As India's soft power project came under severe criticism both at home and abroad, Foreign Minister S. Jaishankar issued a statement asking Indian diplomats to counter the 'one sided narrative' in the Western press about the Modi government's failure to handle the Covid crisis, which caused anger in India (Subramanian 2021). After sixteen years, India reversed a policy of refus-ing humanitarian aid in the face of natural disasters, and was forced to accept donations of BiPAP Machines, oxygen, drugs (faviparivir and remdesivir) and personal protective equipment (PPE, such as coveralls, masks and gowns). In addition to the traditional northern donors – USA, UK, Germany and France – many smaller nations such as Bangladesh, Bhutan, Mauritius, Thailand and Uzbekistan supplied emergency relief to India (Chakraborty 2021). So dire is the crisis that state governments were momentarily freed from New Delhi's red tape on the procurement of foreign funds, to allow them to directly solicit and receive medical aid from foreign governments and multilateral agencies (Dutta 2021). How India attempts to rehabilitate its carefully crafted image after this crisis remains to be seen.

The way ahead in India–Africa and Africa-India studies

The next opportunity to develop a framework for action on India and Africa will be in the Fourth India-Africa Forum Summit, postponed from 2020, as mentioned, because of the COVID-19 pandemic. That will be a Government of India initiative but with substantial African participation at the political and policy levels. By the time such a summit is convened, it would be invalua-ble if there could be some parallel analysis for India–Africa of the review that Sautman and Yan carried out in 'African perspectives on China-Africa links'

(Sautman and Yan 2009). Such African perspectives on India–Africa links would need to draw on the many different dimensions of India's historical and more recent presence in different African countries.

Arguably, it would also be an opportunity to explore whether in due course there could be the development of an India–Africa parallel to the very productive research network on Chinese in Africa/Africans in China (CA/AC). This has played a key role in encouraging: 'cutting-edge research, vibrant deliberations and the exchange of ideas about China-Africa issues by supporting a focused and rapidly growing global network of international scholars, students, journalists, and practitioners' (CA/AC n.d.).

In a small way the current volume is a contribution to the understanding of Indians in Africa and Africans in India. Each chapter has drawn upon the several different disciplines that have been looking at the changing idea of India in Africa, and equally the idea of Africa in India. The real stories of India in Africa and Africa in India are still to be written, but hopefully this book provides a few small steps towards an 'unpacking of the histories, actors, and geopolitical imaginaries underpinning India's worldview and evolving engagements with Africa' (Obi, this volume, back cover; see also Brautigam 2009).

Bibliography

Bagchi, A. 2021. *EAM @Dr. Jaishankar: We would like to be an enlightened power, which not only organises its own rise, but which also facilitates the rise of others*, Twitter, 13 April 2021, https://twitter.com/MEAIndia/status/1381919753745297409, accessed 14 April 2021.

Bhatt, P.M. 2018. *The African Diaspora in India: Assimilation, Change and Cultural Survivals* (London and New York: Routledge).

Brautigam, D. 2009. *The Dragon's Gift: The Real Story of China in Africa* (Oxford: Oxford University Press).

CA/AC. n.d., https://ca-ac.org, accessed 17 June 2020.

Chakraborty, S. 2021. 'Here's the full list of foreign medical aid to India and where they are headed', *Money Control*, 5 May 2021, https://www.moneycontrol.com/news/business/economy/heres-the-full-list-of-foreign-medical-aid-to-india-and-where-they-are-headed-6858141.html, accessed 8 May 2021

Delf, G. 1963. *Asians in East Africa* (Oxford: Oxford University Press).

Dubey, A.K. and Biswas, A. (eds.). 2016. *India and Africa's Partnership: A Vision for a New Future* (New Delhi: Springer).

Dutta, K. 2021. 'Major policy shift: India accepts foreign aid for first time in 16 years amid rising COVID-19 cases', *The Logical Indian*, 5 May 2021, https://thelogicalin-dian.com/trending/major-policy-shift-india-accepts-foreign-aid-for-first-time-in-16-years-amid-rising-covid-19-cases-28098, accessed 8 May 2021.

Gatheru, R.M. 1966. 'Brown man's world', in R.M. Gatheru, *Child of Two Worlds: A Kikuyu's Story* (London: Heinemann), 123–43.

Gill, B. 2019. 'In the shadow of illegality: The everyday life of African migrants in Delhi' (Unpublished PhD thesis, University of Copenhagen).

Hevi, E.J. 1963. *An African Student in China* (London: Praeger).

ICCR. 2020. 'President's message on the seventieth foundation day', *GoI*, 9 April 2020, https://www.iccr.gov.in/sites/default/files/Announcement/ICCR%20 President's%20Message.pdf, accessed 13 June 2020.

ITEC. 2020. *GoI*, n.d., https://itecgoi.in/about_e-ITEC.php, accessed 13 June 2020.

King, K. 2013. *China's Aid and Soft Power in Africa: The Case of Education and Training* (Woodbridge: James Currey).

———. 2019. 'India-Africa cooperation in human resource development: education, training, skills', *MP-IDSA*, Occasional Paper No. 51, April 2019, https://idsa.in/ occasionalpapers/ind-africa-cooperation-op-51, accessed 28 May 2020.

Krishnan, V. 2021. 'India is what happens when rich people do nothing', *The Atlantic*, 27 April 2021, https://www.theatlantic.com/international/archive/2021/04/india-covid19- moral-failure/618702/, accessed 8 May 2021.

Lalwani, V. and Johari, A. 2021. "Bodies after bodies are coming": Death and devastation in Delhi', *The Scroll*, 29 April 2021, https://scroll.in/article/993561/bodies-after-bodies-are-coming-death-and-devastation-in-delhi, accessed 8 May 2021.

McCormick, D. 2008. 'China and India as Africa's new donors: The impact of aid on development', *Review of African Political Economy*, 27/1, 1531–51.

Mangat, J.S. 1970. *A History of the Asians in East Africa* (Oxford: Clarendon).

Mathoo, A. 2014. 'The Modi foreign policy doctrine: India as a smart power', *The Conversation*, 12 June 2014, https://theconversation.com/the-modi-foreign-policy-doctrine-india-as-a-smart-power-27918, accessed 2 January 2020.

Mawdsley, E. and McCann, G. 2011. *India in Africa: Changing Geographies of Power* (Oxford: Pambazuka Press).

MEA. 2018. 'Prime Minister's address at Parliament of Uganda during his State Visit to Uganda', *GoI*, 25 July 2018, https://mea.gov.in/Speeches-Statements. htm?dtl/30152/prime+ministers+address+at+parliament+of+uganda+during+his+s tate+visit+to+uganda, accessed 19 December 2019.

———. 2020. 'About iLearn', *GoI*, n.d., https://ilearn.gov.in, accessed 15 June 2020.

MOE. 2020a. 'Study in India', *GoI*, n.d., https://www.studyinindia.gov.in/NICHE, accessed 15 June 2020.

———. 2020b. 'SWAYAM', *GoI*, n.d., https://swayam.gov.in, accessed 14 June 2020.

Modi, R. and Venkatachalam, M. (eds.). 2021. *India Africa Collaborations for Food Security and Capacity Building: South-South Cooperation* (London: Palgrave Macmillan).

Oginga Odinga, A. 1966. *Two Months in India* (Nairobi: New Kenya Publishers).

Pandey, G. 2021. 'Covid in Varanasi: Anger rises as coronavirus rages in Modi's constituency', *BBC News*, 4 May 2021, https://www.bbc.com/news/world-asia-india-56969283, accessed 8 May 2021.

PTI. 2021. 'We are in the endgame of the pandemic in India: Harsh Vardhan', *The Economic Times*, 8 March 2021, https://health.economictimes.indiatimes.com/

news/industry/we-are-in-the-endgame-of-covid-19-pandemic-in-india-harsh-vardhan/81384488, accessed 8 May 2021.

Roy, A. 2021. '"We are witnessing a crime against humanity": Arundhati Roy on India's Covid catastrophe', *The Guardian*, 28 April 2021, https://www.theguardian.com/news/2021/apr/28/crime-against-humanity-arundhati-roy-india-covid-catastrophe, accessed 8 May 2021.

Sahai, P. 2019. *Indian Cultural Diplomacy: Celebrating Pluralism in a Globalised World* (New Delhi: Vij Book).

Sautman, B. and Yan, H. 2009. 'African perspectives on China-Africa links', *China Quarterly*, 199, 728–59.

Subramanian, N. 2021. 'Counter 'one-sided' world media narrative on govt's pandemic 'failure', Jaishankar tells Indian diplomats', *The Indian Express*, 30 April 2021, https://indianexpress.com/article/india/counter-one-sided-world-media-narrative-on-govts-pandemic-failure-jaishankar-tells-indian-diplomats-7296036/, accessed 8 May 2021.

Taylor, I. 2016. 'India's economic diplomacy in Africa', in A.K. Dubey and A. Biswas (eds.) *India and Africa's Partnership: A Vision for the Future* (New Delhi: Springer).

Thakur, D. 2021. 'India is suffering immensely under the weight of Covid. Now its failures are threatening much of the world', *Stat*, 5 May 2021, https://www.statnews.com/2021/05/05/india-vaccine-heist-shoddy-regulatory-oversight-imperil-global-vaccine-access/, accessed 9 May 2021.

Tirumurti, T.S. 2020. 'Development diplomacy is the spirit of India', in *Modi 2.0: Diplomacy for a New India: Mapping the Way Ahead*, Special Issue (New Delhi: India and World).

Viswanathan, H.H.S and Mishra, A. 2019. 'The ten guiding principles for India-Africa engagement: Finding coherence in India's Africa policy', *ORF Online*, Occasional paper no. 200, 25 June 2019, https://www.orfonline.org/research/the-ten-guiding-principles-for-india-africa-engagement-finding-coherence-in-indias-africa-policy/, accessed 17 June 2020.

Venkatachalam, M., Modi, R. and Salazar J. 2020. *Common Threads: Fabrics Made-in-India for Africa*, ASC series 76 (Leiden: ASC publications).

Worldometers, 2021. 'India: Coronavirus cases', n.d., https://www.worldometers.info/coronavirus/country/india/, accessed 8 May 2021.

Index

and International Day of Yoga
71–2; contradictions in approach
to Africa 74; symbolic ownership
of Gandhi 81; rewriting history
of India-Africa 81; membership
of BJP 81 n.4; as Gujarat chief
minister 82; construction of
Gandhi memorial buildings 82;
link to Gandhi's salt march 82; use
of Gandhi image for Clean India
82; claiming for himself Gandhi
image as spinner 82; political
appropriation of Gandhi 83;
critique of Nehru and Nehruvian
institutions 83; aim for a Hindu
rashtra (nation) 84; continuity of
India's foreign policy but change
in the language and rationale 85;
Modi's extensive visits to Africa
85, 87 n.7; Panchamrit -five pillars
of his foreign policy 86; 66;
promotion of India's civilisational
mission 86; Bharat vs India 86, 86
n.5; towards a Nehru-free India
86–7, 89; spectacle of IAFS III of
2015 87; 18 new Indian missions
in Africa 87; on South Africa as
the land that transformed Gandhi
88; re-enactment of Gandhi's
iconic train journey 89; claim
of African priorities in Indian
education cooperation 116; urges
reform of WHO 139; claims India's
Covid success 145; major errors in
handling Covid 146
Morocco; Chair of Indian Studies 113
Mozambique 2, 3, 31, 46, 112, 136, 142
MPLA 2
Mtikila, Christopher (Reverend); hate
speeches against South Asian
businesses in Dar es Salaam 160
Muasia (Asian) 155
Mufuruki, Ali A.; Tanzanian African
entrepreneur on absence of Indo-
African skill transfer 156; creation

of multi-racial business network
157; business encouragement to
young South Asian, Rahim Mawji
162; transcended Asian-African
racial division 162
Mukherjee, Pranab (former president of
India) 17
Mumbai Consensus; Summers on
Indian development 28; critique
of 35
Muslim community in India; reported
attacks on by Hindu hardliners
36; Hindutva on Muslim rule
in India 60, 83; changes in
textbooks regarding 61; concern
about promotion of IDY 72;
UN campaign to counter
misinformation about role of in
Covid spread in India 143
Mutabuzi, Philbert (chair of joint
Indian-African enterprise in
Tanzania (ACOTA)) 159–60
Mutharika, Bingu wa (former president
of Malawi); on quality of Indian
higher education 101; on his studies
in University of Delhi 170, 174
Mwafrika (African) 155; a Kiswahili
newspaper article on Asian shops
upskilling Africans 155
Mwapachu, Juma V. (African
businessman in Tanzania)
157; experience in Indian high
commission in Delhi and Indian
higher education 164; cofounder
of Confederation of Tanzanian
Industries (CTI) 164; founder
of *Change* business magazine in
Tanzania 164
Myanmar 51

Naidu, Venkaiah (vice president of
India); on impact of South Africa
on Gandhi 88
Nairobi; Indian diaspora domination of
industrial area of 188

Oginga Odinga, Jaramogi (former
    Kenyan vice president);
    appreciation of Indian
    development during ICCR trip 174;
    and Indian scholarship selection
    174
Oil India Ltd.; investment in Africa 46
Olivier, Masonda Ketada (African
    student); murder of in India 180
ONGC Videsh; investment in Africa 46
Operation Samudra Setu; naval
    repatriation of Indian citizens 142
Overseas Citizen of India (OCI) 13;
    East African numbers of 35
Overseas Friends of the BJP (OFBJP)
    in Africa 67; collaboration with
    overseas RSS 68
Oxford, University of: and AstraZeneca
    vaccine 141

Pakistan 61, 72, 158, 191
Pan-African e-Network (PAN) 137;
    121–31 *passim*; as idealised 'South' 18;
    flagship education cooperation 109;
    origins of Pan-African e-Network
    (PAN) with former president
    Kalam 121; Kalam on India's
    unique gift to world of knowledge
    121, 132; African countries 121;
    technological dimensions of 121–2;
    public-private partnership 122;
    first phase 2009–17 122; relaunched
    in 2018 as e-Knowledge India
    (e-VidyaBharati) and e-Health
    India (e-ArogyaBharati)109,
    122–3; iconic example of South-
    South cooperation 123; potential
    of information technology to fix
    health system 123; civilisational
    identity linked with technological
    innovation 124; on PAN's
    exceptionalism 125; PAN as
    non-Western 125; as non-Chinese
    style aid 125; PAN narrative
    exemplifies ideal of India-Africa

solidarity 125; rhetoric of quasi-
    mythological 'South' 125; medical
    dimensions of 126; medical
    teleconsultations and continuing
    medical education 126; child heart
    surgery in Senegal through 127;
    India-Africa medical inequalities
    underlined by 127; technological
    limitations of sharing India's
    comparative advantage in ICT
    through 127–8; ICT as Indian
    model of development cooperation
    128; telemedicine as technological
    'solution' to unequal healthcare in
    India 129; as turnkey development
    solution 130; used Regional
    African Satellite Communication
    Organisation (RASCOM) satellite
    technology for 130; framed as
    'win-win' South-South scenario
    131; PAN a Closed User Group
    131; value of to private Indian
    hospitals 131; as private centralised
    infrastructure 131; as centre-
    periphery, unidirectional model 131;
    concerns about the successor to
    PAN, e-ArogyaBharati 132
Panchamrit; key doctrine of Modi's
    foreign policy 12
Panchsheel; Nehru's foreign policy of
    five key principles 1, 86–7
pandemic; *see* Covid 19; India's Covid-19
    diplomacy
Panjab University, Chandigarh 174Pant,
    Apa (Indian high commissioner
    in Kenya); on mission towards
    diaspora and liberation movements
    172; promoting educational aid 172;
    friendship with Kenyan elite 172
Peace Corps 103
people-to-people relations 43, 116;
    between Indians and Africans 18;
    and knowledge transfer 18; aspect
    of human resource development
    102; Covid impact on 185

Printed and bound by CPI Group (UK) Ltd, Croydon, CR0 4YY

09/06/2025

14685710-0002